CW01647277

Copyright 2021 by Jolene Ejmont | The Best Vinyl Cutters

Names: Ejmont, Jolene Ilse, author
Title: The Complete Guide to Cricut Design Space (for Desktop)
Description: Independently published, 2021
Paperback: 115 Pages
Identifiers: 978-0-6450232-4-4
Subjects: Crafts & Hobbies

Book Design by Jolene Ejmont

THE COMPLETE GUIDE TO

CRICUT DESIGN SPACE

(FOR DESKTOP)

Quick tips & tricks to take you from
Cricut beginner to confident crafter!

WRITTEN BY
Jolene Ejmont
The Best Vinyl Cutters

PLEASE REMEMBER TO LEAVE US A REVIEW

Please remember to leave some constructive feedback on your Amazon purchase as a review and to give the book a star rating.

This feedback will help us to improve future copies of the book and it will also be really helpful for other crafters who might be wondering if this book will be able to help them.

Thank you!

xx Jolene

WELCOME

Hello, I'm Jolene!

In 15 years of crafting I've run an online craft store where I taught in-person classes and online craft-along-workshops.

You could find me inside craft magazines such as Creative Paper, Memory Makers and even on the cover of Scrapbook Creations and Scrapbooking Memories.

I sold my online shop and went to work at a local craft store where my love for the Cricut began. I think it is fair enough to say I became a #vinylcraftaddict.

Soon enough I built an entire business on bringing decades of craft industry reviews and guides to crafter's fingertips.

I'd already been through the trenches with my Cricut years ago and knew how much of a destressor crafting was for me.

I began helping others finally kick that Cricut overwhelm out of the craft room and make crafting feel like a breeze!

FIND US ON SOCIAL MEDIA

Featured In:

TABLE OF CONTENTS

DESKTOP USERS

I. GETTING TO KNOW CRICUT DESIGN SPACE

II. BASIC DESIGN FUNCTIONS

II. BASIC DESIGN FUNTIONS CONTINUED

III. HOW TO USE IMAGES, SVG'S AND SHAPES

IV. HOW TO USE TEXTS AND FONTS

V. PROJECT TUTORIALS

DESKTOP USERS

V. PROJECT TUTORIALS CONTINUED

BONUS RESOURCES

TROUBLESHOOTING GUIDE

CONCLUSION

DESKTOP USERS

HOW TO DOWNLOAD AND INSTALL CRICUT DESIGN SPACE

Step 1

Go to https://design.cricut.com/ to download the Design Space application. If you are on Windows, then you will see a Windows download. If you are on a Mac, then you will see a Mac download.

Step 2

Click on the Download button, and the application will start downloading to your computer. Most of the time, the file will automatically be stored in your Downloads folder, but you may have the option to select where to save it.

Step 3

Double click on the downloaded file and the application will begin installation. A installing window will appear for a minute or two.

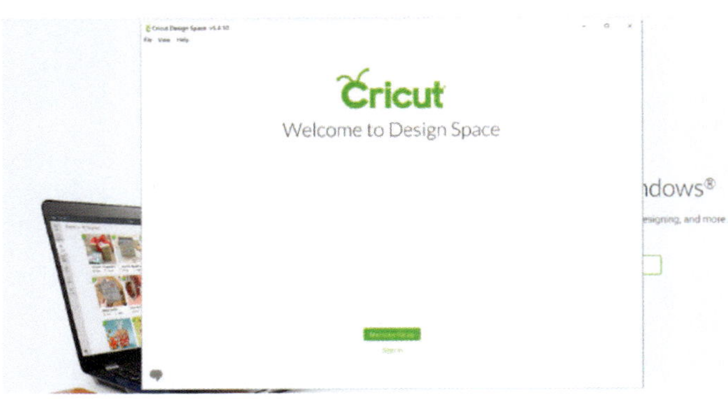

Step 4

Once the desktop app is successfully installed, **a Welcome screen will appear**. If you do not yet have a Cricut ID (account), then create one now. If you have an account, then log in at this point.

HOW TO CONNECT TO YOUR CRICUT VIA BLUETOOTH

Step 1

To connect via Bluetooth, make sure your Cricut machine is powered on. Your Cricut machine must be within 10 feet of your computer.

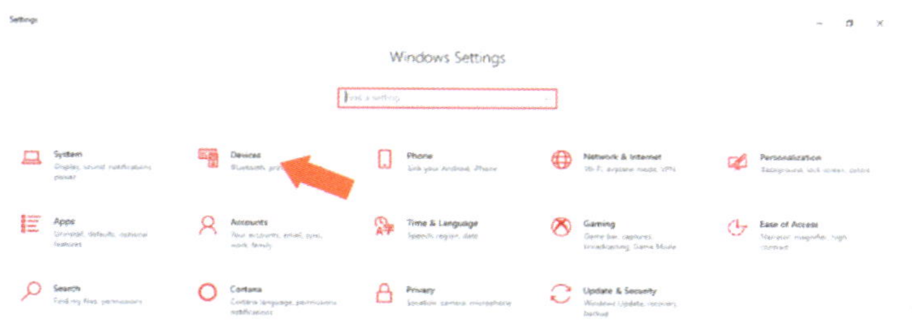

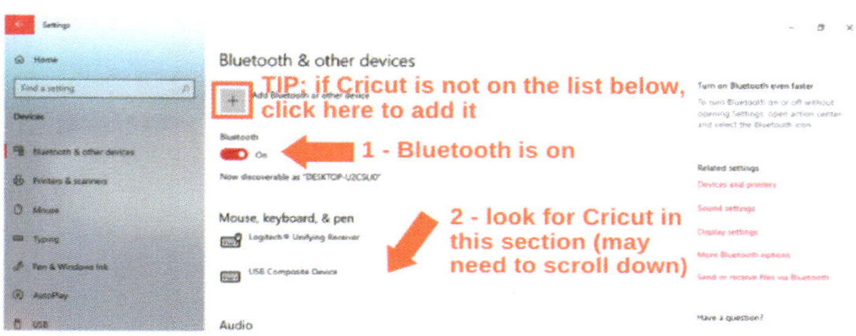

Step 2: Windows PC Users

On your Windows PC, **open Settings** on your computer and **select Devices.**

Make sure **Bluetooth is toggled on** and **select your machine**.

TIP: If you don't see your Cricut in the list of devices, **click on "Add Bluetooth or other device"** and look for it in the list that pops up.

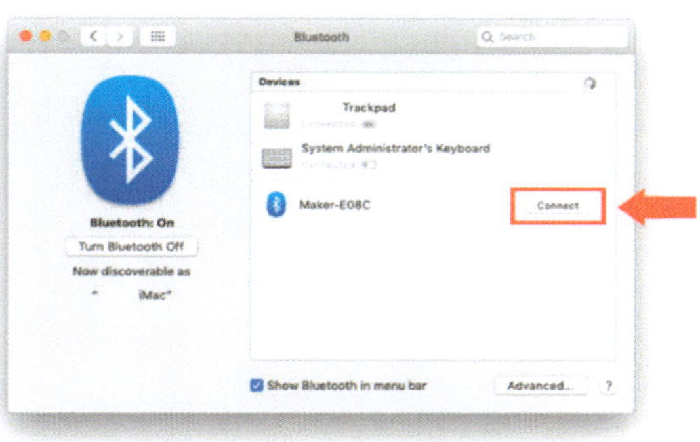

Step 2: Mac Users

On your Mac, **open System Preferences and select Bluetooth**.

Your machine should appear when powered on, and you can **click Connect**.

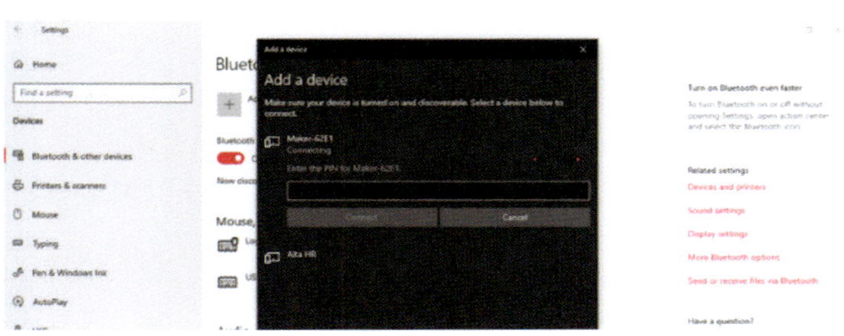

Step 3

If Cricut prompts you to enter a pin, **type 0000 and hit enter**.

HOW TO CLAIM YOUR TRIAL CRICUT ACCESS MEMBERSHIP

Note

Purchasing a Cricut Access Membership through the desktop application is available only in the US, UK, Australia and Canada.

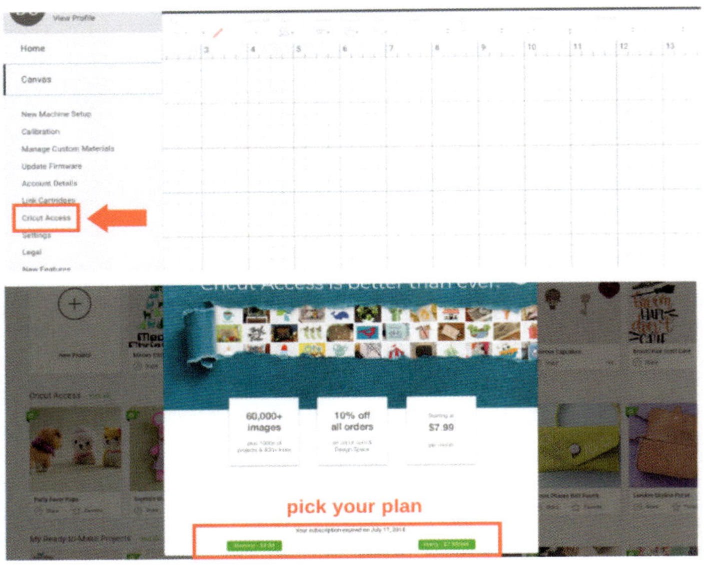

Step 1

Open your Cricut desktop application and sign in to Design Space.

Select the Design Space menu (☰) at the top left corner, then **select Cricut Access**.

Review the plan options and select the appropriate button. Monthly and yearly plans are available and you will be charged after your free trial expires if you choose to continue.

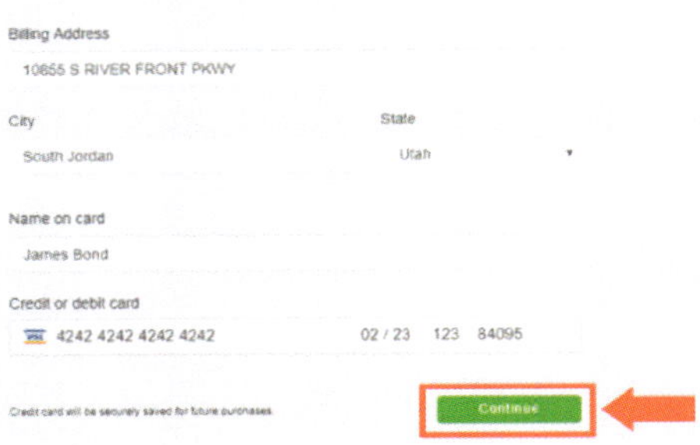

Step 2

Enter and review your credit card details, then click Continue.

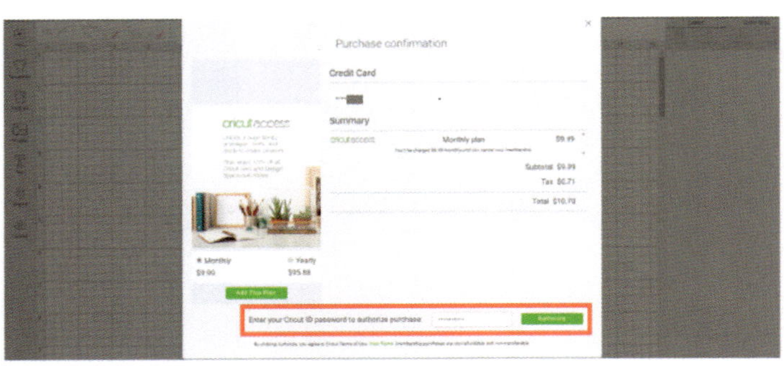

Step 3

Next, authorize your purchase by **entering your Cricut password & selecting the Authorize button**. You will only be charged AFTER your free trial has ended.

HOW TO CREATE A CRICUT PROFILE

You do not need to create a Cricut Profile to use Design Space. If you are going to share projects and are looking to engage with the Design Space Community then creating a profile will be useful.

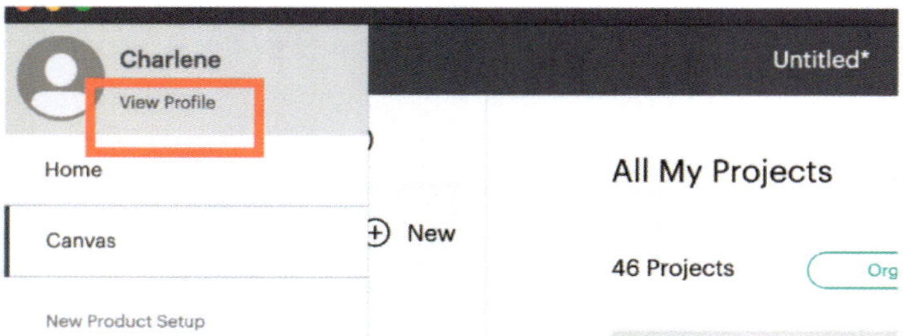

Step 1

To edit your profile **Select the Design Space menu (☰)** at the top left corner, then **select View Profile**.

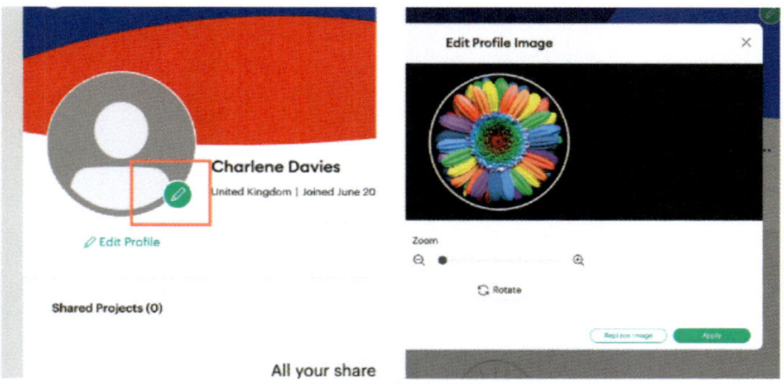

Step 2

To add a profile image, **click Edit Icon. Click upload image** to add an image of choice for your profile picture. Once selected, you can resize or change the image. Next **click Apply**.

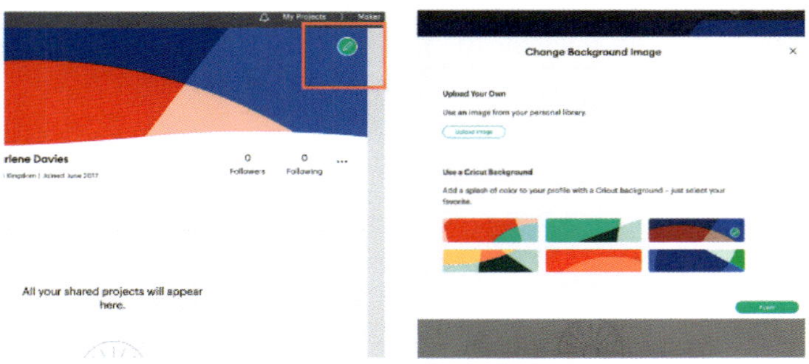

Step 3

To change your Profile Background Image. click the **Edit Icon**. Choose one from Cricut or upload your own. Once you have your new background image, **click Apply**.

Make Projects Public to Design Space Community

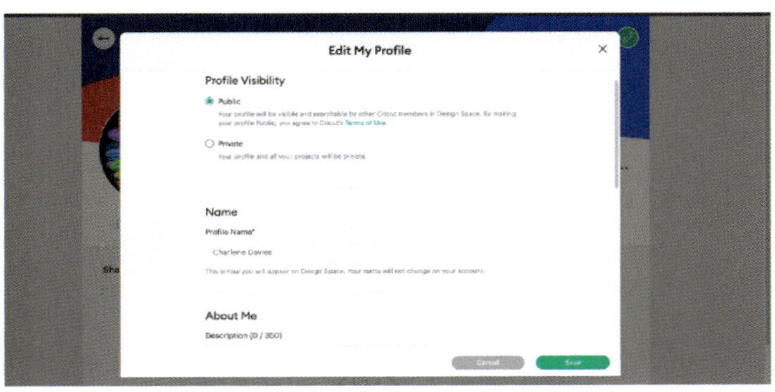

Step 1

Select the Edit Profile. Add any information you would like Cricut Community Member to know. **Click Save**. If you **Click on Make Public in Design Space** this will mean that your projects that are visible on this page will be visible to other users in Design Space.

NOTE: If you wish to remove a project and no longer make it visible, return to the project and click on the toggle for Make Public in Design Space.

HOW TO SELECT YOUR OWN SETTINGS: IMPERIAL VS METRIC ETC.

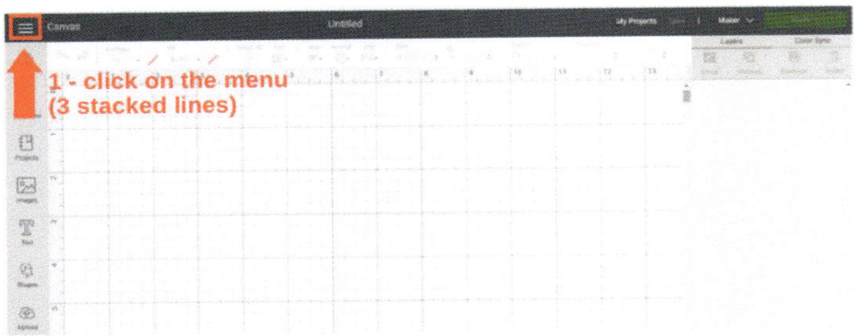

Step 1

Open the Account menu by clicking the icon (three stacked lines in the upper left corner).

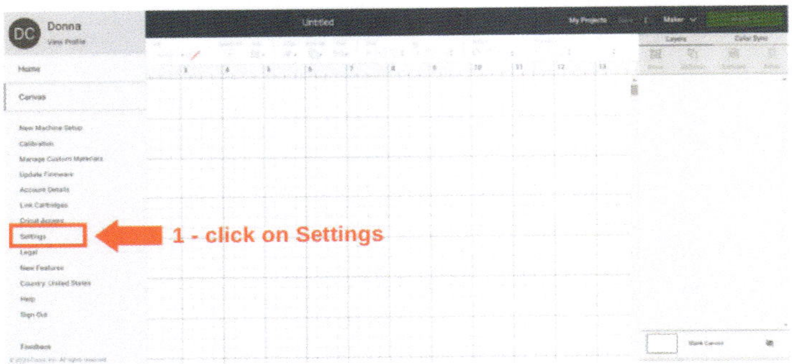

Step 2

Click on Settings in the menu that appears.

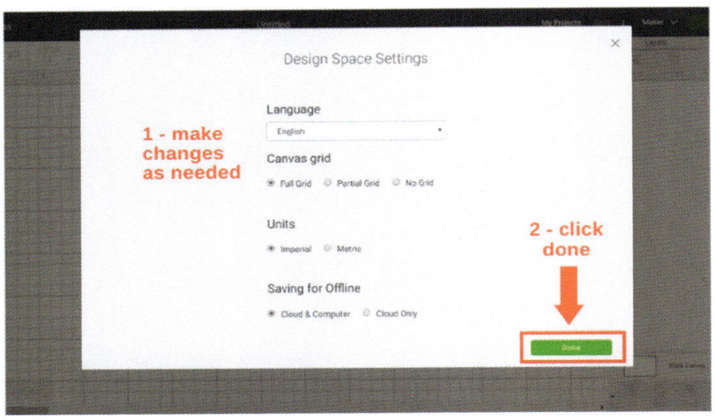

Step 3

In the pop-up window that appears, you can **change settings for:**

- **Language** (English, etc.),
- the **Canvas Grid** (full is default),
- the **Units** (imperial or metric), and
- **Saving for Offline options** (cloud & computer or cloud only).

Step 4

Make your changes and click Done.

Note:

Your Cricut Mats has both imperial and metric measurements on them. Make sure that you use the same measurement units for both your canvas and your mat.

LEARN THE WELCOME PAGE LAYOUT

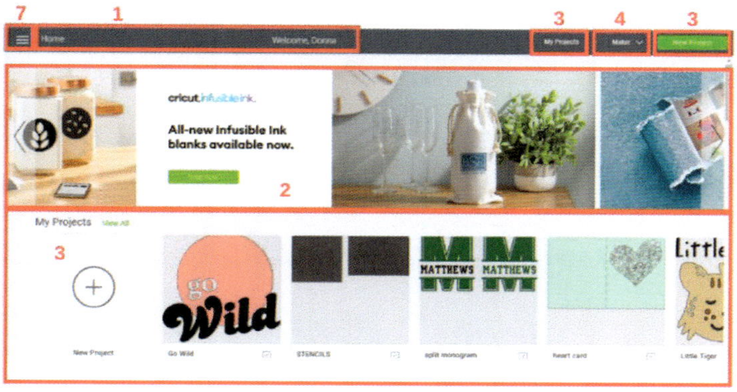

1 - Page Name

You will see either **Home and a welcome message** or **Canvas and the name of the project you're working on** in this section.

2 - Banner

Cricut will show off **special offers, product announcments, tutorials, and maintenance messages** in this section.

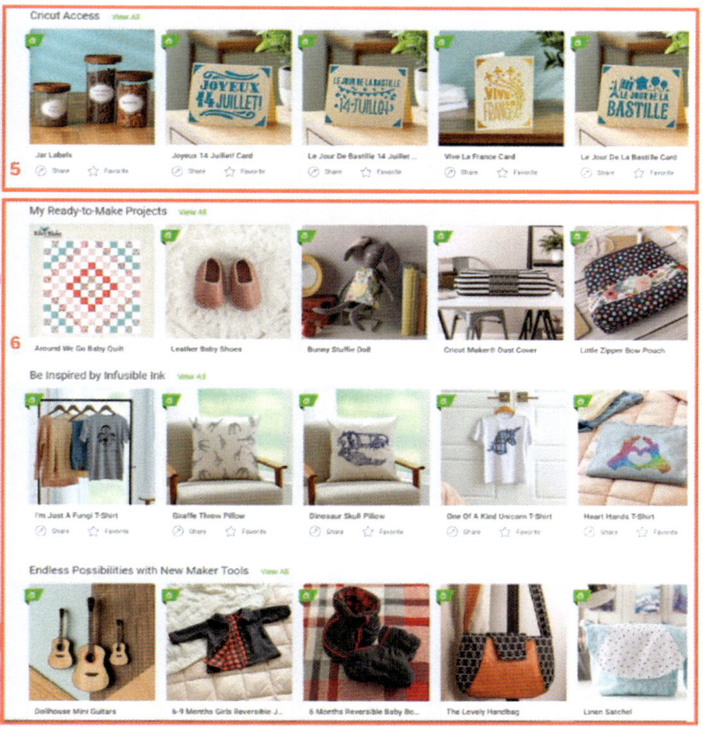

3 - My Projects

You can **access your previous projects or create new projects** in this section. You can also access your projects or create new projects with the **buttons in the header** as well.

4 - Machine Selection

Select your Cricut machine here, if you have more than one.

5 - Cricut Access

You can **view the latest Cricut Access projects** in this section.

6 - Ready-to-Make Projects

You'll find lots of inspiration by viewing the **ready-to-make project sections using various materials and techniques** in this section (Cricut keeps this fresh so you may see different section titles & projects).

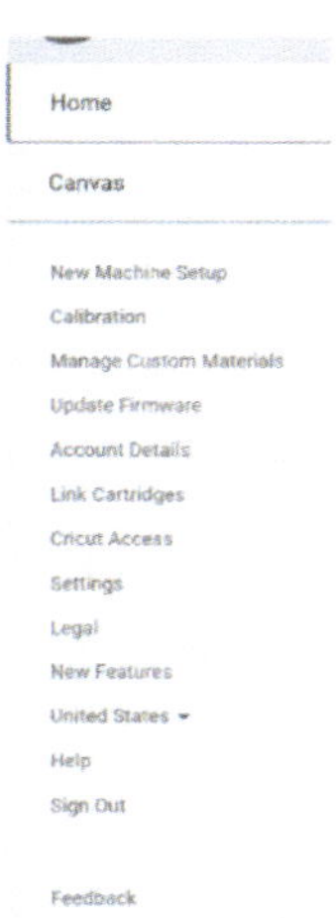

7 - Menu

Click the 3 lines icon at the top left in the header to view the menu, which includes important items like machine setup & calibration, managing materials, updating firmware, account details, link cartridges, Cricut access, settings, and more.

This sign indicates that these images/fonts/projects are included for free in the Cricut Access membership.

HOW TO OPEN AND START A NEW PROJECT

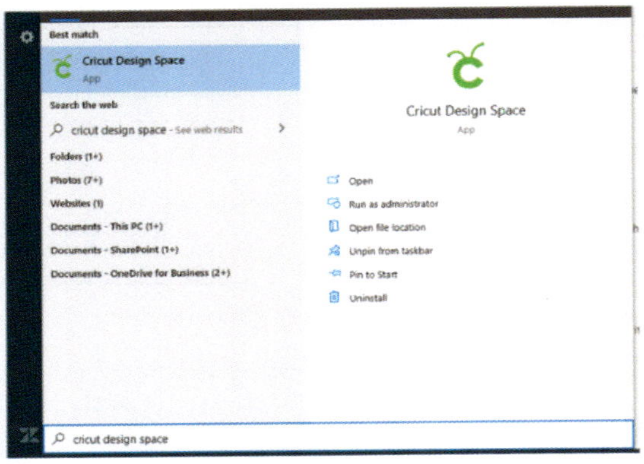

Step 1: Windows PC Users

Open Cricut Design Space by:

1. Double-clicking the shortcut icon on your desktop or single clicking the icon on your taskbar. - OR -
2. Selecting it from the start menu or searching the start menu for it.
3. If prompted, sign in with your Cricut ID.

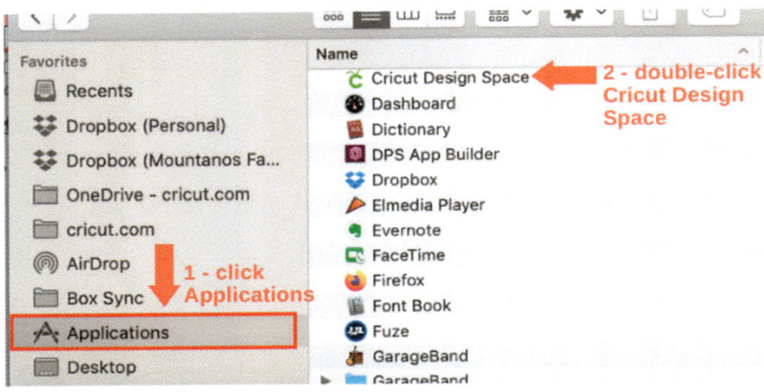

Step 1: Mac Users

Open Cricut Design Space by:

1. Opening the finder and selecting Applications.
2. Locating the Cricut Design Space application and double-clicking it.
3. If prompted, sign in with your Cricut ID.

Step 2

Click the New Project icon in the middle of the "My Projects" section **or the green New Project button** in the upper right corner (they both do the same thing).

Step 3

Now you have a new canvas, ready for you to add images, shapes, text, and other fun projects!

LEARN THE CANVAS LAYOUT

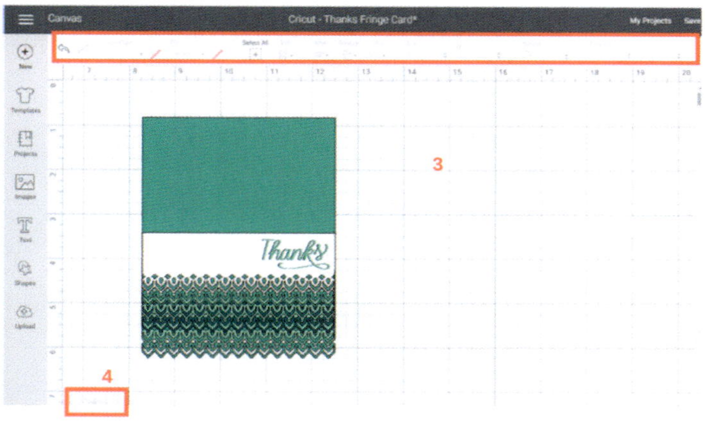

1 - Help

To get help at any time, **click on Help in the top menu bar** and then click Help from the dropdown menu. You'll be taken to the Cricut help website.

2 - Design Panel

The Design Panel on the far left is where you can **add images, shapes, text, open a new project, and much more**. See page 8 for more info.

3 - Edit Bar

The horizontal bar of functions along the top of the canvas. See page 9 for more.

4 - Zoom Box

To zoom in or out on an object, **use the small zoom box floating near the bottom left of the screen**. The plus button will zoom in, and the minus button will zoom out.

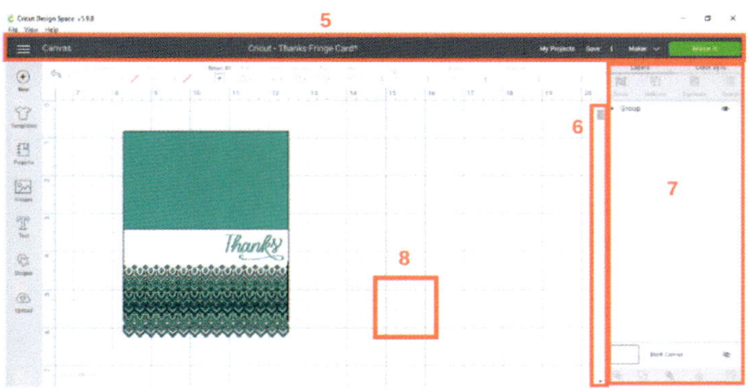

5 - Header

The Header consists of **canvas settings** on the far left, **the name of your project** in the center, access to your **existing saved projects**, a **save button**, **linked machine** (Explore, Maker or Joy), and the **Make It button**.

6 - Scroll Bars

You can find **scroll bars on the bottom and the right-hand side** of the canvas.

7 - Layers Panel

The Layers Panel features all the primary functions needed to edit any image, such as **Group, Ungroup, Duplicate, Delete, Slice, Weld, Attach, Flatten, and Contour**. See page 10 for more info.

8 - Margins

Every canvas consists of **1-inch margins**. These margins and grid match your Cricut mat and can be used as a guide for placement and design. The margins are marked on the left-hand side and top of the Canvas. Note: You can switch from imperial to metric settings if you wish.

Cricut Access Project: Thanks Fringe Card

DESIGN PANEL OVERVIEW

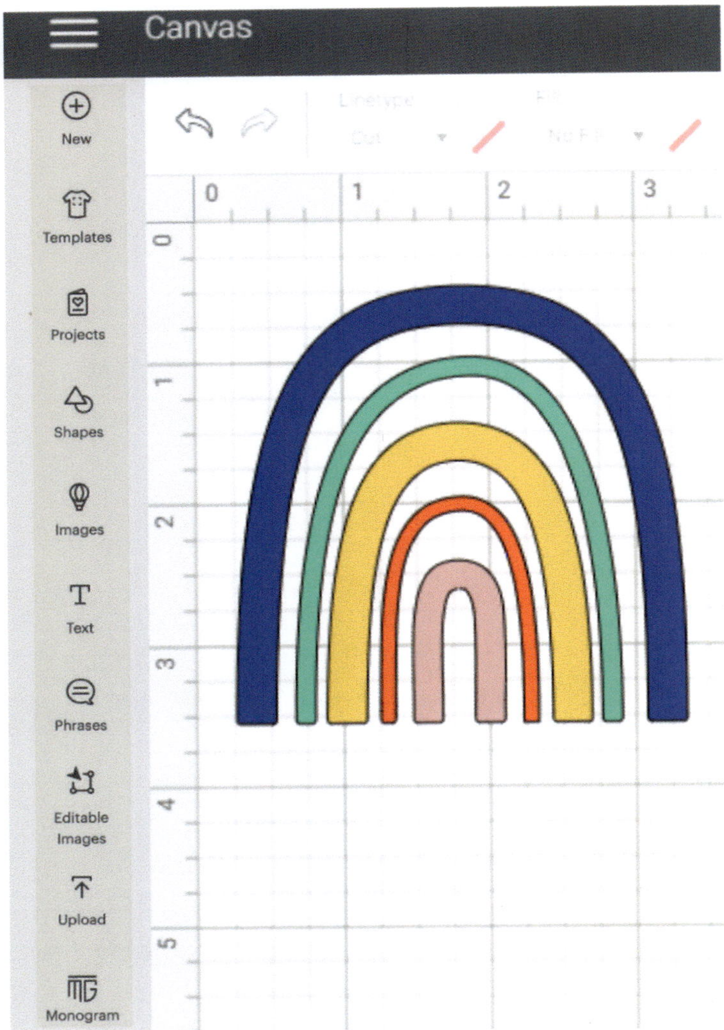

New

The New button **creates a new canvas**.

Templates

Templates are used **to help give you a size reference** and help you to visualize your project. To learn more about templates see page 44.

Projects

The Projects button **allows you to find professional ready-to-make crafts** with imagery and usually some instruction.

Images & Editable Images

When you click on Images, **you will find over 100,000 image designs**. This includes Cricut Access images (if you have a subscription) as well as images that you can purchase individually. To learn more about images see pages 46-60.

Editable Images are images that you can edit text, font, size, and colors.

Text

Text tool allows you to **type text, change your fonts, create curved text &** more. Learn more about text on pages 61-79.

Shapes

The Shapes button gives you **access to free basic shapes** for use in Design Space, such as circles, square, hexagons, and more.

Phrases

The Phrases button lets **access the large library of pre-designed Phrases** in Design Space.

Upload

The Upload button lets you **upload your own SVG images, JPEG or PNG printable images, and patterns**. There is no cost to upload your own designs.

Monogram Maker

Create Monogram projects easily when selecting from a variety of design options. Only Cricut Access subscribers can send to make however all users can try creating with the Monogram Maker.

Cricut Access Image: Rainbow #M143D7070

EDIT BAR OVERVIEW

Undo & Redo

Undo or Redo a **recent action**.

Operation

Linetype is essential in telling your Cricut what you want it to do. This is where you modify your images so Cricut knows if you want the image on your canvas to be **cut, scored, engraved, drawn, etc.** To learn more about linetypes see page 32-33.

Fill

You can **fill shapes and images with either a solid color or with a pattern**.

Select All / Deselect

You can either choose to select all your layers and elements or you can choose to deselect your selection.

Edit

Option to either **Cut, Copy or Paste** an element/layer.

Offset

Create larger or smaller layer of your design usually used as a shadow layer. Use with text, images, or a combination!

Align & Arrange

Arrange: Move the arrangement of the layers. You can move back/forward or send it all the way to the back/forward.

Align: A quick way to align or distribute your elements to keep things neat & tidy.

Flip

Flip your design **horizontally or vertically**

Size

Manually enter **exact measurements for width and height**. Click on the lock symbol to change the width or height independently from the other.

Rotate

Turn your design. You can **rotate it up to 360 degrees**.

Text

You will get an **additional edit bar when working with text** where you can choose the font, size, curve, alignment, etc.

Position

Tells you where your design is located on the canvas.

Cricut Access Image: Wale and Baby Silhouette #M14C7D0A7

LAYERS PANEL OVERVIEW

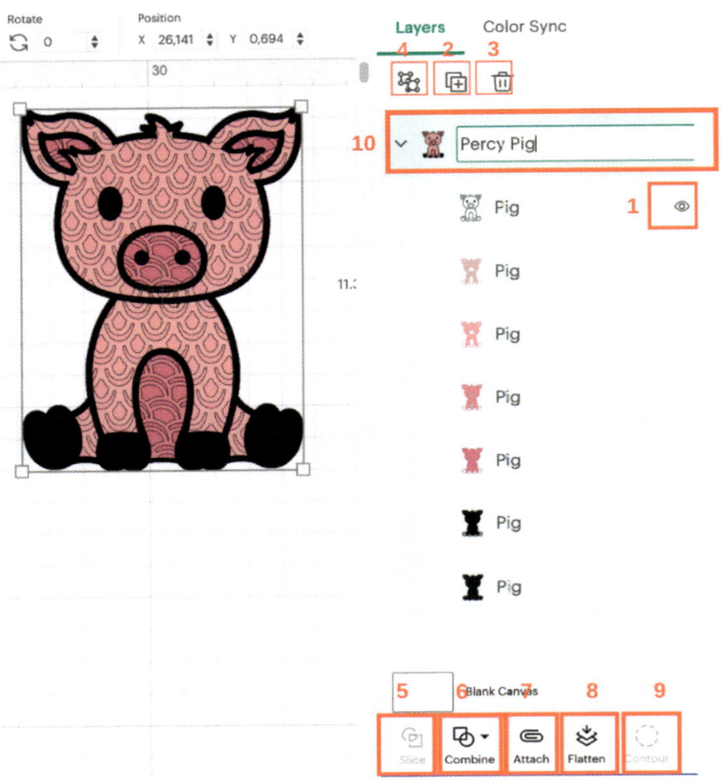

1 - Show/Hide (Eye Icon)

To hide an image or layer from your workspace without deleting it, click the Eye icon in the Layers Panel whenever any image / layer is selected. Click the eye icon again to show the image.

2 - Duplicate

To duplicate any element on the canvas, **select an element** and **click Duplicate** to make a copy of it.

3 - Delete

To delete any element on the canvas, **select an element** and **click Delete** to permanently delete it.

4 - Group & Ungroup

Group multiple layers, images, or text together so that they move and size together on the Canvas or ungroup them. For more on group & ungroup, see page 34.

5 - Slice

Split two overlapping layers into separate parts. For more on slice, see page 41.

6 - Combine

Previously known as Weld. **Use Combine to join multiple layers together to create one object, removing any overlapping cut lines.** For more on Combine and the different effects, see pages 40-42.

7 - Attach

Attach to hold your objects in position on the mat. For more on attach, see page 38.

8 - Flatten

Flatten turns any image into a printable image. For more on flatten, see page 37.

9 - Contour

Hide or unhide contour lines or cut paths on a layer. For more on contour, see page 42.

10 - Rename Layer

Rename the layer by **double-clicking on the layer, a text box will show so you can change the name by typing in your text.**

Cricut Access Image: Pig #M4162BB17

HOW TO FIND FREE IMAGES AND PATTERNS

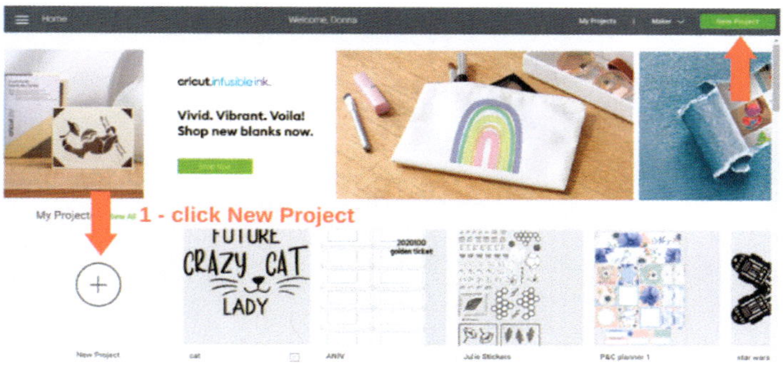

Step 1

Sign in to Design Space and **select New Project**.

You can find free images, patterns, fonts, and projects in Cricut Design Space.

Free Images

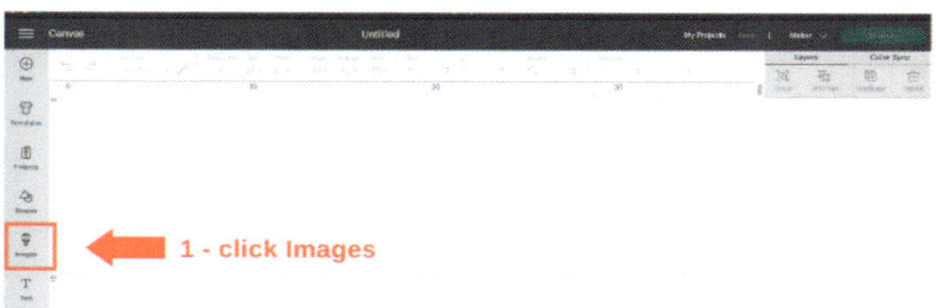

Step 1

Click Images on the design panel to the left of the Canvas.

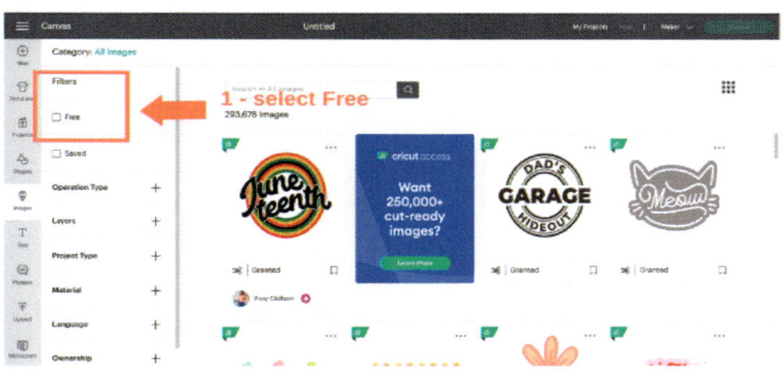

Step 2

Click on **Browse All Images**, then **click "Free" in the Filter menu** that pops up. This will display all the free Cricut images.

Free Patterns

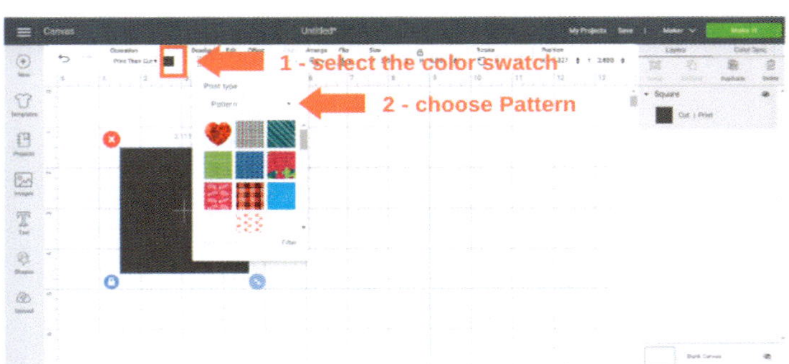

Step 1

Insert an image or text and **change the Operation type to Print Then Cut. Select the color swatch and choose Pattern** from the Print Type menu to see all the free patterns.

HOW TO FIND FREE FONTS AND PROJECTS

Free Fonts

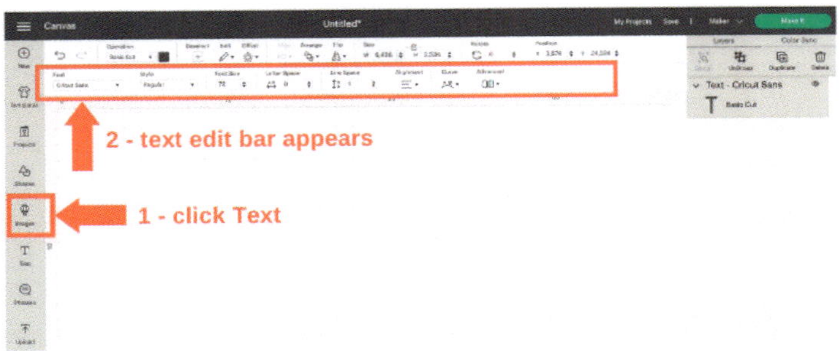

Step 1

Click Text on the design panel to the left of the Canvas. The Text Edit bar will appear at the top of the screen along with a blank text box on the canvas.

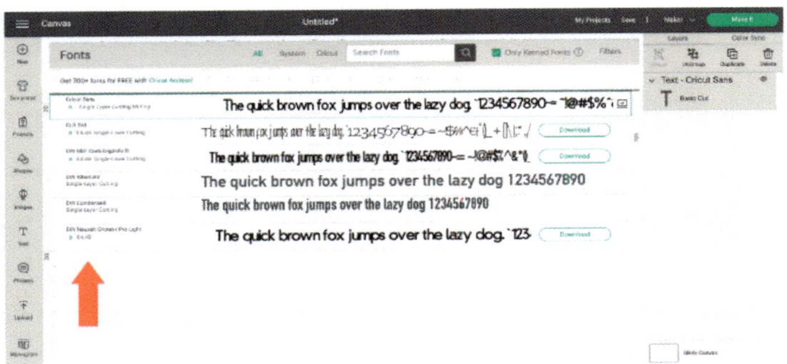

Step 2

Click on the Font drop-down menu. The fonts that you have installed on your computer or that are free will not have a price below the font name.

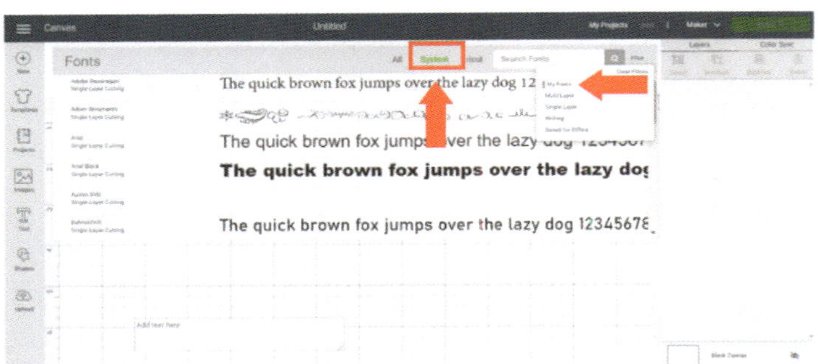

Step 3

You can also **select System at the top of the Font drop-down menu** to see all the fonts installed on your computer or select Filter from the top right to view them as well.

Free Projects

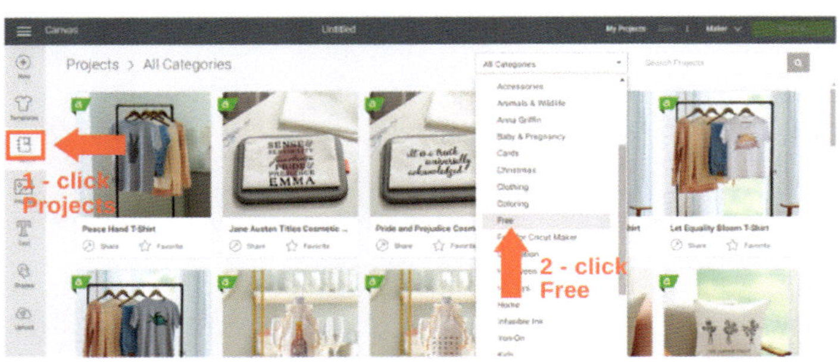

Step 1

Click Projects on the design panel to the left of the Canvas. **Select the dropdown menu at the top** and scroll down and **click on Free**.

LEARN THE CUT SCREEN PAGE LAYOUT

Cut Screen #1 Mat Settings

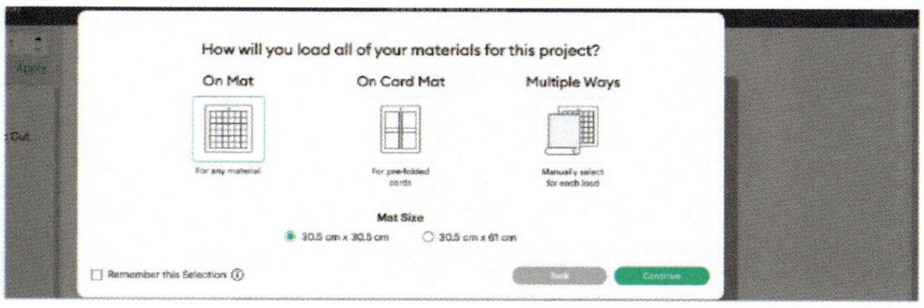

Step 1

Select which **cutting mat type and size** you will be using. **Click Continue.** Select Remember this Selection if you want this as the default for cutting.

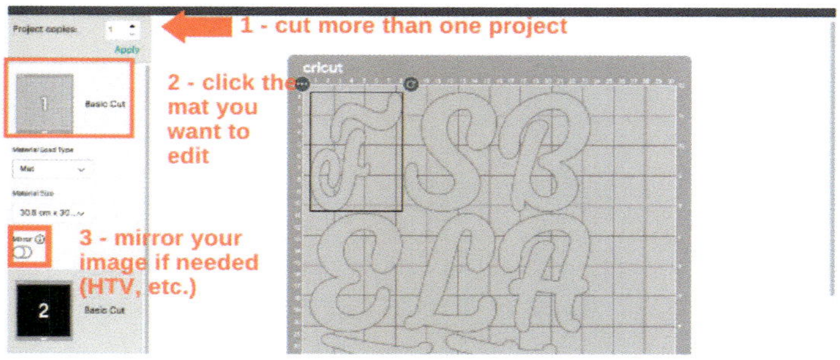

Step 2

Cut the project multiple times by **increasing the project copies**. **Click each mat image** to select it & make any changes. Mirror your image (use to cut HTV (Iron-On) by **clicking mirror** under each mat. You can also change the **Load Type**.

Step 3

Change the material size and mat load type that you're using. **Click material size dropdown and select the closest material size** or **load type to change the mat**. **Click Continue** when done.

Cut Screen #2 Material Settings

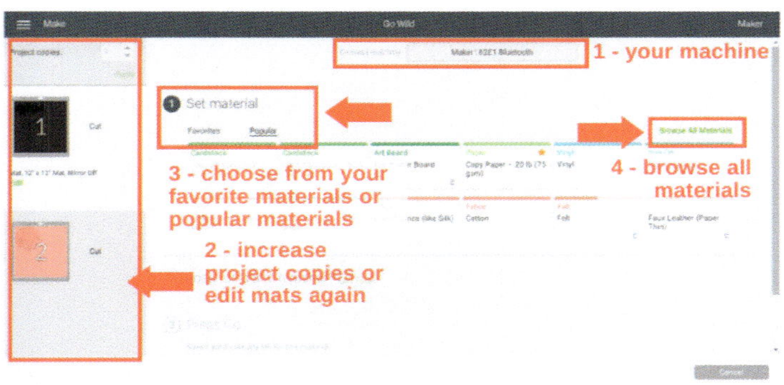

Step 1

If your Cricut is on and connected, it will automatically connect & show at the top. You can still **increase the number of times you cut this project** or **edit your mats** on the left. **Select your materials from your favorite or popular materials** in the tabs or **click Browse All Materials**.

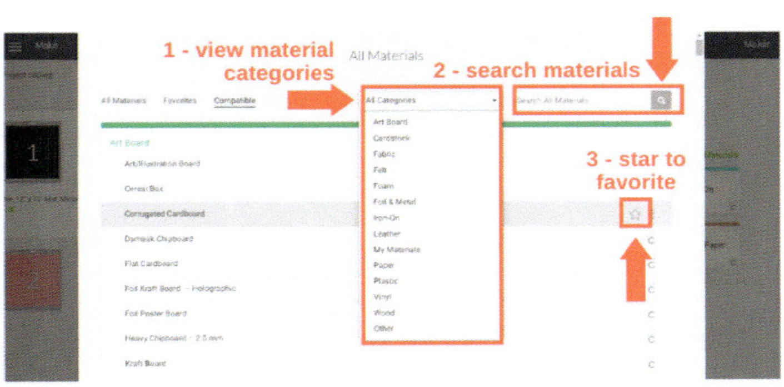

Step 2

You can **view materials by category with the dropdown menu**, **search for any material in the search bar**, and **use the star icon to favorite items** for faster access (will show up in the favorites tab next time).

LEARN THE CUT SCREEN PAGE LAYOUT

Cut Screen #3 Pressure Settings

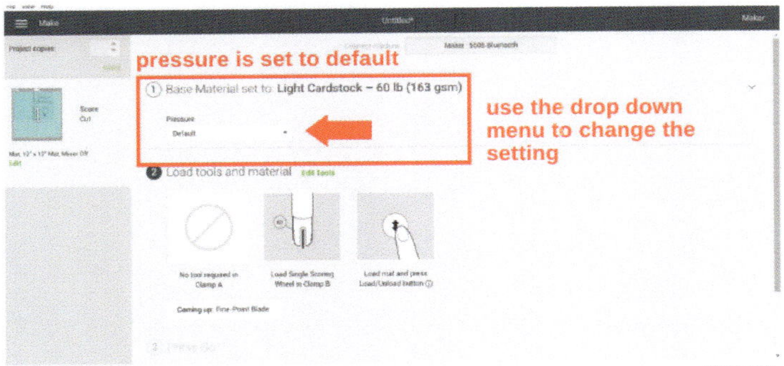

Step 1

Pressure refers to the force that the blade will apply to the material. **Your machine will automatically set the pressure** according to type of material you select. **The pressure will be set to default.**

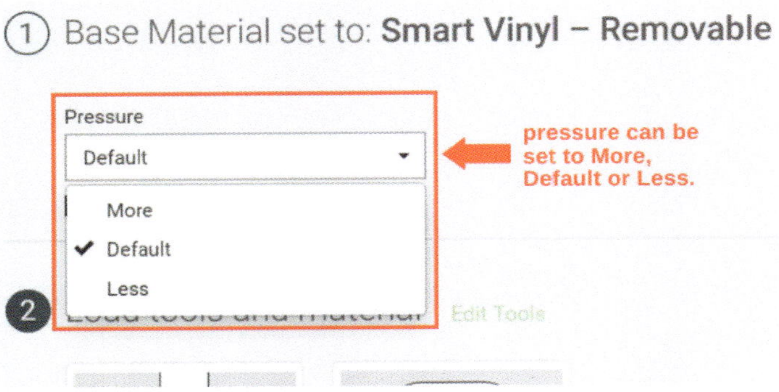

Step 2

You can **change the pressure to More or Less.**
Changing the setting is personal and can be due to simple trial and error. E.g. I like to cut my glitter materials with pressure set to More to get a deeper, cleaner cut.

Cut Screen #4 Tool Settings

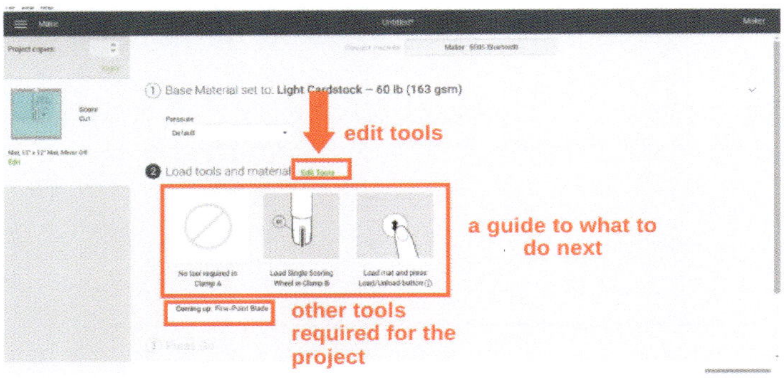

Step 1

Next Design Space will tell you to **load the tools and materials**. It might also have reminders here (e.g. place your iron-on vinyl shiny side down).
You can **change the tool selection** (if required) by clicking on **Edit Tools**.

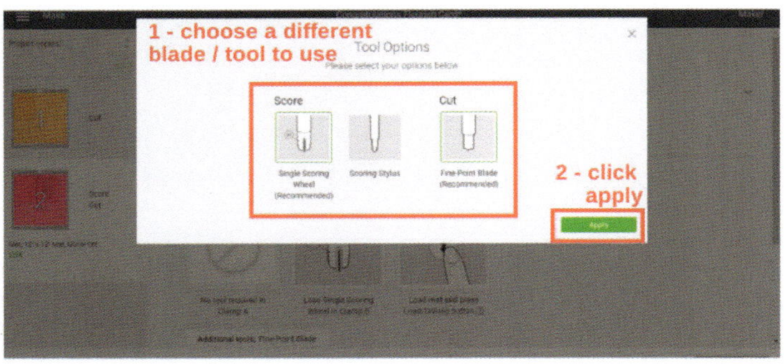

Step 2

You can edit tools. E.g. if you don't have a scoring wheel, you can edit the tools to tell the machine to use a scoring stylus instead.
Click on the tool you would like to use. Click apply, load up your mat and tools, and click Go.

HOW TO REPOSITION ITEMS ON MAT PREVIEW OR MOVE TO ANOTHER MAT

To Reposition Items on the Mat

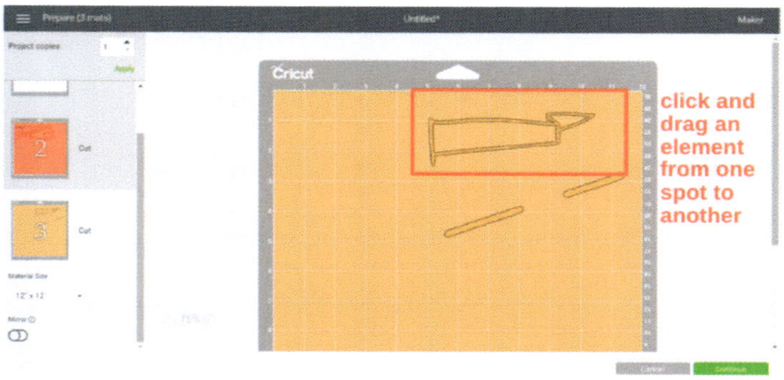

Step 1

You can move items around on the mat if you're using scrap material, for example, and want it to be in a specific spot on the mat. After you click "Make It", **click on the item you want to move and drag it to the position you want** using the grid as a guide.

To Move Items to Another Mat

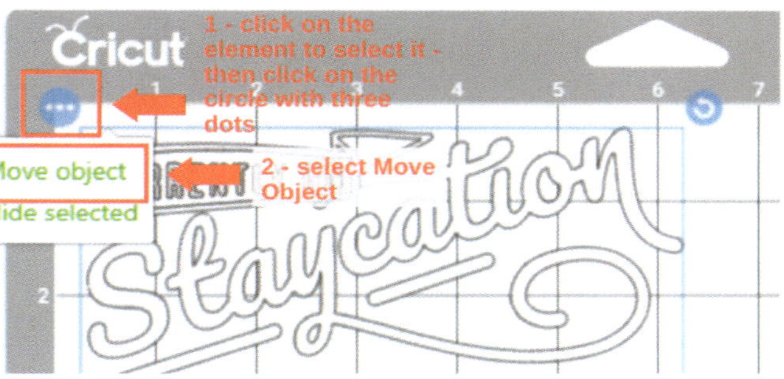

Step 1

You can move items to a different mat to cut them from a different color material if you want. After you click "Make It", **click on the element you want to move** and **click on the three dots and choose "Move Object."**

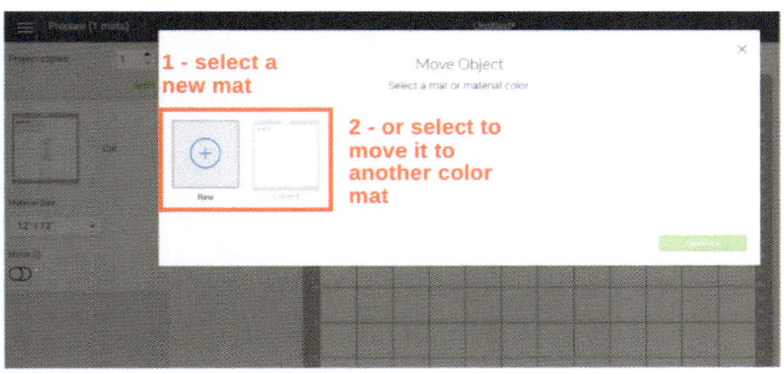

Step 2

Choose an existing mat you wish to move the item to or create a new one. If you create a new one, you will be asked to choose which color should represent the material you are cutting.

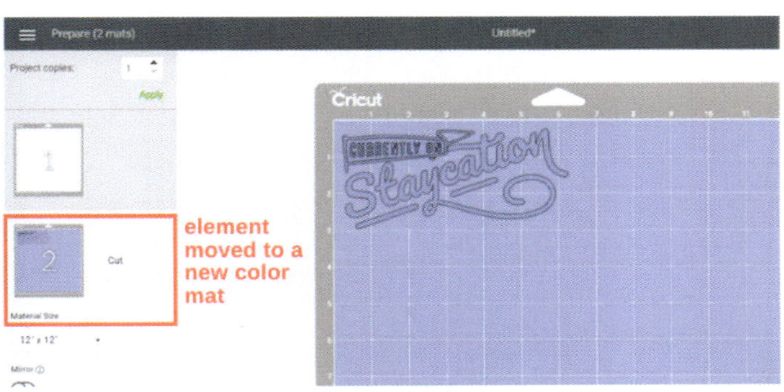

Step 3

Once you've chosen your mat or created a new one, **click the "Confirm" button** and your object will now appear on its new mat, and you can continue with your cut.

Cricut Access Image: Currently on Staycation #M16D115A0

MATERIAL SETTINGS AND PRESSURES

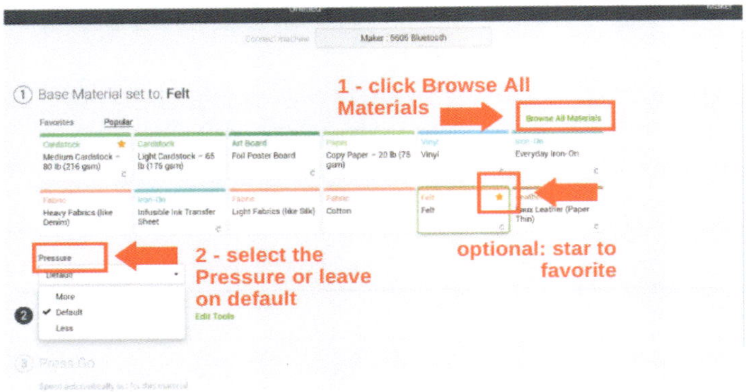

Step 1

Once you **choose Make It** from your canvas you will be asked to **set your Material and set Pressure**. If your material is not listed here **click Browse All Materials** and locate the one you're looking for. You can also **click on the star** to add a material to your Favorites.

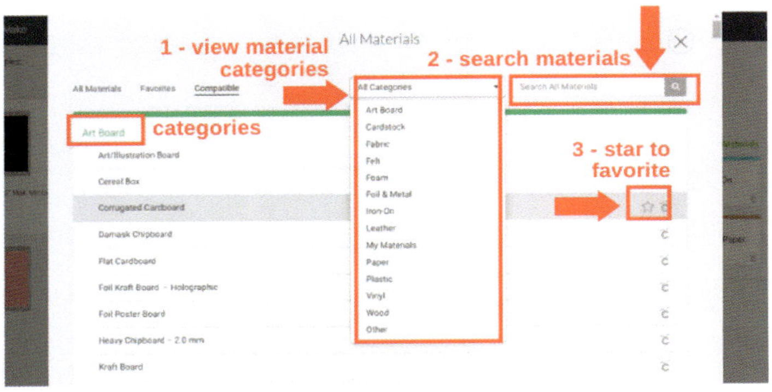

Step 2

Once you click on Browse All Materials, you will be able to **view materials by category with the dropdown menu**, search for any material in the search bar, and use the star icon to favorite items that you use often.

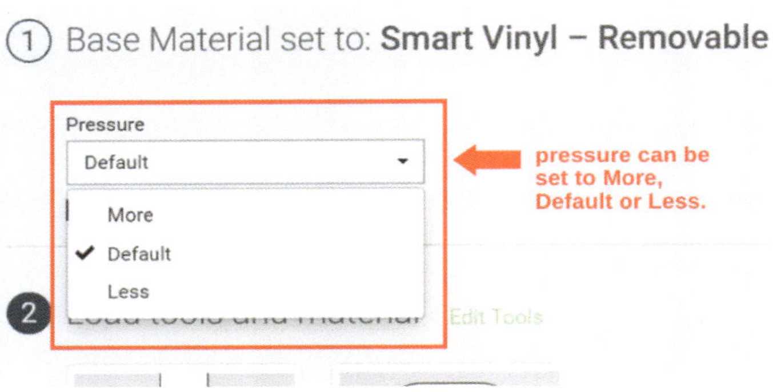

Step 3

Pressure: the force that the blade will apply to the material. **Your machine will automatically set the pressure to match the material you select.** The pressure will be on default, but you can change it to More (to increase) or Less (to decrease).

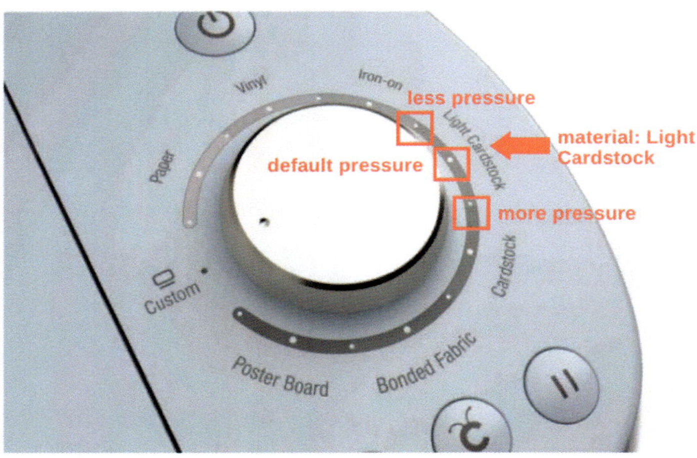

Explore Air Series

The **Explore Air series has a Smart Set dial** located on the machine. **Rotating the dial will set your material and pressure**. The bolded dot located in the center of each material option is the default pressure. The other two indicate less or more pressure. If you choose Custom you will be able to edit your options in Design Space.

HOW AND WHEN TO USE CUSTOM MATERIAL SETTINGS

You can change the default material settings according to your preference. You can change the individual tools, pressure and number of cuts for a specific material. You can also add a new material here which is handy when it is not listed in the material list.

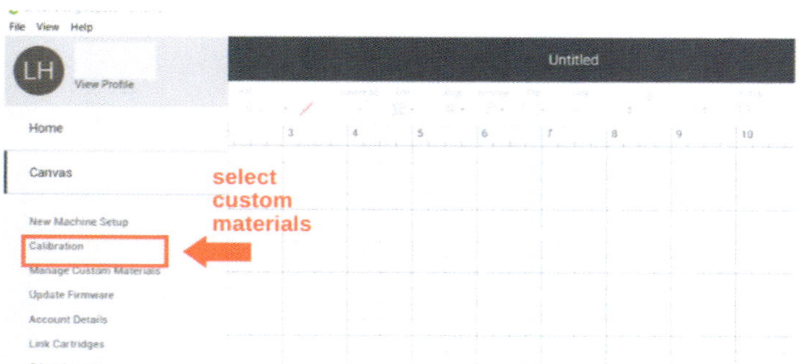

Step 1

In the upper left corner of your screen **click the three lines** to open the fly-out menu. Next click **Manage Custom Materials**. Select **Cricut Device**, once selected the Custom Materials list will appear.

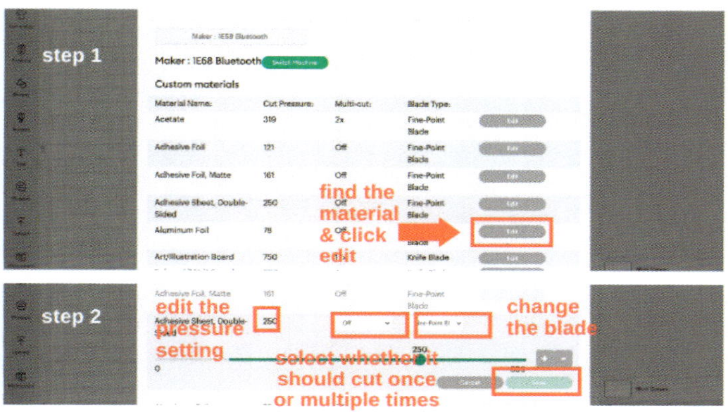

Change Existing Settings

Scroll through to the material you would like to adjust and **click Edit**. A box will open where you can **edit the Pressure, Blade and the Number of Cuts**. Click Save.

***Note:** You can not edit knife blade settings.

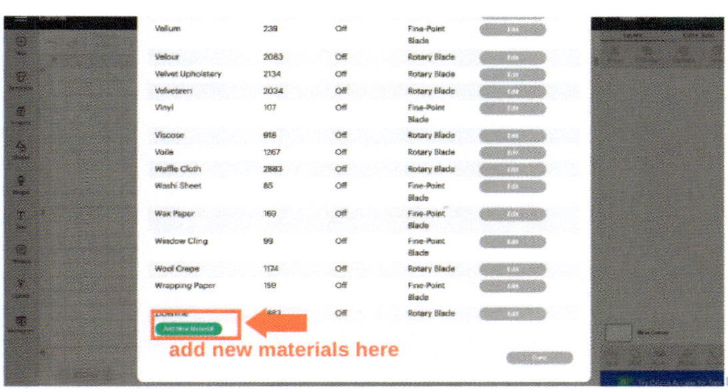

Add a New Material

Click Add New Material. Name your material and click Save. Next create the **settings** (pressure, blade and number of cuts) **for your new material**.

***Note:** You might have to do test runs to find the best settings to use.

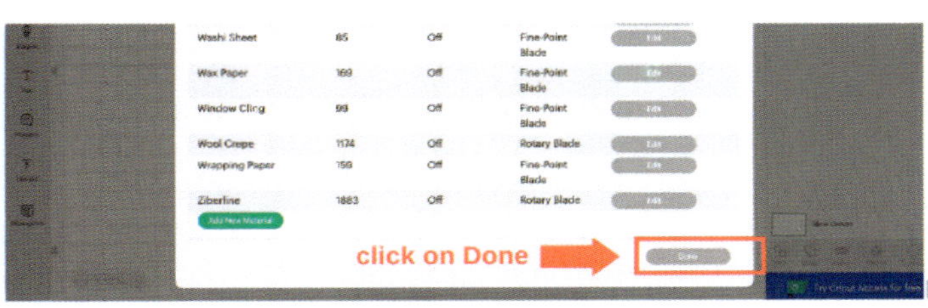

Step 3

When you're **finished editing** your materials you can scroll to the bottom and **click Done**.

HOW TO FAVORITE THE MATERIALS YOU USE MOST OFTEN

Note: Setting your favorite material eliminates the need to search for it when you get to the cut screen. Which means you can work faster and more efficiently.

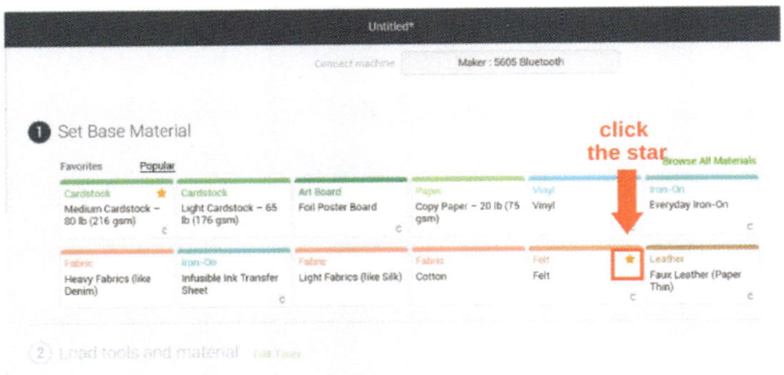

Step 1

On the Cut Screen, if your favorite material is one of the twelve that appear in the most popular list, you can hover over it and click the Star here and it will turn yellow and be immediately added to your favorites.

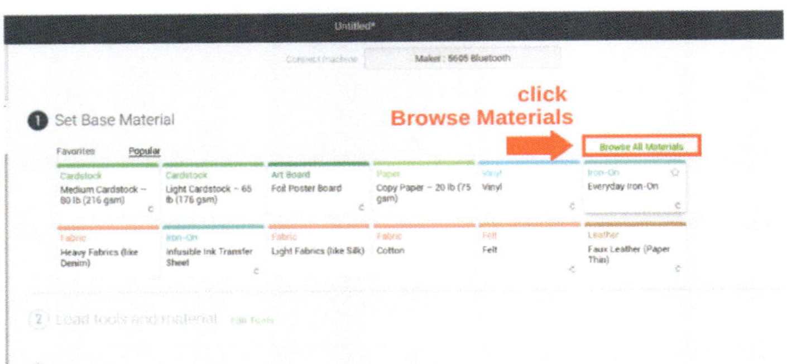

Step 2

If it's not one of the popular materials, simply **click Browse All Materials** and a list of all the available materials will appear.

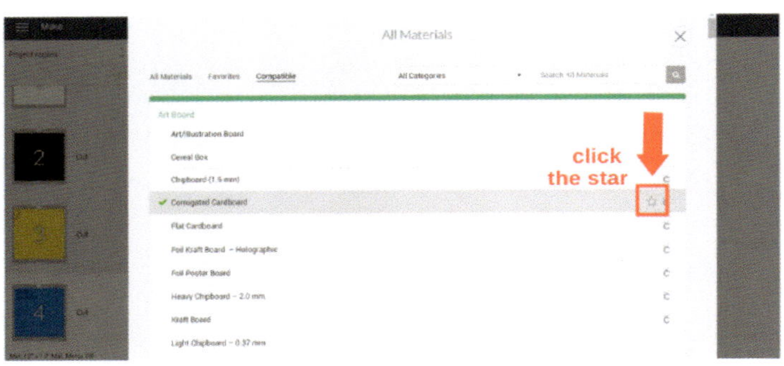

Step 3

Either scroll through the material options or use the search bar to find the material you're looking for. Once found, hover over it and **click the Star** and it will turn yellow and be added to your favorites.

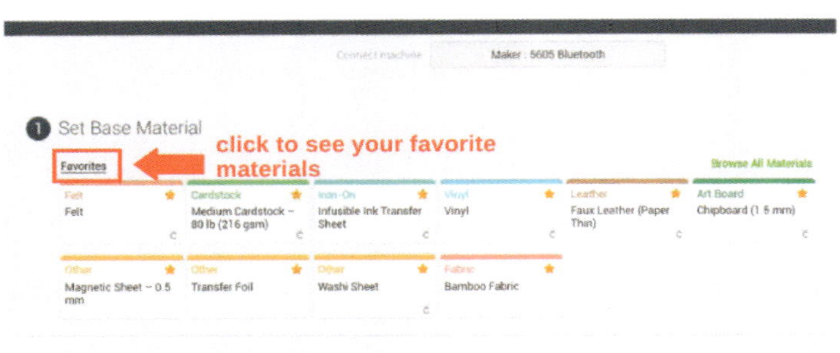

Step 4

After you set your favorite materials, every time you get to the Cut Screen, your Base Materials will now default to your favorites instead of the popular ones.

HOW TO SAVE YOUR WORK AND VIEW SAVED PROJECTS

Step 1

Once you have created your project, you will need to save it so you can open it again later if you want. **Click Save** in the top bar. You can tell if something is unsaved if an asterisk * appears next to the name at the top of the window.

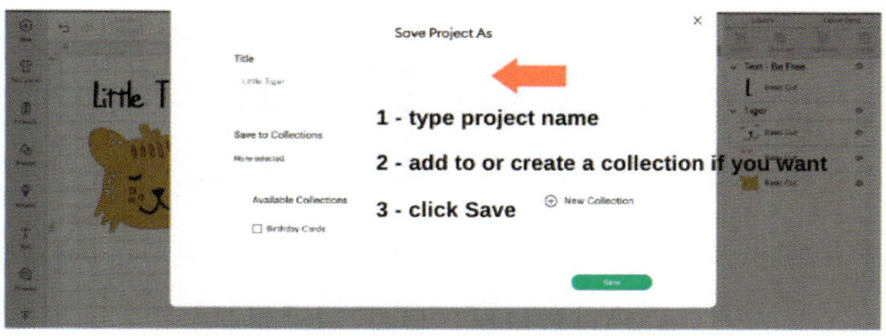

Step 2

Type a name for your project, decide if you want to add it to a collection or create a new collection and **click Save**. Wait while Cricut saves your project.

Step 3

Once saved, **a blue confirmation box will flash near the top of your screen** and the new name will appear at the top of the window.

Cricut Access Image: Tiger #M144644E8
Cricut font shown: Be Free

To View Your Projects

Step 1

To view your Saved Projects, **click the My Projects link** in the top right corner of your window, or click the Projects icon on the left side of the window and select "My Projects" from the Projects drop-down menu.

HOW TO SAVE PROJECTS FOR OFFLINE

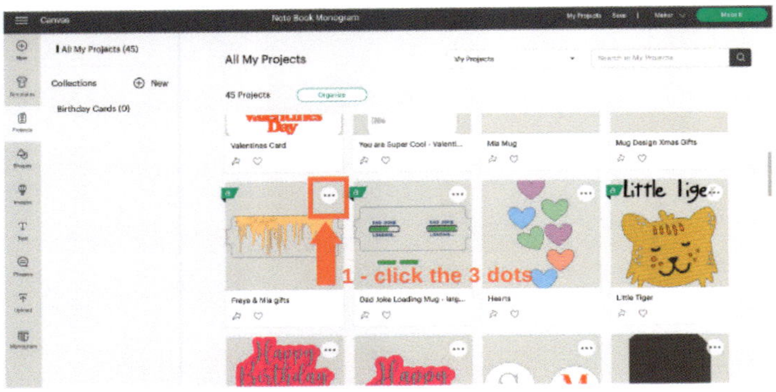

Step 1

Save your work as described on page 8. **Click on My Projects**, find the project you just saved, and **click the three dots** at the top right corner of the project.

Step 2

In the panel that appears, **click Save for Offline**.

Step 3

Once saved for offline successfully, **a blue confirmation box will flash near the top of your screen** and a checkmark appears by the project.

Notes

- There is currently no way to batch save all of your projects for offline. You must click each one and select "Save for Offline" individually.
- If you are working offline, the next time you go online a pop-up will appear asking you to select a version to keep (the offline version or the online version).
- Any images you have in a project from Cricut Access will expire after 30 days if you do not go online at all during those 30 days (even if you have monthly access). So be sure to set a reminder to go online at least once every 30 days.
- You cannot upload anything new while offline, so be sure to save all images you want in a project / canvas before going offline.

WORKING OFFLINE IN DESIGN SPACE

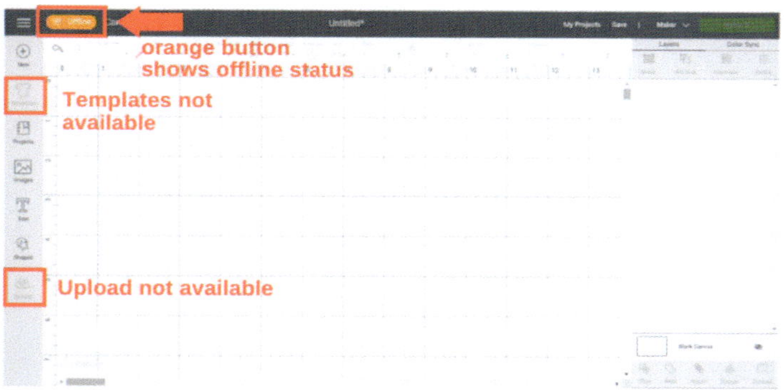

Note

Cricut made it possible for Design Space to be used offline, which is perfect when you are not connected to the internet. While many of the tools are the same, there are a few differences to be aware of when cutting offline.

- When offline, an orange button at the top will notify you that you're working offline.
- The Templates tool will not be available.
- The Upload tool will not be available.

Saving Images for Offline Work

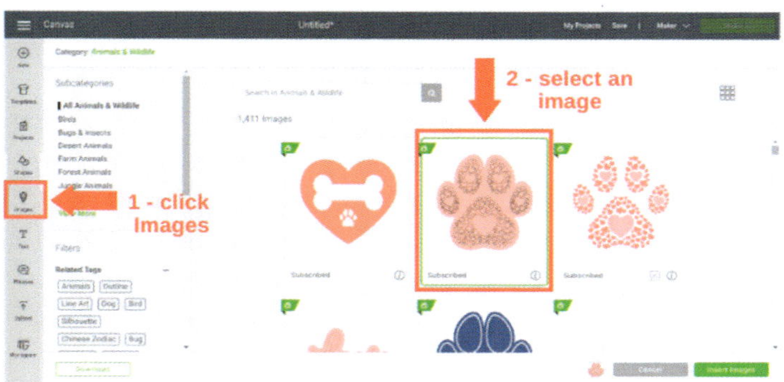

Step 1

Click the Images button and find an image you want to work with offline.

Select an image by clicking on it (a green box will appear around the image to show it's selected).

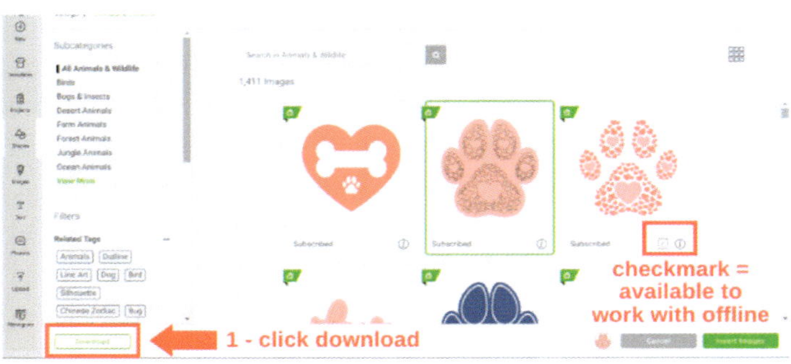

Step 2

While the image is selected, **click the Download button** in the far left corner.

Once downloaded **a small checkmark will appear under your image** to show that it is available to be edited and cut offline.

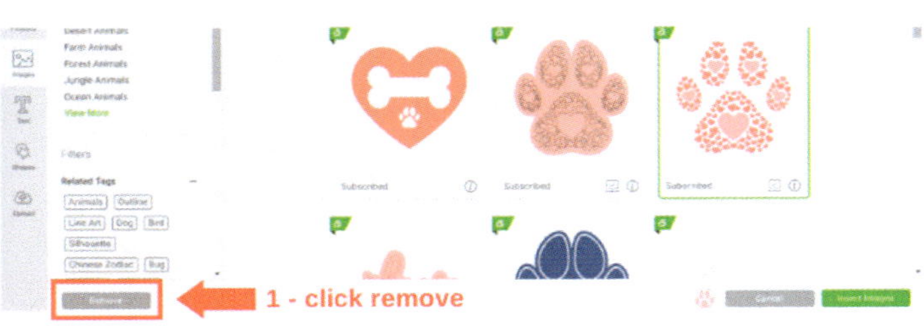

Step 3

You can remove an image you previously downloaded by **selecting it and clicking the remove button** in the far left corner.

WORKING OFFLINE IN DESIGN SPACE

Saving Fonts for Offline Work

Note

- System fonts are already stored on your computer, so they do not need to be downloaded.

Step 1

Click the Text button and **type any text on your screen** (it doesn't matter what font you use to type).

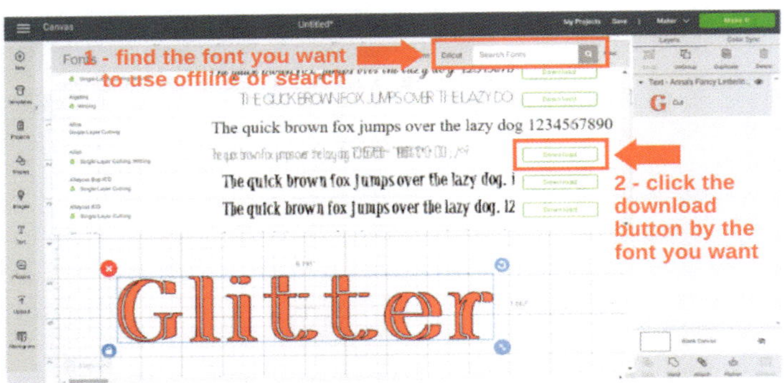

Step 2

Open the font selection menu in the text edit bar and scroll to the font you want to use offline (or search by name in the search box). **Click the Download button** beside the font you want to use offline.

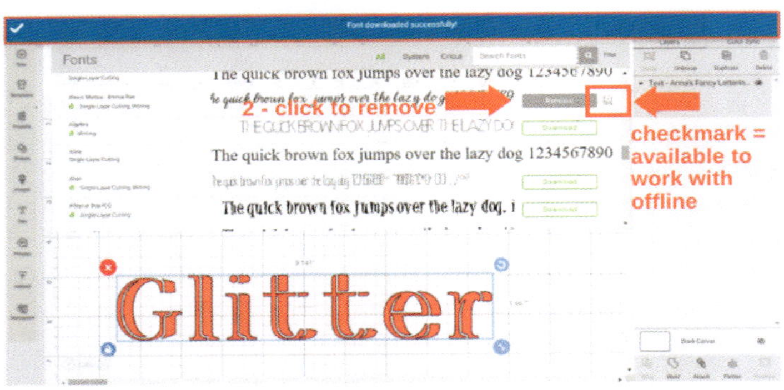

Cricut Font Shown: Anna's Fancy Lettering - Carson

Step 3

Once clicked, a blue success message appears at the top of the canvas and **a checkmark will appear to confirm** that it is saved for offline use.

You can remove a font you previously downloaded by **clicking the remove button beside the font.**

Saving Projects for Offline Work

For full step-by-step instructions, see page 20.

HOW TO SHARE LINKS TO PROJECTS

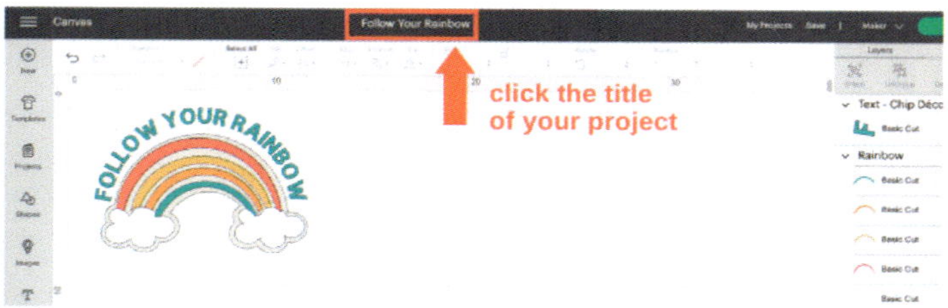

Step 1

Once you have saved your project, click the Title of your project in the Header bar of your canvas.

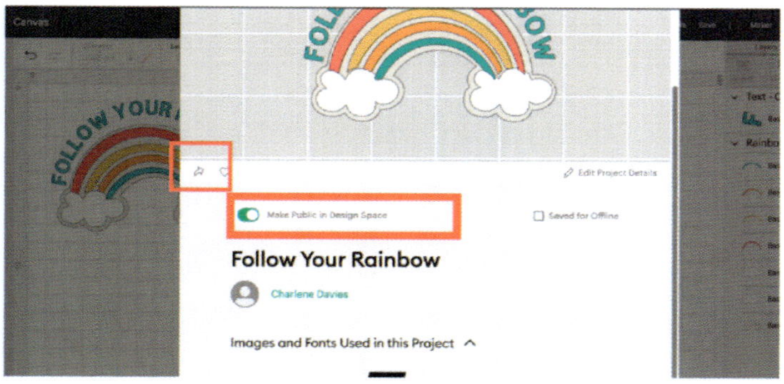

Step 2

If you would like your project visible to users of Design Space, click on Make Public in Design Space. Agree to Cricut T&C's.

In the pop-up window, **click the curved arrow.**

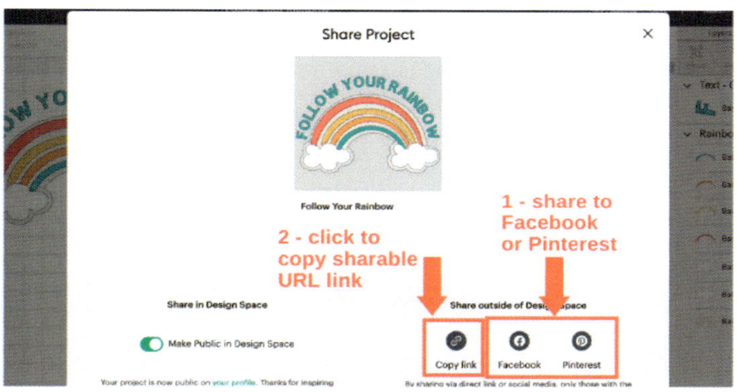

Step 3

A pop-up window will show links to **share to Facebook or Pinterest.** You can also **click on Copy Project Link.** After you click it, it will be in your clipboard, so you can open an email and **paste the link** in (right click & paste or use the shortcut CTRL + V on PC or CMD + V on Mac).

Sharing Projects from Blank Canvas Option

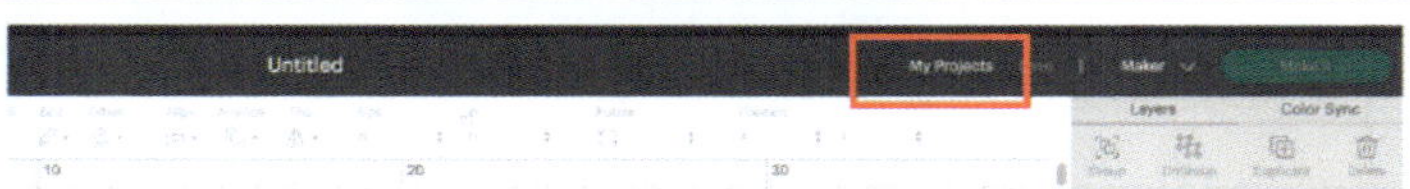

Step 1

If you have a blank canvas, click on **My Projects** (as per steps on page 19 to view your projects).

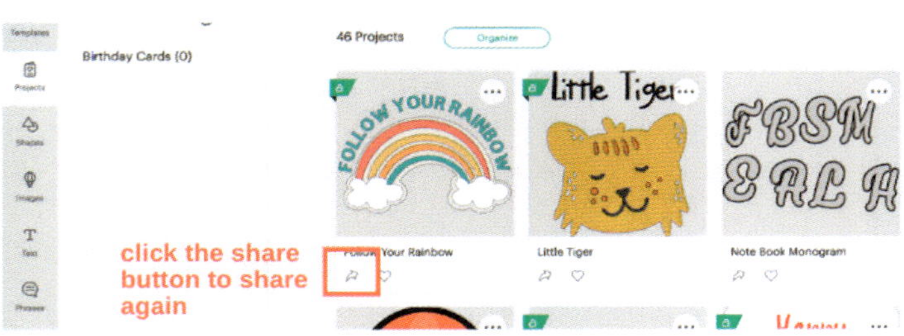

Step 2

Click on the **curved arrow to share** your project and follow the step 3 above to select how you wish to share your project.

Cricut Font Shown: Chip Decor - Chipboard *Cricut Access Image:* Rainbow #MB66F2E5

HOW TO CALIBRATE YOUR MACHINE

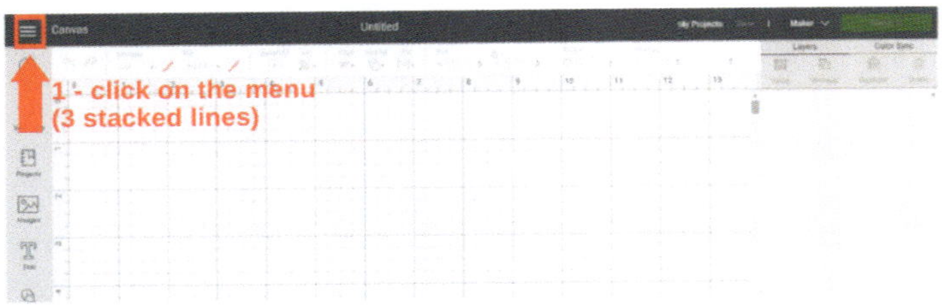

Step 1

Open the Account menu by clicking the icon (three stacked lines in the upper left corner).

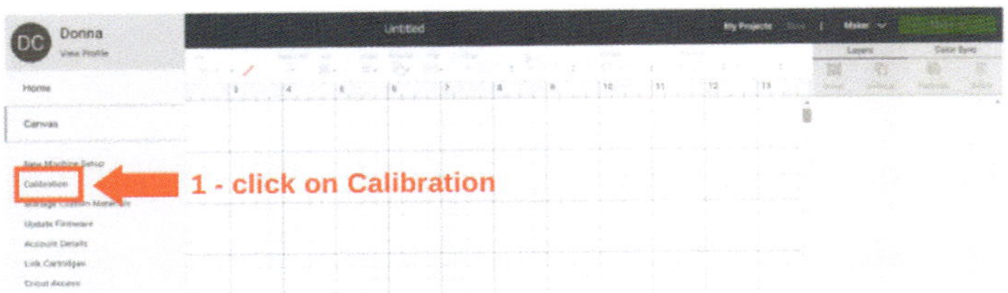

Step 2

Click on Calibration in the menu that appears.

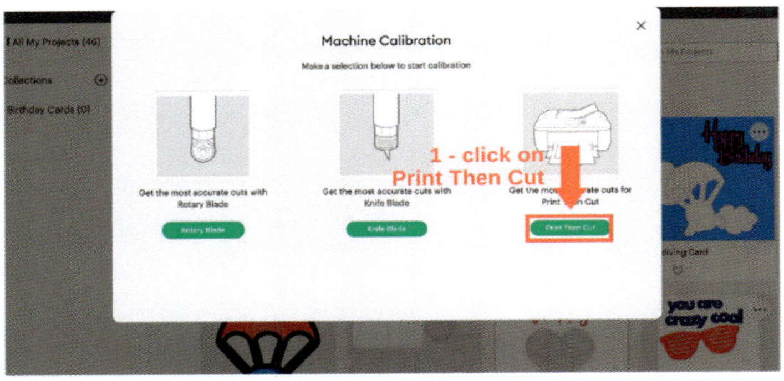

Step 3

In the pop-up window that appears, you can calibrate for different tools. **Select the Print Then Cut button** for this example.

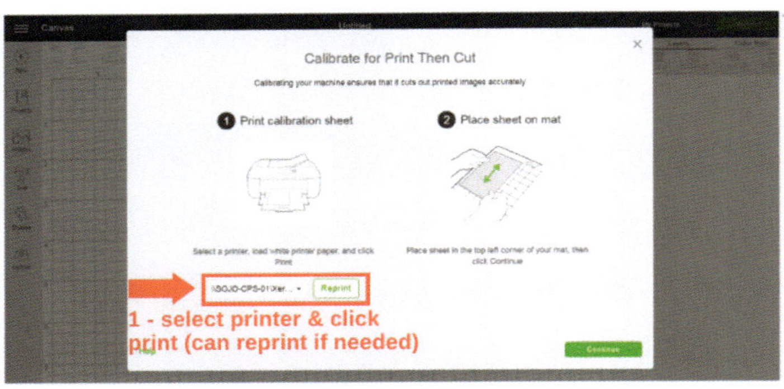

Step 4

Select the printer you would like to use, then **click Print. Place the printed calibration sheet on your mat,** positioning it in the top left corner of the mat. **Click Continue**.

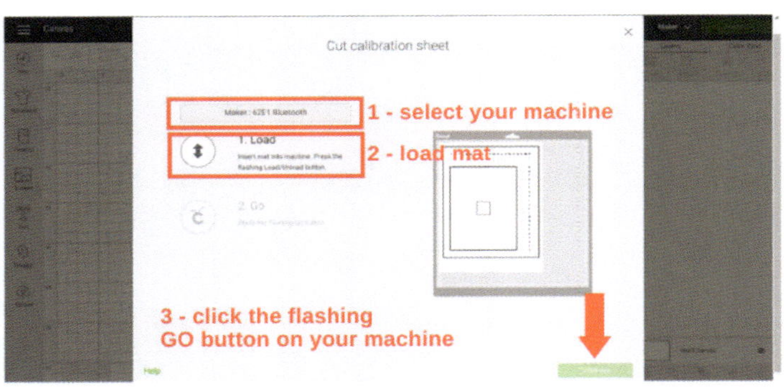

Step 5

Select your machine from the drop-down menu, **load the mat**, and **press the flashing Go button.**

HOW TO CALIBRATE YOUR MACHINE

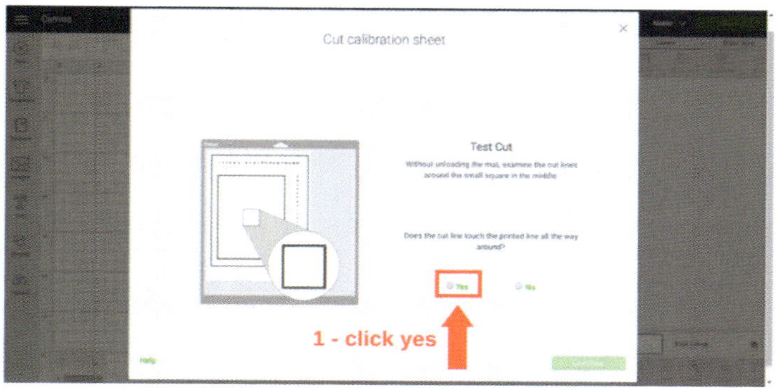

Step 6

Your machine will scan the sheet for calibration marks then cut around the small square near the center of the sheet. **Without unloading the mat, look at the cut** to see if the cut touches the printed line all the way around. **If it does, select Yes in Design Space, then Continue.**

<u>NOTE:</u> **If you select No**, Design Space will proceed to the next step in an effort to get the cut closer to the line. Once that is complete, you will be guided through the calibration once more to fine-tune it.

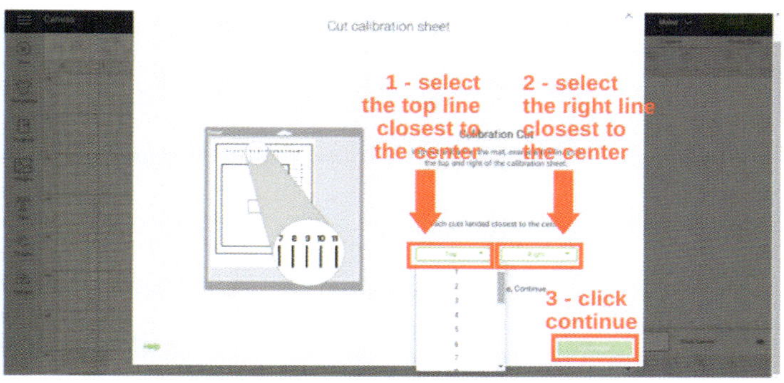

Step 7

The machine will begin the calibration cuts along the top and side of the page. Once done, **without unloading the mat, look closely at the lines along the top and side of the page.** Some will not touch the printed lines, and others will. **Select the Top then Right dropdowns to indicate the line number or letter with cuts closest to the center of the line.** When you are done, **click Continue**.

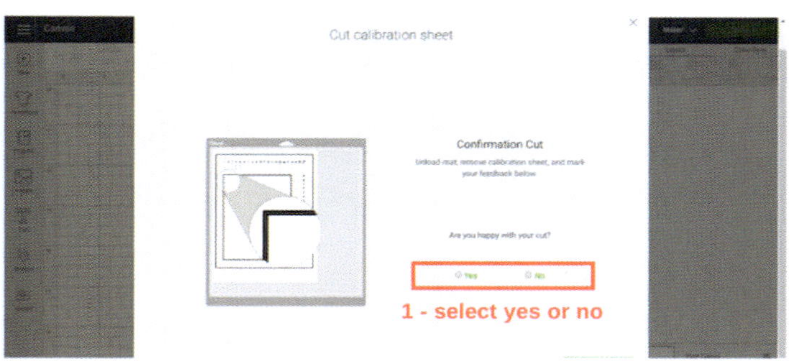

Step 8

The machine will then perform a confirmation cut around the large rectangle. When it is done, **unload the mat, remove the calibration sheet and respond to the final question.**

- If you are happy with the cut, **select Yes**, then Continue to proceed to the final calibration screen.
- If you **select No**, you will be guided through the calibration process again to refine it.

When finished, **click Save & Close to save your calibration settings.**

HOW TO LINK CARTRIDGES

If you had an older Cricut machine that used cartridges, you can still use them with Cricut Explore and Maker in Design Space. To link them you will need to use either your Cricut Explore machine or a Cartridge Adapter.

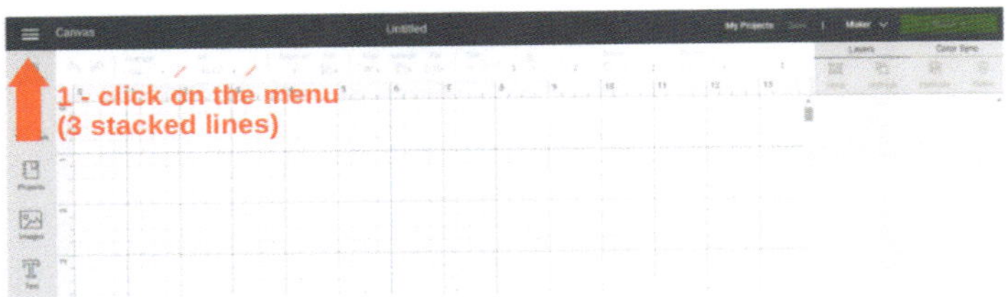

Step 1

Open the Account menu by clicking the icon (three stacked lines in the upper left corner).

Step 2

Click on Link Cartridges in the menu that appears.

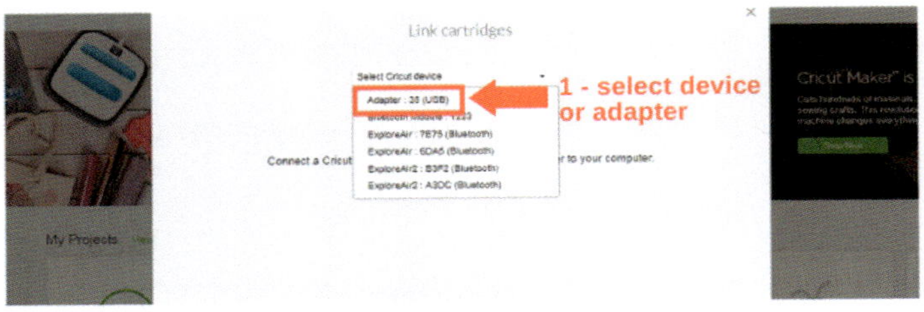

Step 3

Select your device from the drop-down menu. Cartridge adapters will show up in the list as Adapter.

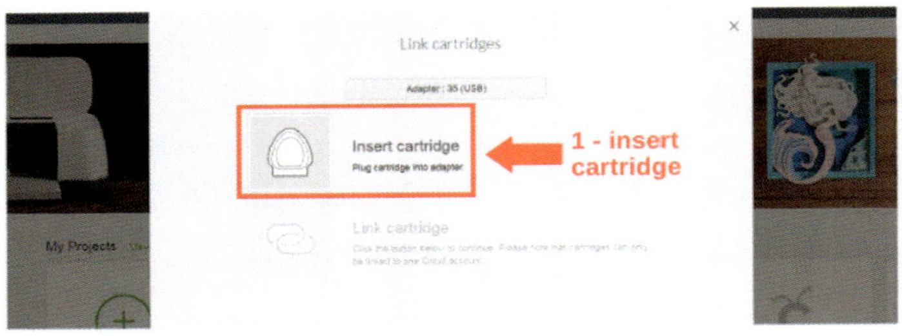

Step 4

When instructed, **insert the cartridge** into the Explore cartridge port or plug your cartridge into the adapter. Design Space will detect the cartridge.

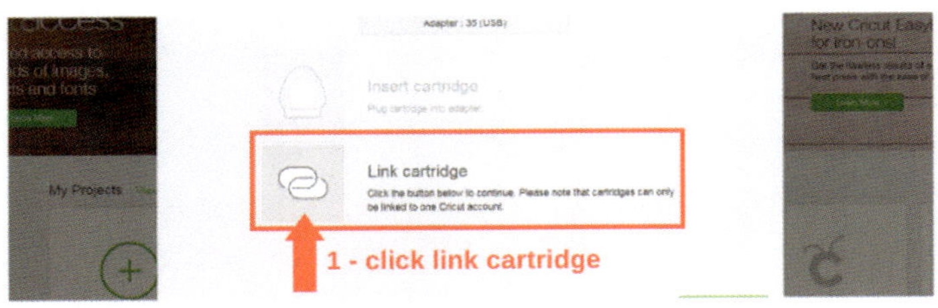

Step 5

When the cartridge has been detected, **click the Link Cartridge button** to initiate the linking process.

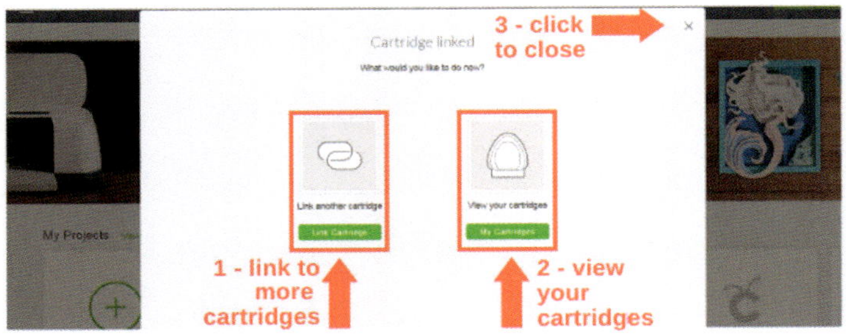

Step 6

Once complete, **remove the cartridge.** You can **link other cartridges, view your cartridges,** or click the X in the upper right corner to **return to Home or Canvas.**

HOW TO GET RID OF THE GRID LINES ON THE CANVAS

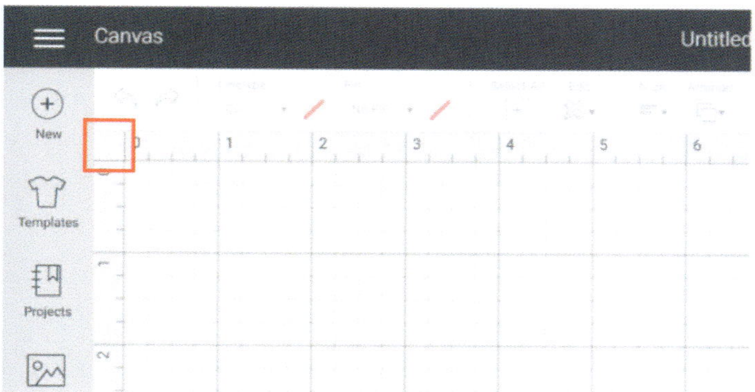

Note

The square in the top left corner of your canvas controls the grid lines. It is grey and unlabeled. You may want to take a screenshot at some point so removing the grid lines makes it nice and clean or you may have a busy design that's easier to see with less grid lines.

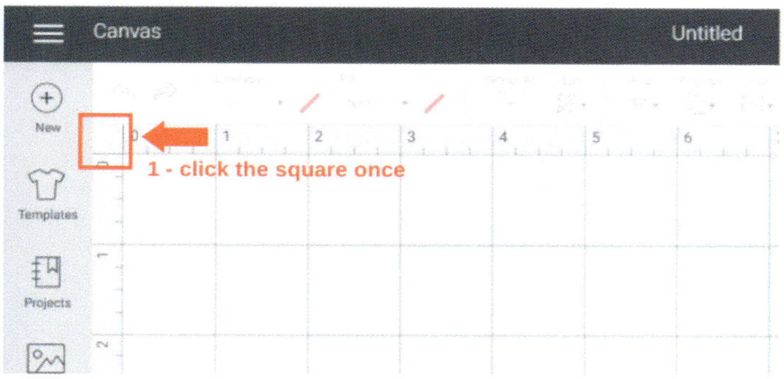

Step 1

Click on the square in the top left corner of your canvas once and the grid lines at each quarter of an inch will disappear, leaving just the lines at each inch.

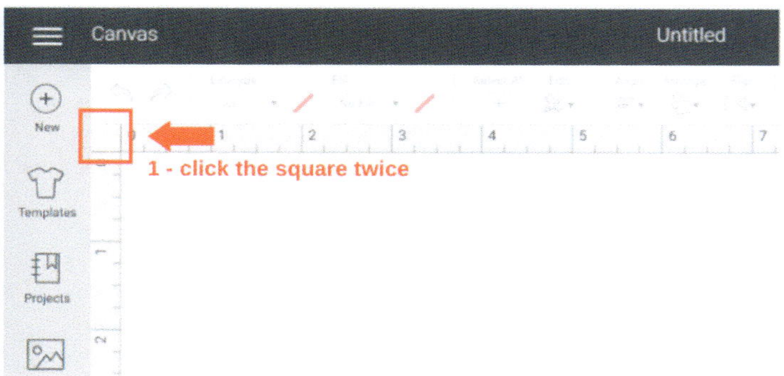

Step 2

Click on the square in the top left corner of your canvas twice and all the grid lines will disappear.

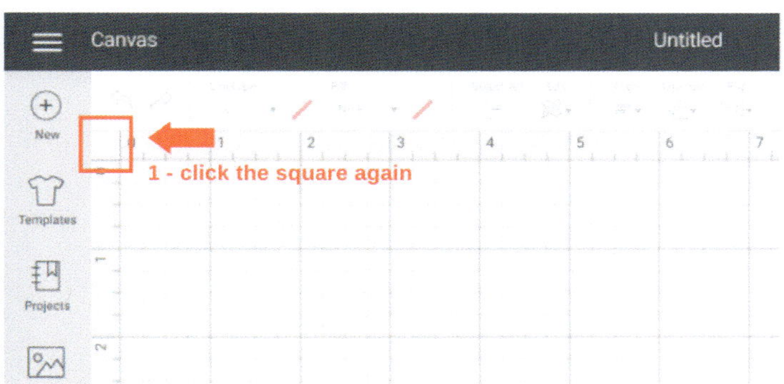

Step 3

Click on the square in the top left corner of your canvas again and all the grid lines will return to normal.

HOW TO HAVE TWO WINDOWS OPEN: CREATE ON ONE & CUT ON OTHER

If you have several projects you want to work on but you know that one may take a long time to cut since it's very complex, you don't have to just wait for it to finish. You can actually open a new window in Cricut Design Space so you can start your first project and then design your second project while the first is running through your machine.

Step 1

Create your first project.

Cricut Access Project: Anna's Lovely Layers II Lace Medallion Card

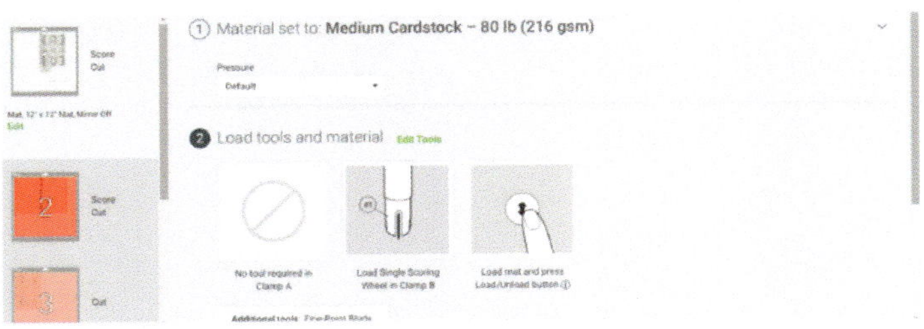

Step 2

Start setting up your first project to cut on your machine.

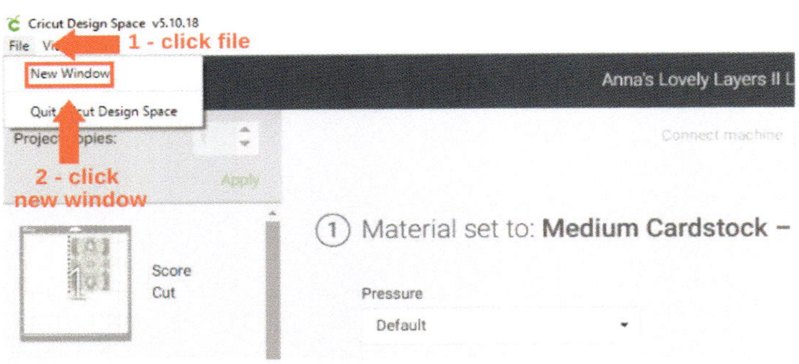

Step 3

Once you load your mat and click the Go button to start cutting your first project, **click on File in the top bar** then **click New Window.**

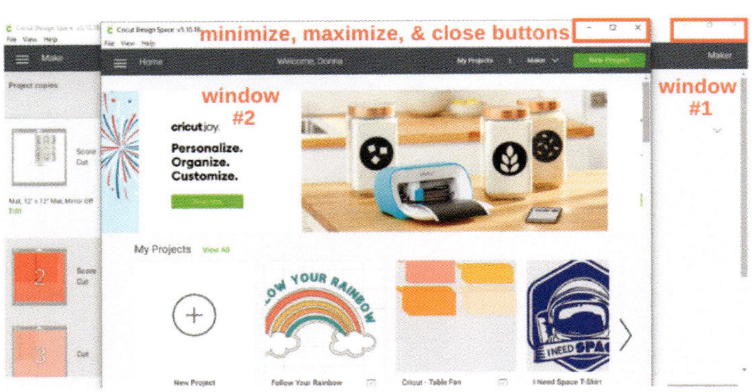

Step 4

A new window of Cricut Design Space will open on top of the first one so you can start designing another project while the first one finishes. **Use the minimize, maximize, or close buttons** in the upper right corner to switch between windows.

HOW TO UPDATE YOUR SOFTWARE AND CUTTING MACHINE FIRMWARE

Updating Cricut Design Space

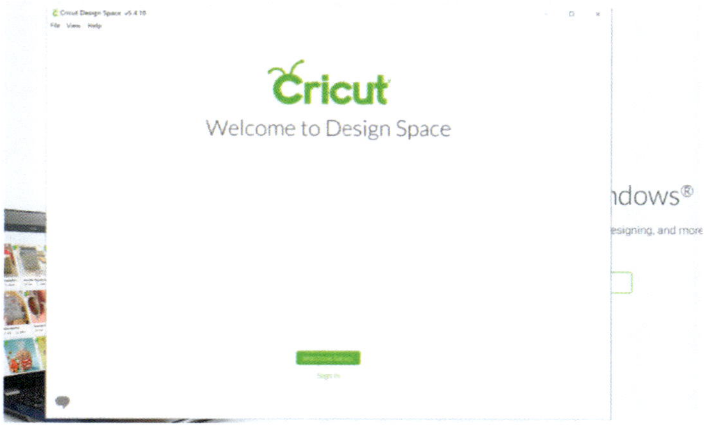

Step 1

Cricut Design Space should automatically update, however if you receive an alert to manually update, **quit / exit the application**.

Go to https://design.cricut.com/, sign in to your account, and **download & install the desktop application.**

Updating Your Machine Firmware

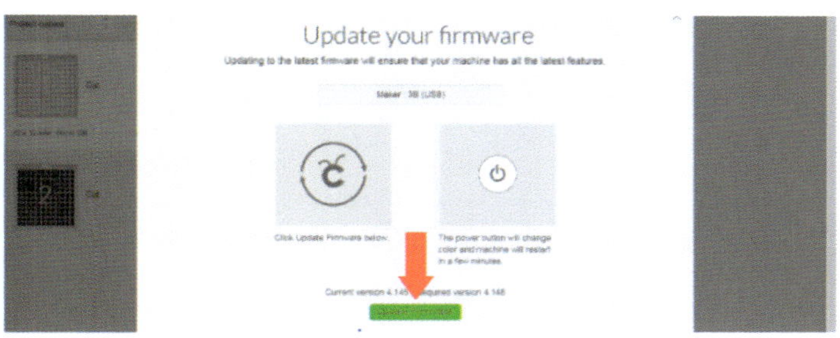

Step 1

You will receive an alert when a firmware update is necessary. In the window that pops up, **click Update Firmware** to proceed.

Step 2

The firmware update process will begin. A progress bar will appear on the screen and **your machine's power button will turn red (if connected via USB) or purple (if connected via Bluetooth)**, indicating that an update is in progress.

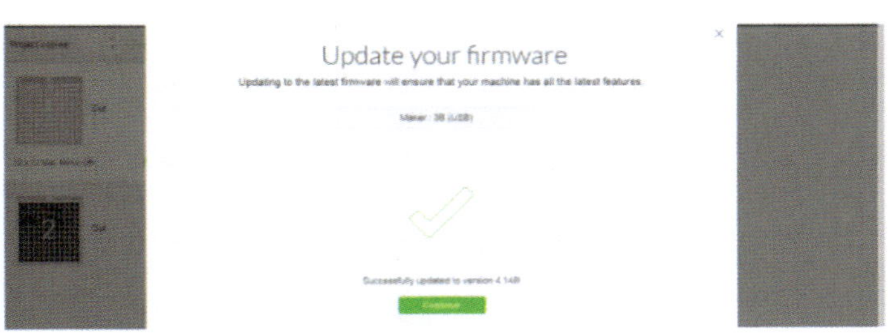

Step 3

When the update is complete, **your machine will automatically turn off and back on**, and you will receive a message that the update was successful.

HOW TO RESIZE YOUR PROJECTS

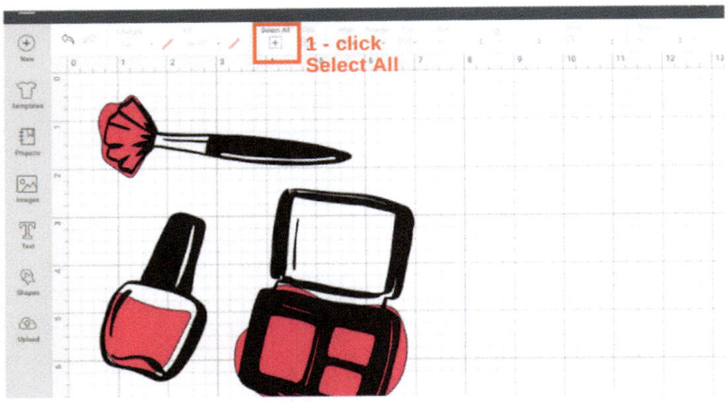

Step 1

Insert, upload, or create an image on your canvas in Design Space and **click Select All** in the Edit Bar.

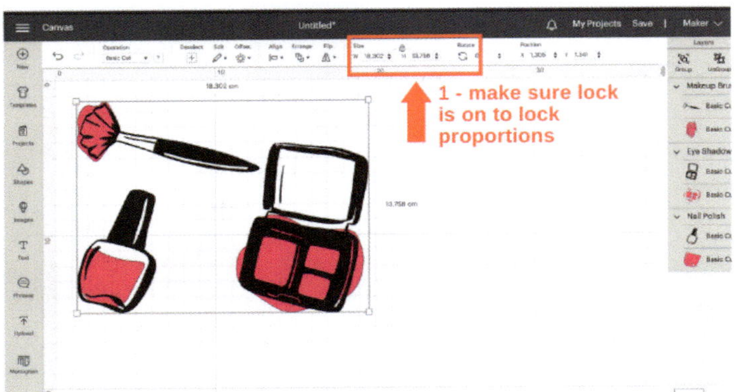

Step 2

Note the size at the top of the window (it also appears above and to the right of the selection itself.)

Make sure the lock icon between the width & height is locked (you will see "lock proportions" when you hover over it.)

Step 3

Resize by doing one of the following:

1. Type the proper size in either the W or H field at the top of the screen.
2. Use the resize icon in the lower right corner of the selection box. Just click, hold, and drag to resize.

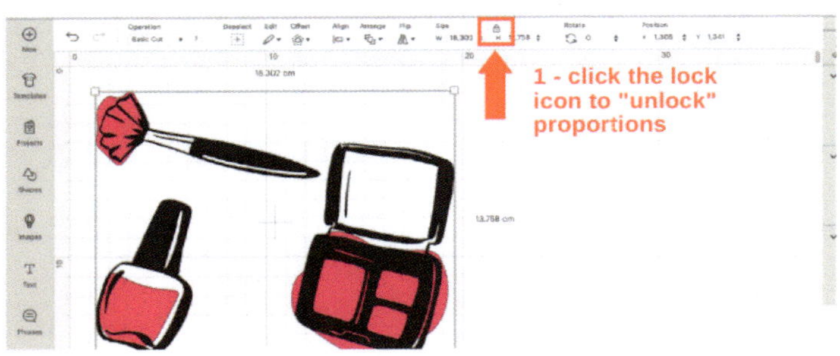

Note

If you want to resize something and NOT keep in it proportion (you want it wider, but not taller, for example), you can **click the lock icon by the width & height in the Edit Bar.**

Cricut Access Images: Nail Polish #M127B499C; Eye Shadow Case #M127B5C78; Makeup Brush #M127B4980

HOW TO CHANGE COLORS

Step 1

Colors represent separate cutting mats, so **you can change colors based on what materials you're using.**

Add an image to your canvas and **select a layer** to change colors.

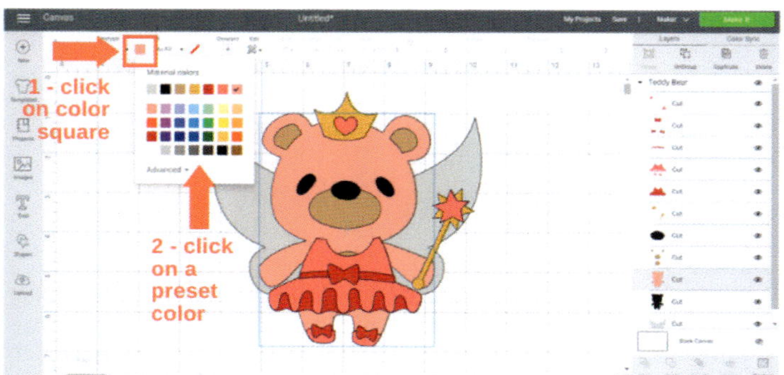

Step 2

Click on the color square next to Operation to choose a new color from the preset colors shown.

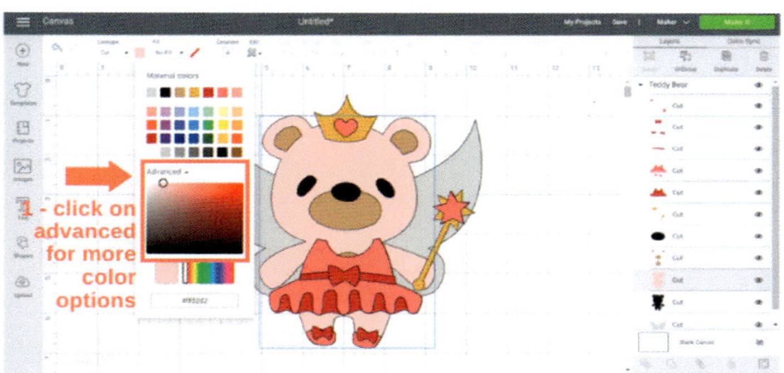

Step 3

You can also **click on Advanced to choose a more specific color** than the premade sample colors visible by dragging the bar and your mouse on the color image shown. You can also manually enter a hex code in the box if you know it for a specific color.

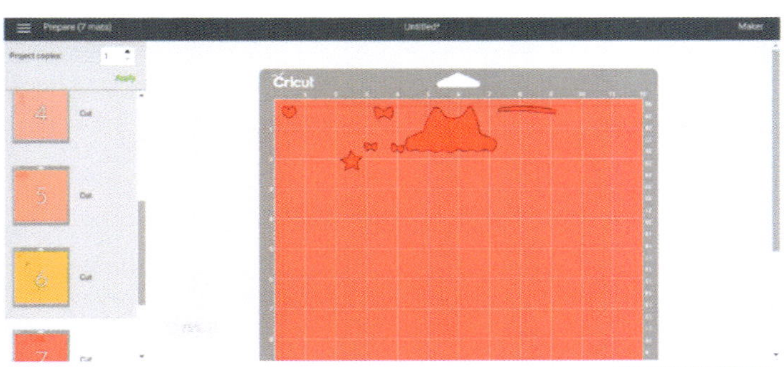

Step 4

Continue clicking each layer and changing colors until you're happy with the result.

When you **click Make It** to start cutting your project, **you'll see each color on it's own mat.**

Cricut Access Image: Teddy Bear #M41F47

OPERATION DEFINED

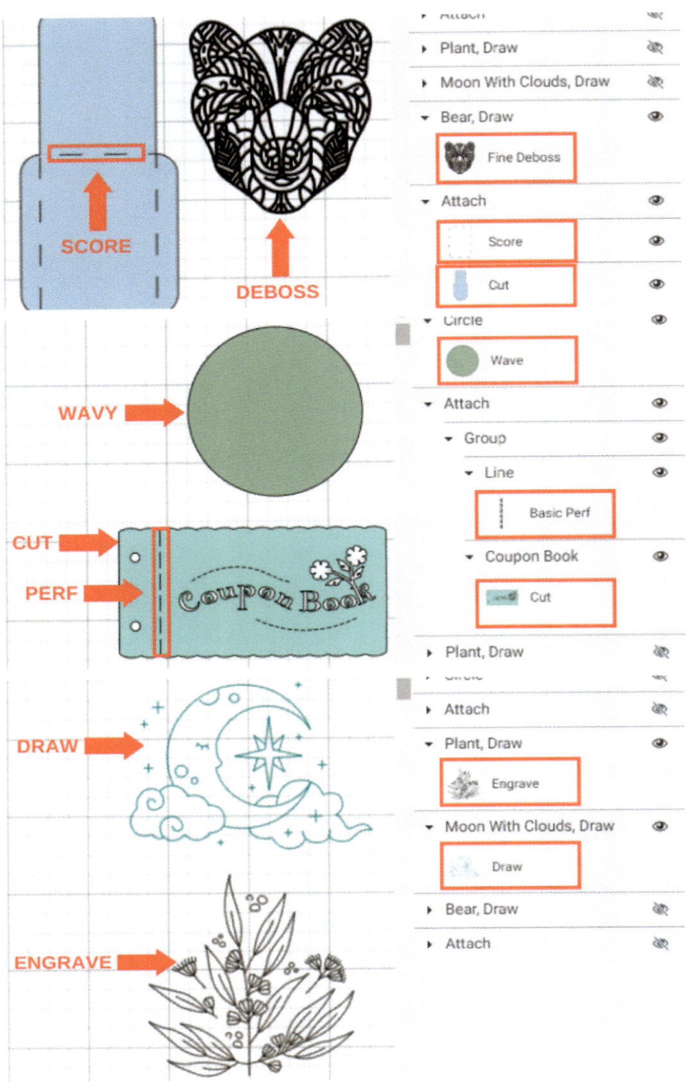

Print-then-Cut

The Print-then-Cut operation will print the image using your home printer then it will cut around the images (Cricut Explore and Maker machines only)

Draw

The Draw operation will **draw a single width line OR the outline** of the shapes or images. Requires a pen.

Score

The Score operation will **allow you to fold your project** easier by scoring your material. Requires a scoring stylus/wheel (Cricut Explore and Maker machines only).

Engrave

The Engrave operation will **engrave on metal and wood**. Requires an engraving tip (Cricut Maker & Maker 3 only).

Deboss

The Deboss operation will **create depressions** in materials like cardstock, wood, and leather to add dimension. Requires a debossing tip (Cricut Maker & Maker 3 only).

Perf

The Perf linetype will create even perforation lines for clean, even tearaways. Perfect for tear-out booklets, raffle tickets, etc. Requires a perforation blade (Cricut Maker & Maker 3 only).

Wavy

The Wave linetype will **cut a curvy waved edge** on your image. Requires a wavy blade (Cricut Maker & Maker 3 only).

Foil

The Foil operation (Fine, Medium & Bold) will **add a foil accent** on your image. Requires a Foil Transfer Tool + Foil Sheets (Cricut Explore & Maker machines only).

Cut

The Cut linetype will **cut the edges** of the shapes or images.

Cricut Access Images:
Envelope #M41856
Bear, Draw #M1279F562
Coupon Book #M44920
Moon With Clouds, Draw #M17CD2424
Plant, Draw #M166EBECB

HOW TO CHANGE OPERATION

Operation is essential in telling your Cricut what you want it to do. This is where you modify your images so Cricut knows if you want the image on your canvas to be cut, scored, engraved, drawn, etc. The operation menu is also where you can customize the color you want the image to be. This can help represent the color of your material to visualize your project. **Different operations will be available depending on your type of Cricut.**

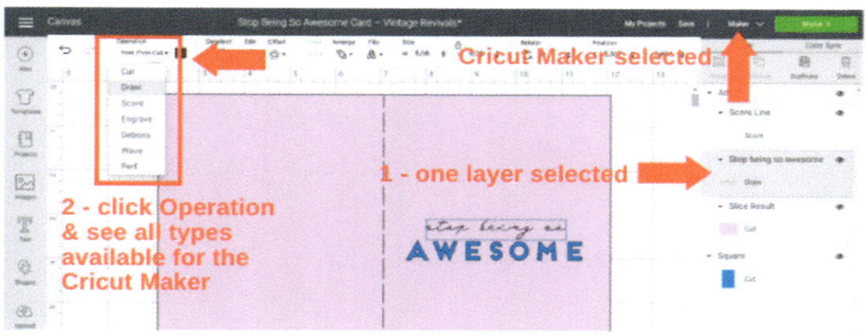

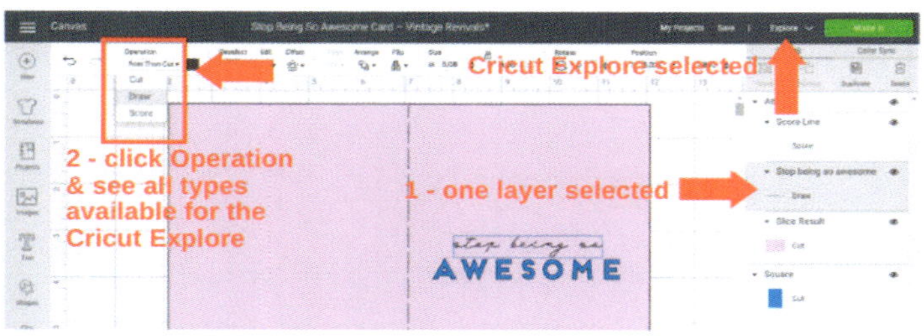

Step 1

Add elements or a project to the canvas and select the layer that you want to change operation for. **Click on Operation** in the Edit Bar to see all available operations for your particular machine.

- The top image is for the Cricut Maker.
- The bottom image is for the Cricut Explore family.
- Cricut Joy not shown, but you will only have Cut & Draw or Foil operations available.

Notes

Available linetypes by machine:

Cricut Joy: Cut, Draw, Foil

Cricut Explore (all versions): Cut, Draw, Score, Foil

Cricut Maker: Cut, Draw, Score, Engrave, Deboss, Wave, Perf, Foil

- Use Cut for the fine point, deep cut, fabric, knife (Maker only), or rotary (Maker only) blades.
- Use Draw to write with pens and markers. Click the box to the right to choose the color and thickness.
- Use Score to score with the Stylus (Maker or Explore) or Scoring Wheel Tools (Maker only).
- Use Engrave to use the Engraving Tool (Maker only).
- Use Deboss to use the Debossing Tool (Maker only).
- Use Wave to use the Wavy Edge Tool (Maker only).
- Use Perf to use the Perforation Blade Tool (Maker only).
- Use Foil to use the Foil Transfer Tool. Choose fine, medium or bold tip.

Cricut Access Project: Stop Being So Awesome Card - Vintage Revivals

HOW TO GROUP AND UNGROUP

How to Group

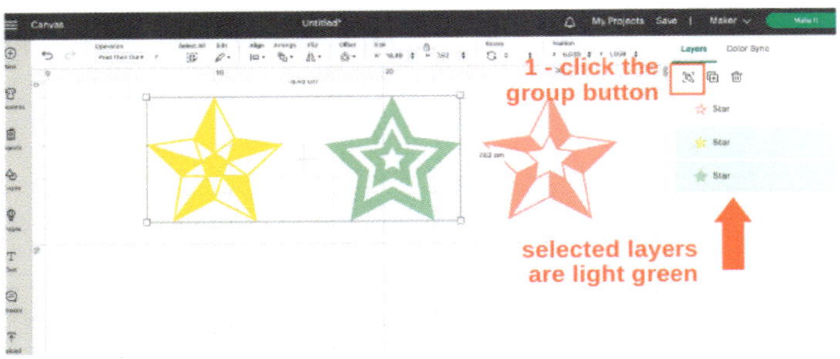

Step 1

Select the layers you want to group by either:

1. In the layers panel, **click on each layer you want to select while also holding the CTRL key (CMD key on Mac).**
2. **Left-click on the canvas and hold down your mouse button while dragging** over everything you want to select.

Step 2

You can tell the layers are all selected because they will be gray in the Layers Panel. **Click the Group button** at the top of the Layers Panel.

You'll see your new Group in the Layers Panel.

How to Ungroup

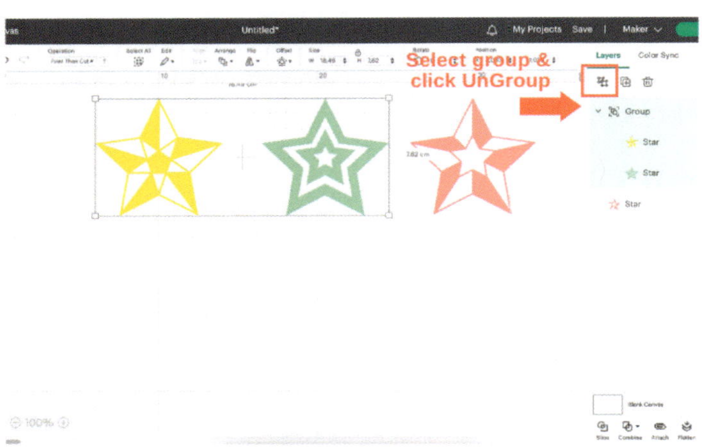

Step 1

In the Layers Panel, **click on the group** of items that you wish to ungroup, and **click on the Ungroup button** at the top of the Layers Panel.

Cricut Access Images:
Star #M9A60CC9
Star #M9A60CDC
Star #M9A60C9C

HOW TO ARRANGE LAYERS: BRING TO FRONT OR SEND TO BACK

Note

Arrange lets you change the order in which the images are layered on the canvas.

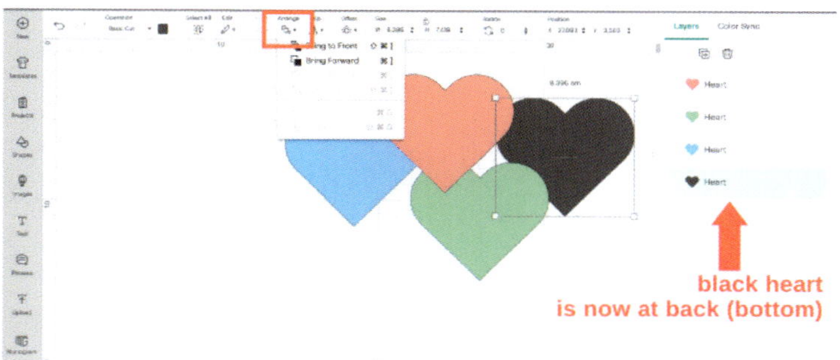

Send to Back

Select the layer in the Layers Panel & **click Arrange** in the Edit Bar. Click **Send to Back** to move that layer to the back (bottom) layer. *Black heart went from the top to the very bottom layer.*

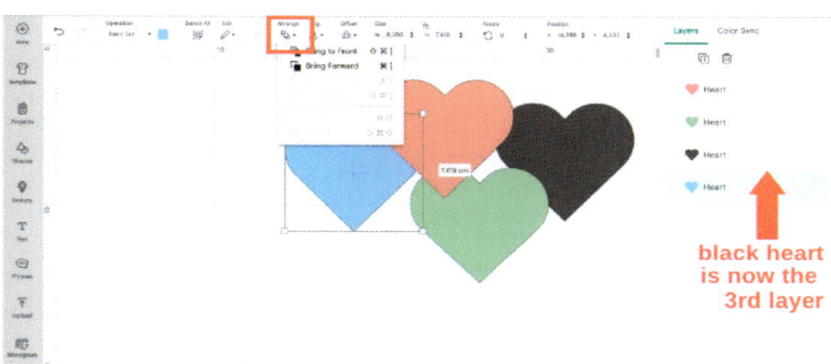

Move Backward

Select any layer but the last one in the Layers Panel & **click Arrange** in the Edit Bar. Click **Send Backward** to move that one 1 layer down. Black heart went from the bottom to the 3rd layer.

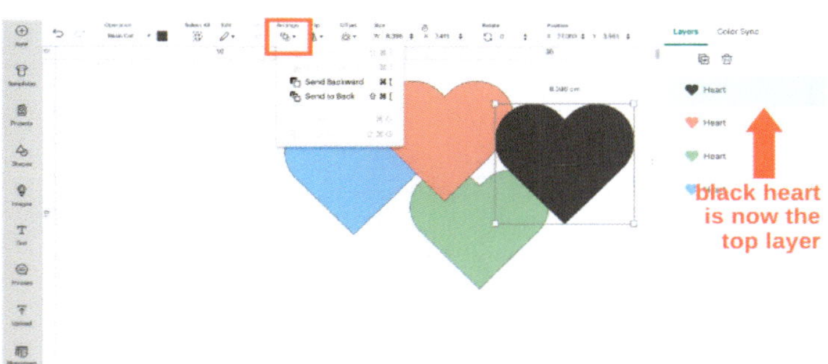

Send to Front

Select any layer but the top one in the Layers Panel & **click Arrange** in the Edit Bar. Click **Send to Front** to move that layer to the top (1st layer) layer. *Black heart went from the 3rd layer to the top layer.*

Move Forward

Select any layer but the top one in the Layers Panel & **click Arrange** in the Edit Bar. Click **Send Forward** to move that one 1 layer up. *Blue heart went from the bottom layer to the 3rd layer.*

HOW TO ALIGN AND DISTRIBUTE OBJECTS

Step 1

Add two or more elements to the canvas that you want to align or distribute evenly.

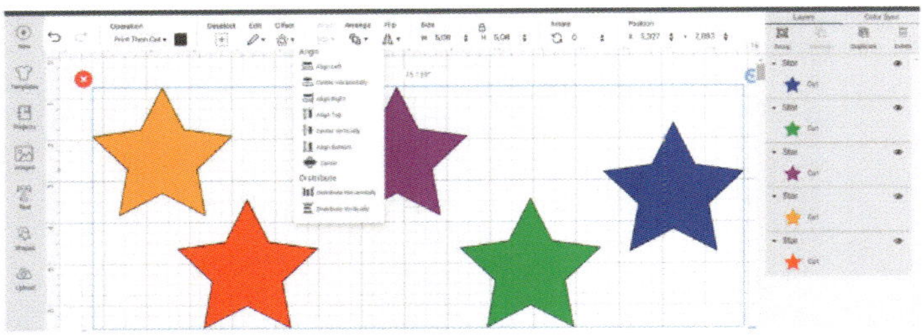

Step 2

Select those elements and **click Align** in the Edit Bar to see all the ways you can align or distribute.

Examples of Different Alignments & Distributions

Cricut Shapes: Stars

HOW TO FLATTEN AND UNFLATTEN

How to Flatten

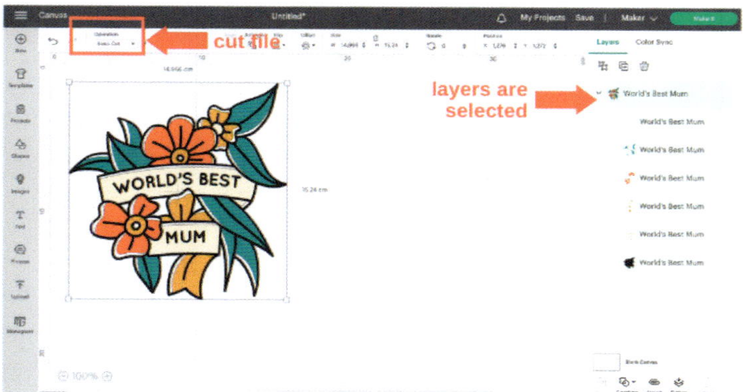

Step 1

Flattening is how you change a layered SVG image or cut file to a Print Then Cut image.

Import an SVG image (see Page 50-51) **or find a layered cut file** in Cricut Access and **select the image layers**.

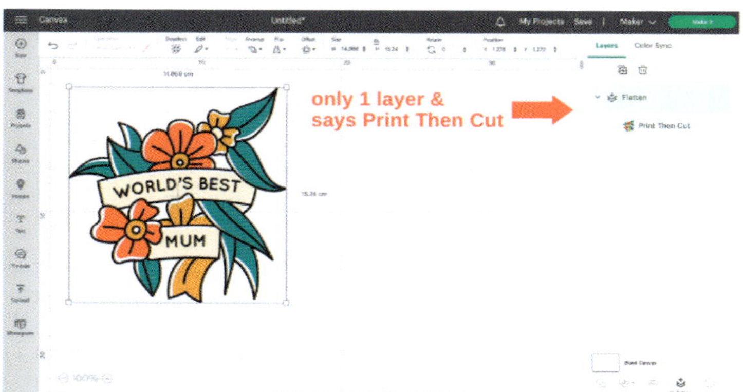

Step 2

Once your selection is made, **click the Flatten Tool** in the Actions Panel.

The image will change appearance and you will also see this reflected in the Layers Panel to Print Then Cut.

How to Unflatten

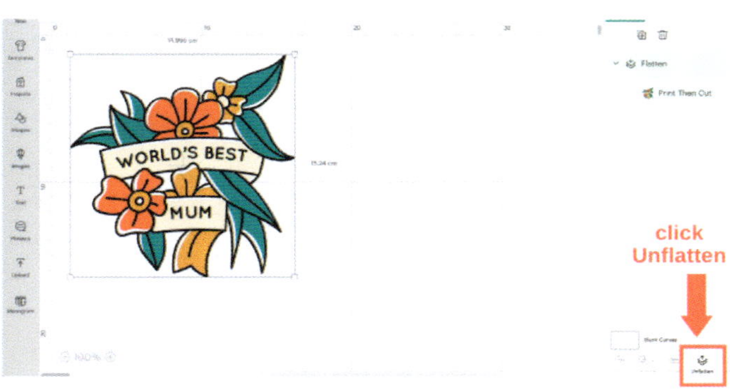

Step 1

You can unflatten at any time by **clicking the Unflatten Button** in the Actions Panel.

If you have unflattened and it still shows Print Then Cut in the Layers Panel, check your fill in the Edit Bar and make sure it says No Fill. This will turn it back into the original SVG (cut file) and in the Layers Panel, it will be shown as a cut line again.

Cricut Access Image:
World's Best Mum with Flowers #M13F6D14F

HOW TO ATTACH

What is Attach?

You can **use the attach tool to hold all the items you want grouped together so they stay exactly the same way on the mat as they look on your canvas**.

Without using attach, here you can see the elements are separated on the mat instead of together the way they were on the canvas.

Be sure to use the Attach Tool anytime you add Draw, Score, Perforation, Deboss, Engrave, or Foil Operation. You will also use attach anytime you want to hold the image placement on your mat.

Step 1

Select all elements that you want to attach by left clicking and holding the mouse button down while dragging across the elements OR by clicking all the elements in the Layers Panel (click each layer & hold CTRL to select another - CMD if on Mac).

Once everything is selected, **click the Attach button** at the bottom of the Layers Panel.

With attach, here you can see the elements are together on the mat exactly how they were on the canvas.

Cricut Access Image: Hooray It's Your Birthday #M175909A7

HOW TO COMBINE SEPARATE IMAGES TO CREATE ONE SHAPE

When you Weld or Combine one item with another they fuse together to make one item. When you want to eliminate the cut lines between two images or letters you would use the Combine function to weld. Like Attach, Weld keeps your project together on the canvas and on the mat when you cut.

Step 1

You can use the Combine Tool to join letters together or simplify an image by combining elements. Start by **inserting your images** onto the canvas.

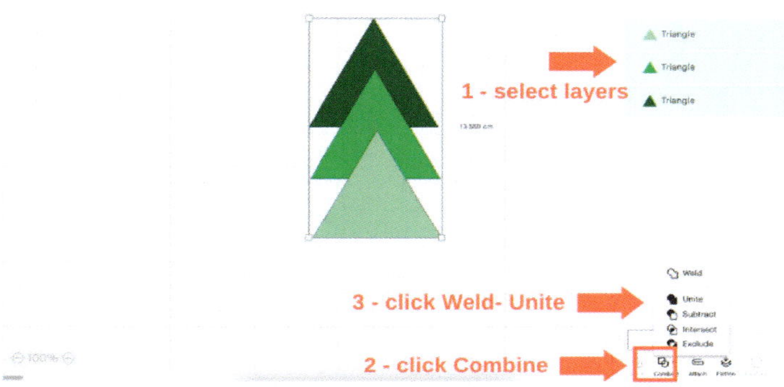

Step 2

Select the images you want to weld then **click the Combine Button** in the Actions Panel. Now select **Weld.**

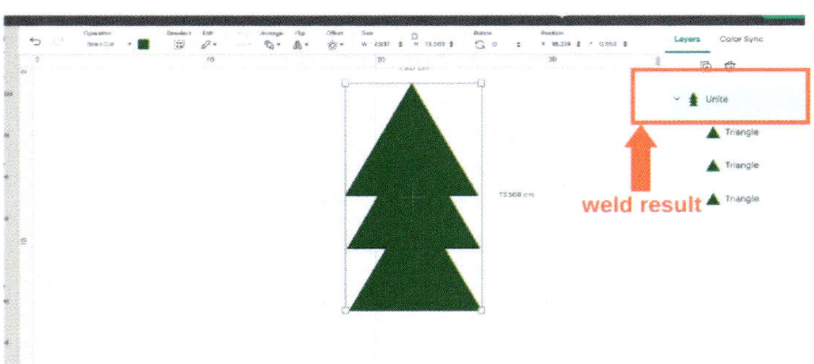

Step 3

After you click the Weld Button, **your images will be merged into one image** [it will remove unnecessary lines] and will change to one color. You can see the result in the Layers Panel.

Note

- You cannot unweld images even if you have closed your project and opened it again later. However, if you use the Unite option in Combine you can undo the action, click on Combine and selecting Undo Unite. The images will return to their original state. Read more about the other Combine actions on page 42.

Cricut Shapes: Triangles

THE COMBINE FUNCTIONS EXPLAINED

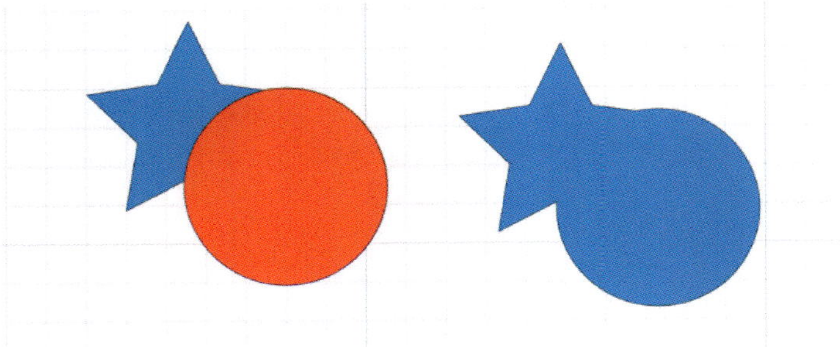

COMBINE -WELD

Select two shapes and click on **Combine - Weld**. The two images/shapes **create one shape. This cannot be undone.**

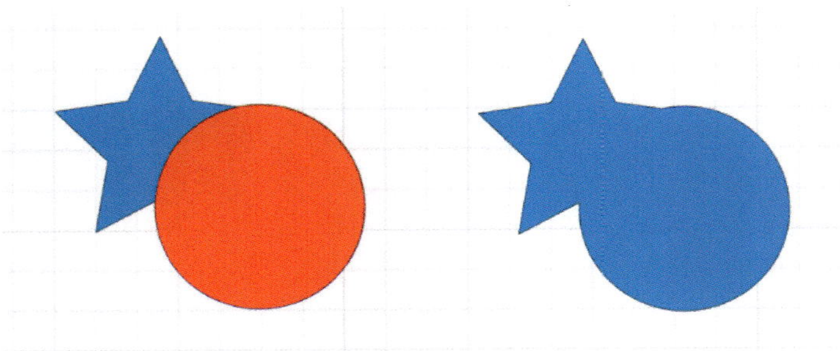

COMBINE -UNITE

Select two shapes, and click on **Combine - Unite to create one shape similar to Weld however you can undo this action** even after saving and reopening your project. To **undo click on Combine and Undo Unite**

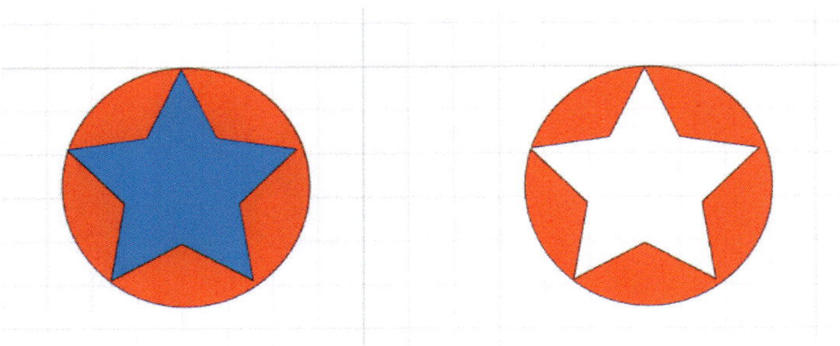

COMBINE -SUBTRACT

Select two shapes, and click on **Combine - Subtract**. The result is similar to slice however the original shape is automatically removed. To **undo click on Combine and Undo Subtract**

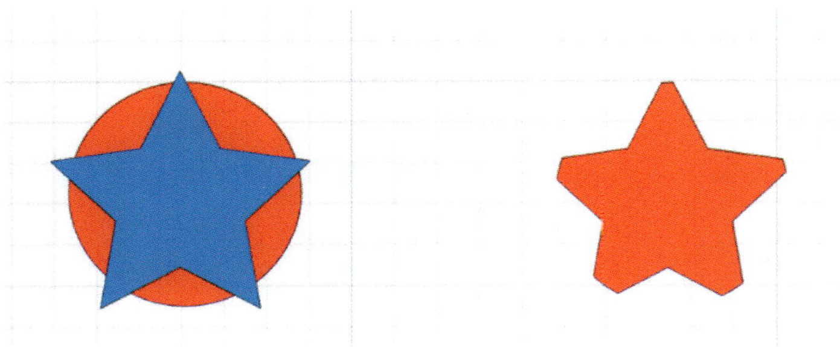

COMBINE -INTERSECT

Select two shapes, and **click on Combine - Intersect**. You will be left with a design where the parts of the two shapes overlap/intersect. To **undo click on Combine and Undo Intersect**

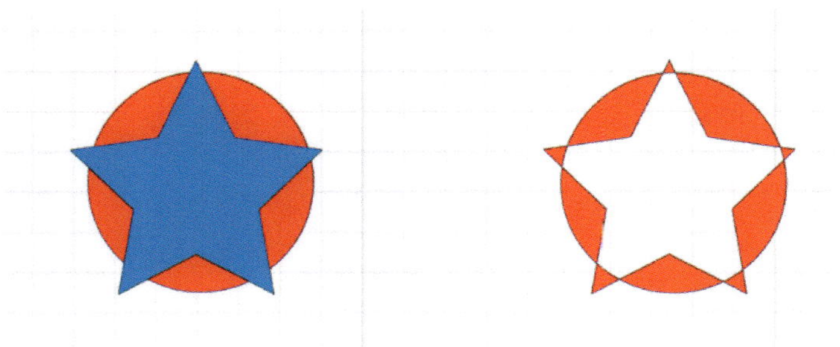

COMBINE -EXCLUDE

Select two shapes, and click on **Combine - Exclude**. This removes the parts of the shapes that overlap. To **undo click on Combine and Undo Exclude.**

Cricut Shapes Shown: Star and Circle

HOW TO COMBINE SCRIPT FONTS TO CONNECT THE LETTERS

NOTE: When using a script font, Cricut Design Space automatically welds your letters together. The un-welded word on the left becomes welded once you hit Make It in the upper right.

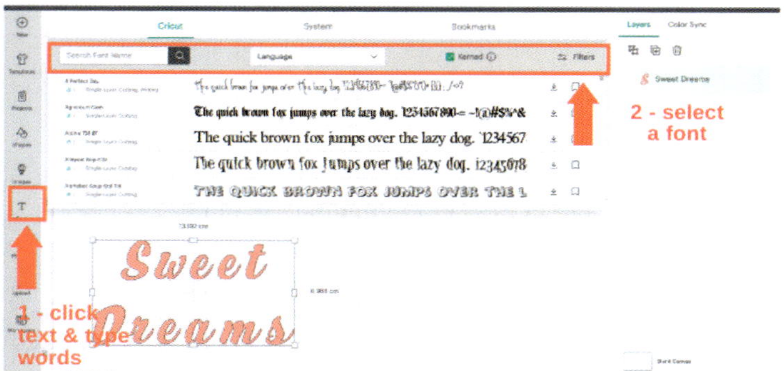

Step 1

Click text to add a text box to the canvas. In the Text Edit Bar at the top, use the Font dropdown menu to **select the font of your choice.**

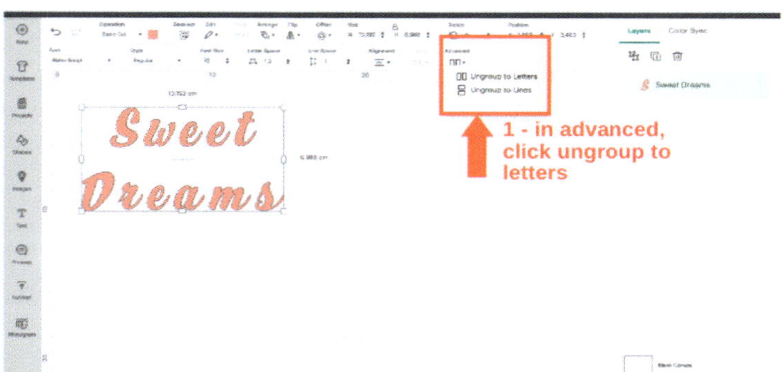

Step 2

In the Text Edit Bar, **click the dropdown menu in the Advanced section and click on Ungroup to Letters.**

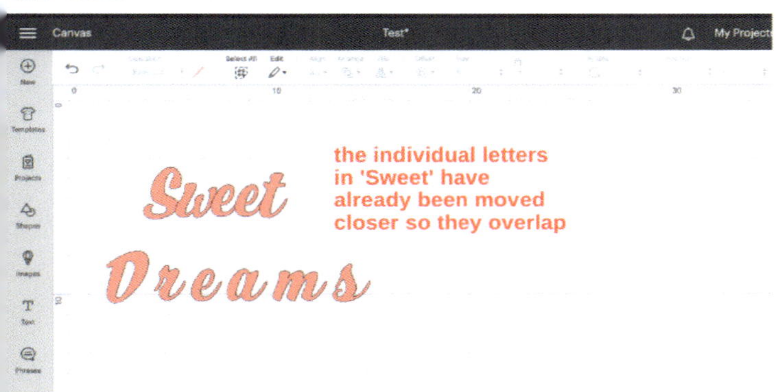

Step 3

Now that the letters are ungrouped, **move each one individually so it is just barely touching the ones next to it.** You may need to **use the Align tool** to make sure your text is straight. You can also use the grid on the canvas to visually align the letters.

Step 4

Once you are satisfied with the text and have all letters touching as if they were naturally written, **select all and weld the together using the Weld tool.** The words will now cut as one seamless piece.

Cricut Font Shown: Retro Script

HOW TO SLICE

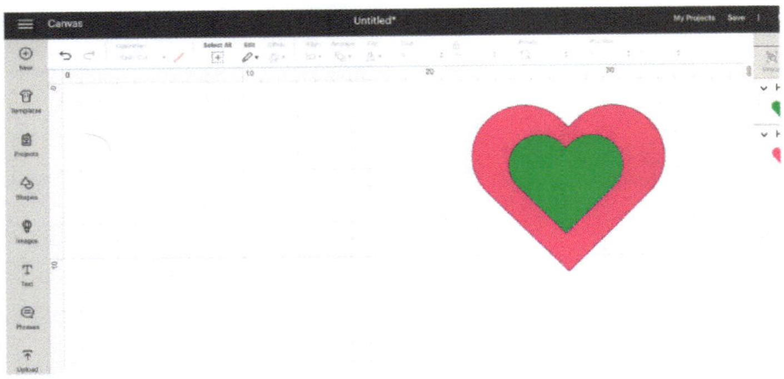

Step 1

You can use the slice tool to create split monograms and other creative shapes. Start by **inserting your images** onto the canvas **so that they are overlapping**. In this case, we're going to cut out the green heart out of the purpleheart.

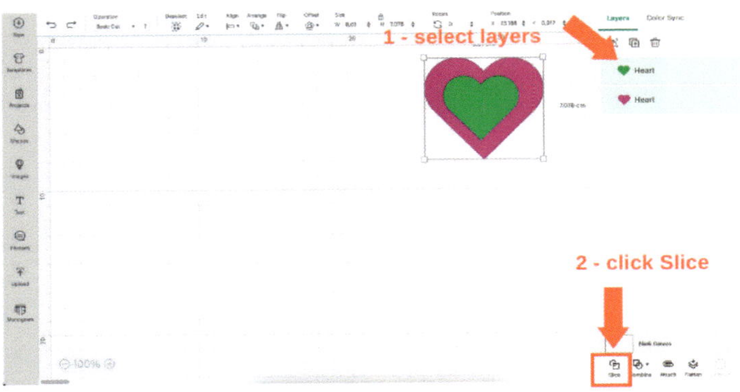

Step 2

Select the images you want to slice (the purple heart & green heart) then **click the Slice Button** in the Actions Panel.

Step 3

After you click the Slice Button, **new layers called "Slice Result" will appear** in the Layers Panel. You can move, hide or delete these if you don't need them.

Final Result

When you move the layers you will see your final Slice Result.

Note

- You can slice both images and text.
- Layers in groups can be sliced if you select just the individual layers, not the entire groups.
- If text is multi-layered and one layer is hidden, you can use the Slice tool. However, if you ungroup text from its shadow layer, it becomes an image and will no longer work with the Slice tool unless the text is ungrouped to individual letters.

HOW TO USE CONTOUR

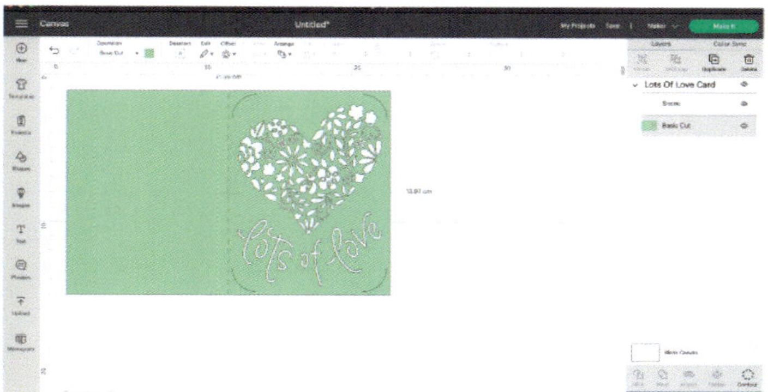

Step 1

You can use the Contour Tool to remove cut lines from a project. For example, to change this card to a different occasion like a birthday, we can remove "lots of love" and add our own words. Start by **inserting your image** onto the canvas.

Step 2

Click Contour in the Actions Panel and **a new window will pop up**.

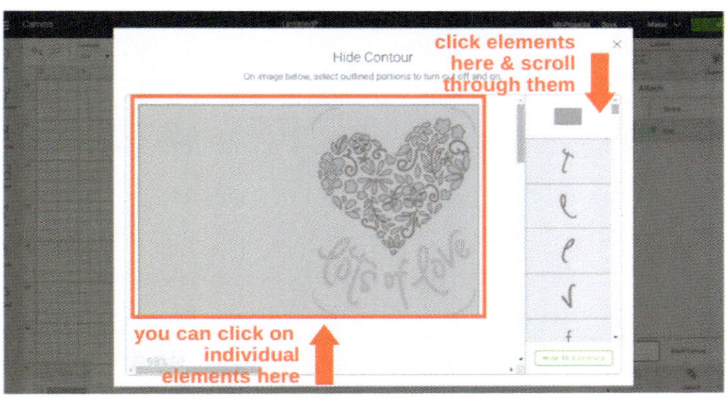

Step 3

Select all the shapes/cut lines you want to remove from the project. You can click right on the design in the box or click on each item & scroll through in the right column.

Close the window using the X in the top right corner when you're done.

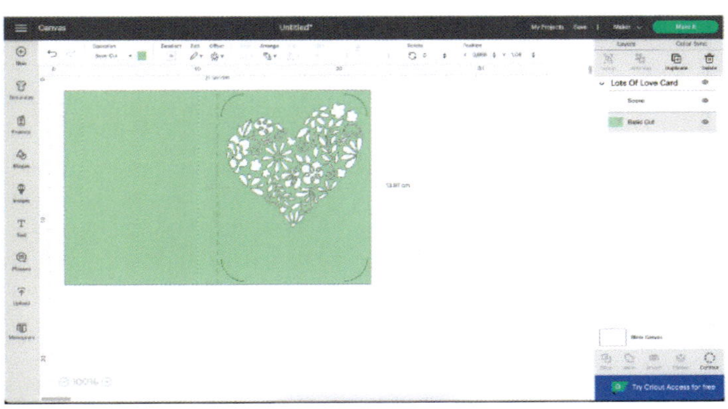

Step 4

Your final result will now be shown.

You can easily add the shapes back into your project by clicking Contour again and selecting shapes to add back.

Cricut Access Images: Lots Of Love Card #M10AC448C

HOW TO USE COLOR SYNC

Color Sync

You may import an SVG file that has more colors in the file than you want. Each color cuts on a different mat, so to reduce the number of colors used, and therefore how many mats of material you need, use the Color Sync panel to consolidate some colors.

Step 1

Add your image to the canvas and then **click on Color Sync** at the top of the Layers Panel to see the colored layer groups.

Step 2

To reduce the number of colors, **drag and drop any colored layer in the Color Sync panel to another colored layer**. Hold the image layer and drag up or down. Here, we combined the 2 yellow layers into one.

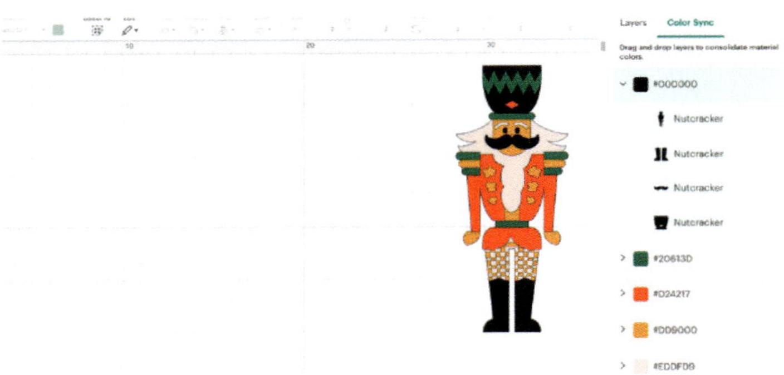

Step 2

Repeat this process for any colors you want to combine. Here we've gone from 9 colors (mats) to 5 colors. You can reduce down to one color if you want, it may vary per image that you're working with and what materials you want to use.

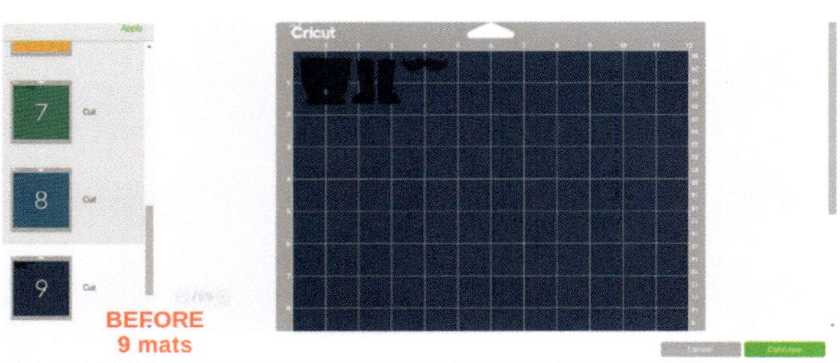

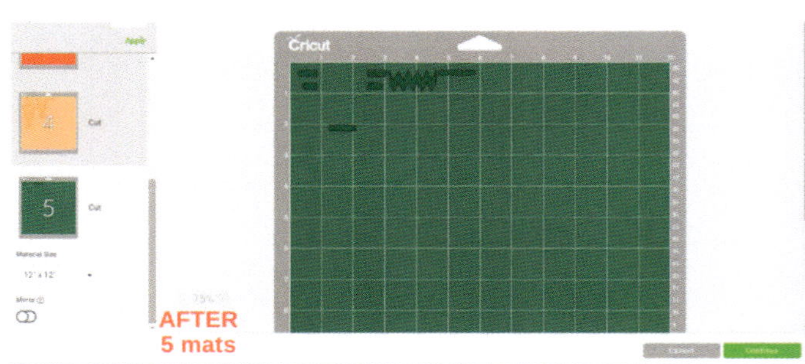

Cricut Access Image: Nutcracker #M11B6F121

HOW TO USE A TEMPLATE

You can choose from multiple template designs that will help you visualize your final project and provide size reference.

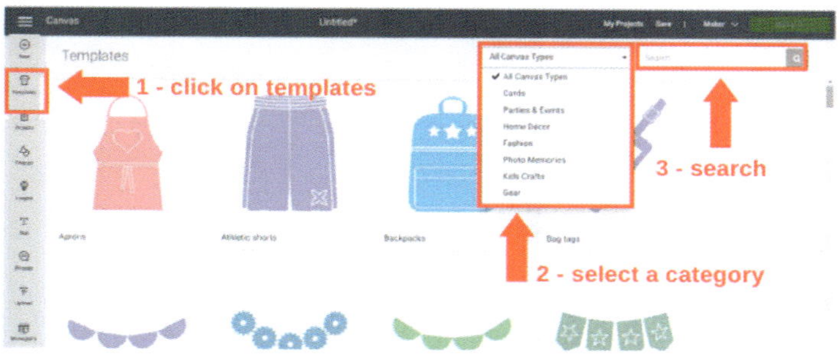

Step 1

Select the Templates tool in the Design panel to the left of the Canvas. You can **scroll through the templates**, **select a category** to filter the templates, or **search** to find a specific type of template.

Step 2

When you select a template, it will be added to the Canvas screen. **An alert will appear**, stating that Templates are intended for reference only and will not be saved with your project.

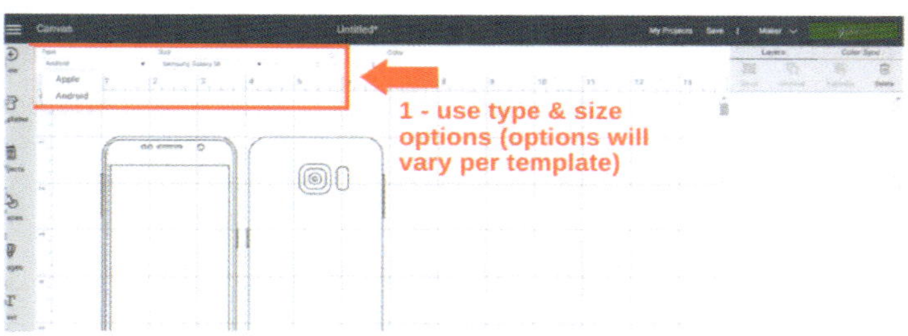

Step 3

Use the Type and Size options in the Template Edit bar to **select a version of the template that is closest to the item you will be using.**

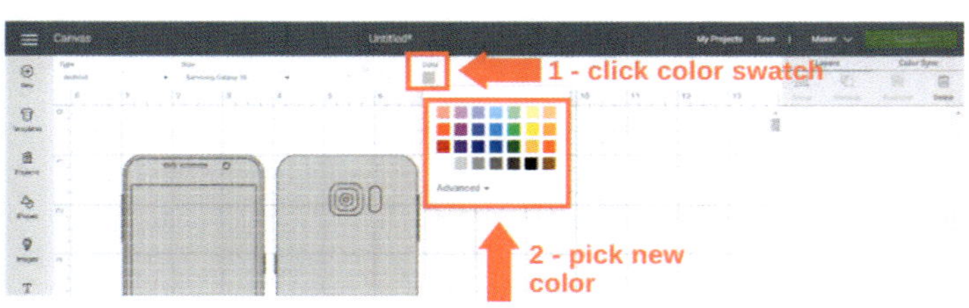

Step 4

You can also change the color of the template by **clicking the color swatch** in the Template Edit Bar.

Cricut Access Image: I Craft So Hard I Sweat Glitter #M12406100

Step 5

Add text and images to your project as needed, using the template as a guide for the layout. **When done, you can delete the template by selecting it** at the bottom of the Layers Panel and **clicking delete** at the top of the Layers panel.

HOW TO ADD OR CHANGE PATTERNS

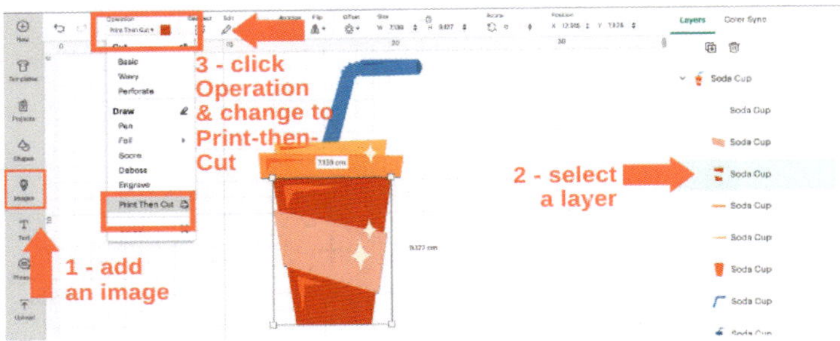

Step 1

Add an image to your canvas and **select a layer** to add a pattern to. **Click Fill** in the Edit Bar and **change to Print** instead of No Fill.

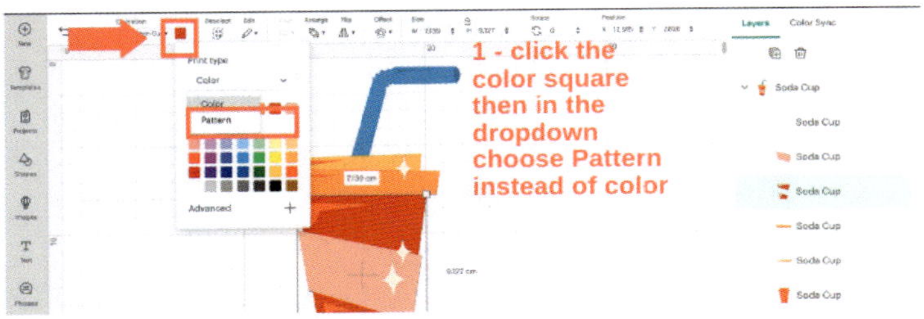

Step 2

Click the color square next to Fill. In the dropdown menu, **select Pattern** instead of color.

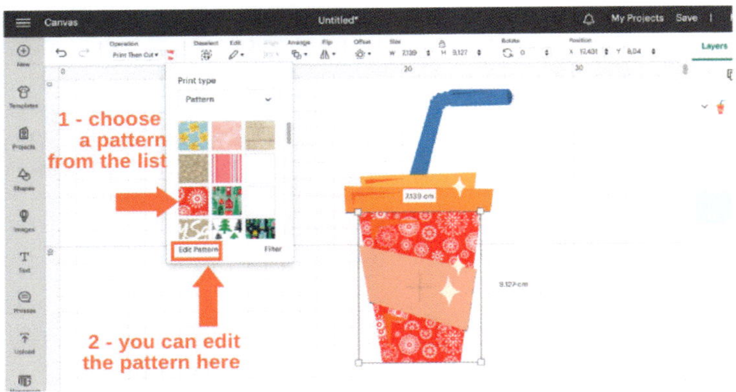

Step 3

Choose a pattern from the list of swatches shown.

You can edit the pattern further by **clicking Edit Pattern**. This includes changing the scale, rotation, flipping it, or moving it horizontally or vertically.

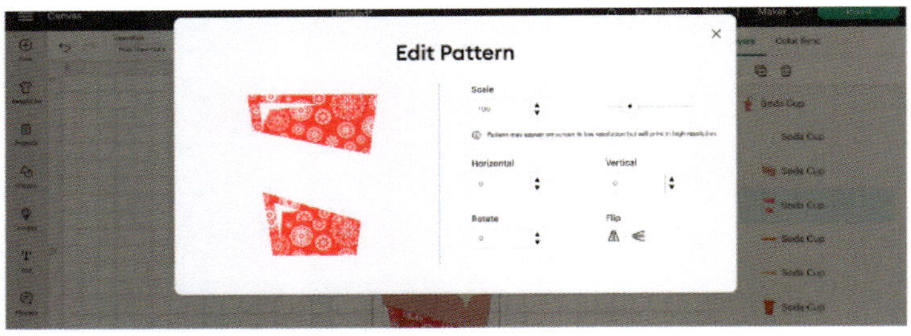

Step 4

Once you **click Edit Pattern**, you can change the scale, rotation, flip it, or move it horizontally or vertically to change the look of the pattern.

Cricut Access Image: Takeaway Soda Cup #M14280639
(colors were changed before showing pattern change)

Note

You can also upload your own image or photo to use as a custom pattern (.jpg, .gif, .png, or .bmp files). **Click Upload** in the design panel, **select Upload Pattern**, **select the image** on your computer & **click Open.** Then you'll **name your pattern**, add tags (optional) and **click Save**. Then add a pattern like normal & **click filter to see all your patterns.**

HOW TO FILTER AND SEARCH FOR IMAGES IN THE IMAGE LIBRARY

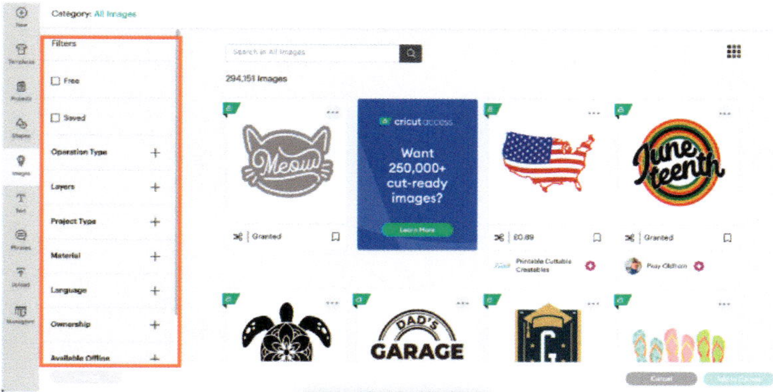

Image Filter

When you click Images to view the Image Library, it can be overwhelming, but there is a great way to narrow down what you're browsing for, without searching for something specific using the search bar. **Look to the Filter on the left side of the screen.**

- You can expand each section by clicking the + to see the options in that section.
- Click any of the checkboxes to select them and you'll see the images change.
- All the filter options are shown below (you'll have to scroll in Design Space to see them all).

Filters — Clear

Categories — All >

FREE
- Free

SAVED
- Saved

OPERATION TYPE
- Cut Only
- Draw Only
- Print then Cut
- Cut + Draw

LAYERS
- Single
- Multi

PROJECT TYPE
- 3D
- Cards
- Phrases
- 12oz/355ml Regular Ceramic Mug Designs
- 15oz/425ml Regular Ceramic Mug Designs

OWNERSHIP
- Purchased
- Uploaded

AVAILABLE OFFLINE
- Downloaded

LICENSED CONTENT
- Marvel
- Sanrio

MATERIAL
- Chipboard
- Infusible Ink
- Iron-on
- Leather
- Paper/Cardstock
- Sticker Paper
- Vinyl

LANGUAGE
- Arabic
- ASL
- Chinese
- Danish
- Dutch
- English
- Finnish
- French
- German
- Hawaiian
- Hebrew
- Italian
- Japanese
- Korean
- Norwegian
- Portuguese
- Russian
- Spanish

HOW TO UPLOAD IMAGES INTO DESIGN SPACE: JPEG, PNG, GIF, BMP

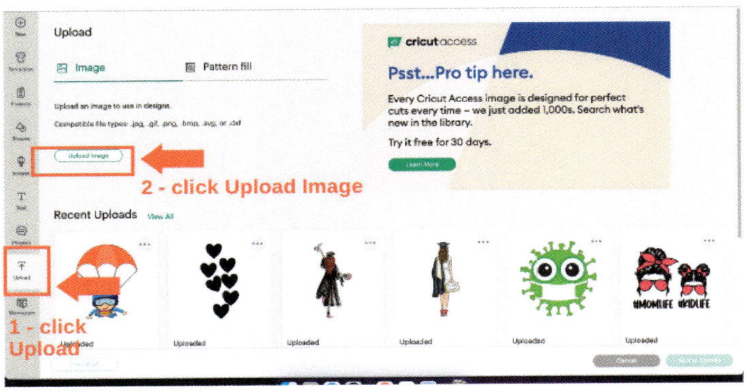

Step 1

Click Upload in the Design Panel on the left and then **click Upload Image**.

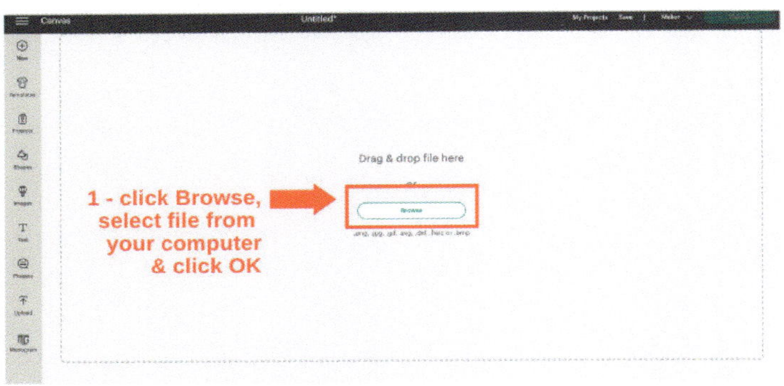

Step 2

Click Browse in the popup window that appears and then you can **select an image from your computer**. You can upload JPEG, PNG, GIF, or BMP images.

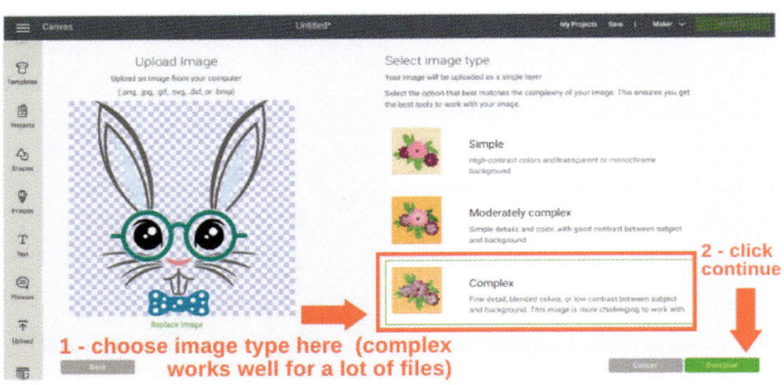

Step 3

Select an image type based on what your image looks like. Complex works for most images, so you can select that if you're not sure which to use. **Click the continue button** next.

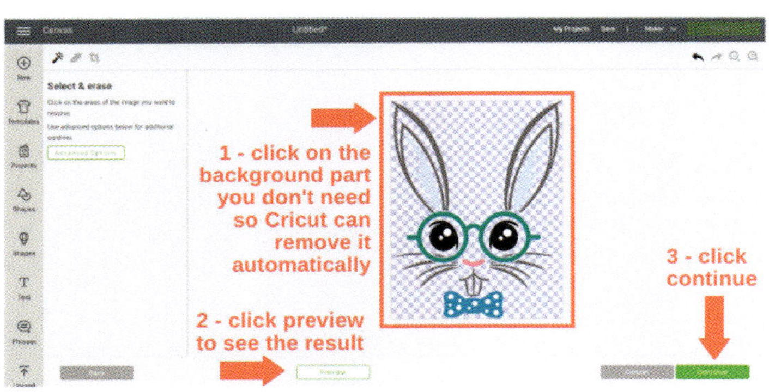

Step 4

Click on the areas of the image you don't need (the empty background area) and Cricut will automatically remove it. You can **click the Preview button** to see how it looks. There are advanced options available on the left if you need them.

HOW TO UPLOAD IMAGES INTO DESIGN SPACE - CONTINUED

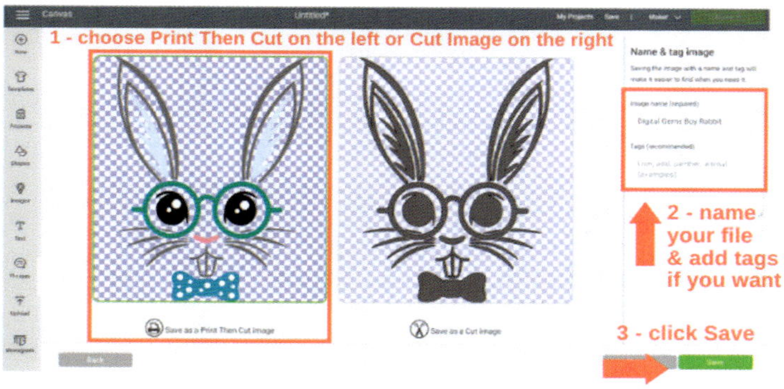

Step 5

Select either a Print Then Cut project (left) or a Cut project (right). Name your file in the box on the right side and **add tags** to help you find your image later (optional). When finished, **click the Save button**.

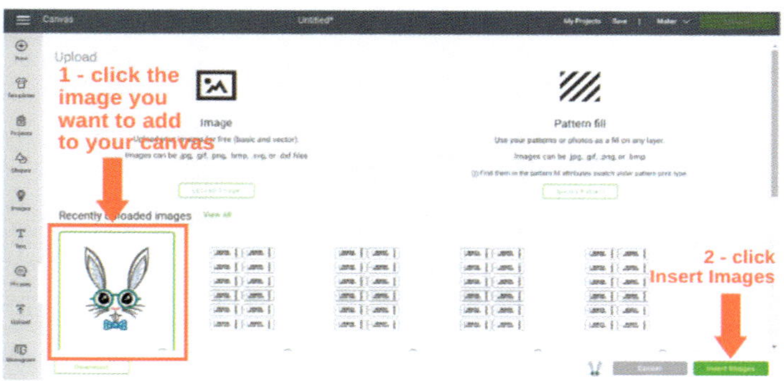

Step 6

Click the image you just uploaded and then **click Insert Images**.

Step 7

Your new image is now on your canvas, ready to add text or other items for your project.

Notes

- If you purchase files from Etsy or other sites, the files may be in a zip file and will need to be unzipped before you can upload them to Cricut Design Space.
- Once you have uploaded several images, you can insert them into your project at once by selecting multiple images in Step 6 above.

Commercial Use Image (PNG, SVG, EPS, & DXF) from The Hungry Jpeg (seller is Digital Gems): https://thehungryjpeg.com/product/3516732-rabbit-faces-svg-png-eps-dxf-files

HOW TO USE EDITABLE IMAGES

You can choose from multiple Editable Image designs that you can change to suit your needs. You may need to pay for Editable Images depending on if you have Cricut Access or not.

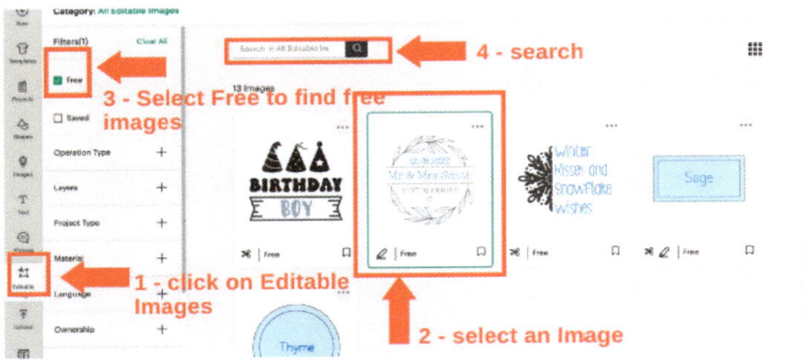

Step 1

Select the Editable Images tool in the Design panel to the left of the Canvas. You can **scroll through the images. Select Free** to filter the templates for free images, or **search** to find a specific type of image.

Step 2

When you select an image, it will be added to the Canvas screen.

Step 3

To **edit the image**, **select the relevant layer** you want to change. We are changing the color by **clicking on the Color tool**, and **selecting your color**. You can also change the other layers in the image by repeating the steps.

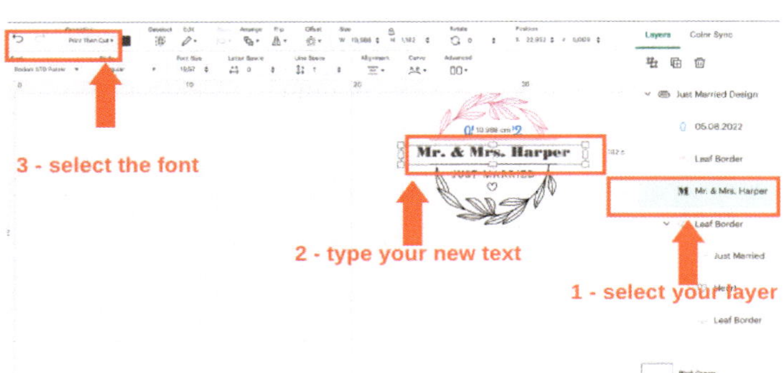

Step 5

To edit the text, click on the text layer and **type the text** that you want. You can **change the font** by clicking on **Font and selecting your font.** You can also change color.

Cricut Access Image: Mr. & Mrs. Smith Just Married #M41494270 *Cricut System Font: Bodoni STD Poster*

HOW TO REMOVE A BACKGROUND, CROP AND CLEAN UP AN IMAGE

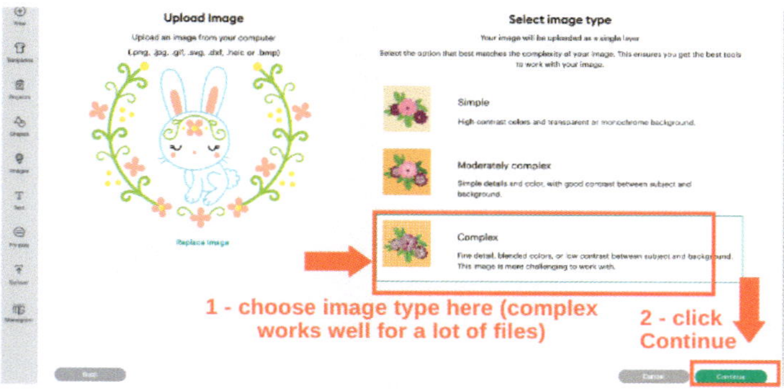

Step 1

Find and save an image from the web. **Click Upload** and select the downloaded image file. Next select the best option (Simple, Moderately Complex or Complex) from the Image Type list. if you are unsure **select Complex. Click continue.**

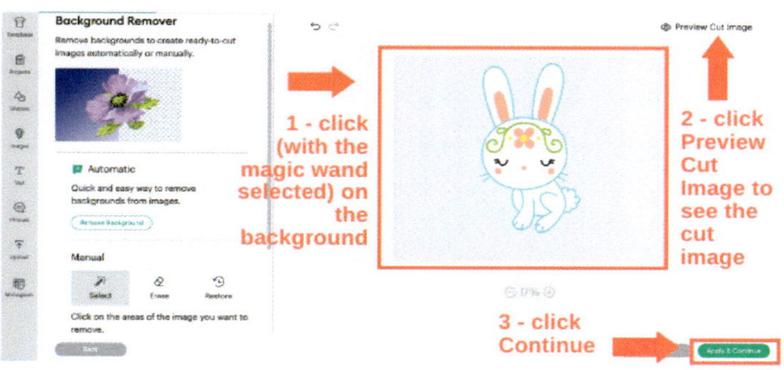

Step 2

If you have **Cricut Access** you can **click on the Remove Background button** to remove the background automatically. **Use the Wand tool and click on the background of the image** to remove it manually (*this works for solid backgrounds only*). You can **click the Preview button** to see the result.

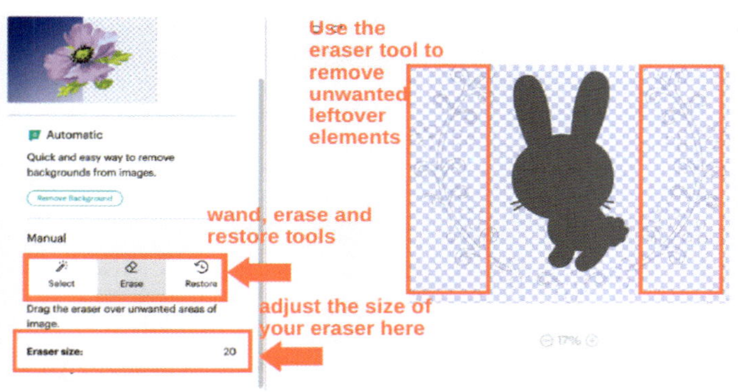

Step 3

Remove unwanted elements by using the **Erase Tool to get rid of the remaining pieces** that you do not want in the image after using the wand to remove the background.

Step 4

Click on Zoom to make sure that you have erased all unwanted pieces (it is easier to see as it will be in grey mode). **Click Apply and Continue** it as either a Cut File or a Print Then Cut File (see pg 85).

Commercial Use Image (PNG, SVG, EPS, & DXF) from Design Bundles (seller is Bunnycup):
https://designbundles.net/bunnycup/595609-bunny-laurel-svg-clipart-graphic

HOW TO UPLOAD SVG FILES

What is an SVG File?

An SVG is a Scalable Vector Graphic. The benefit of using an SVG file is you can resize the image larger or smaller and it will not lose its resolution. Unlike an image which is one layer only, an SVG file often has multiple layers allowing you to easily cut different color vinyls.

Where to Find SVG Files

You can find many **free SVG files in Google Images** or places such as **Pinterest**.
You can also **purchase SVG's** online. Popular places to browse for SVG files include Etsy, Design Bundles, The Hungry JPEG, So Fontsy, LoveSVG, Creative Market, Creative Fabrica, Miss Kate Cuttables, Printable Cuttable Creatables, and more!

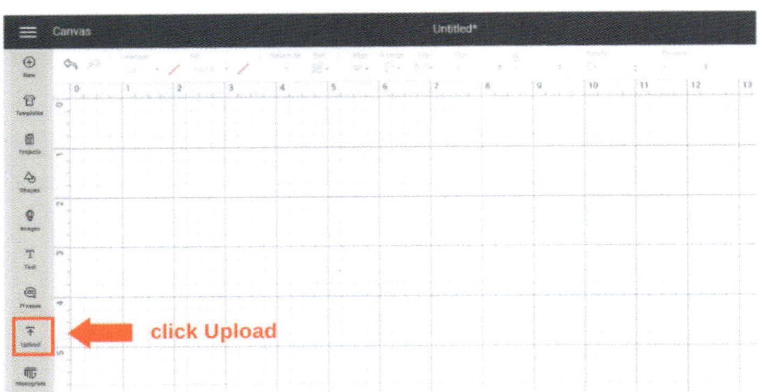

Step 1

Open Design Space. On the left side of the canvas **click Upload**.

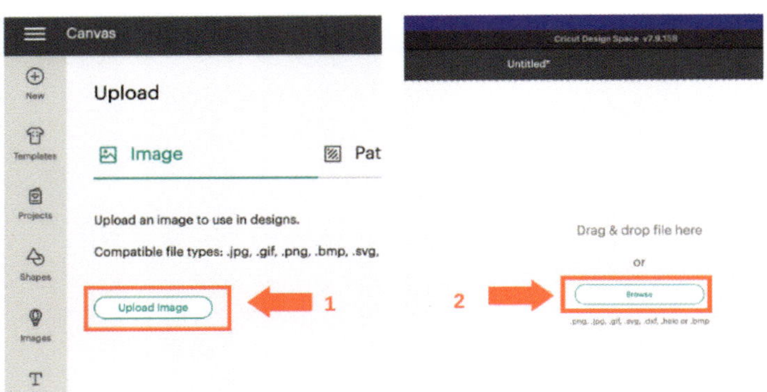

Step 2

On the Upload page **click Insert Image**. Then either drag and drop your file onto the screen or **click Browse** to find and **select the downloaded SVG File.**

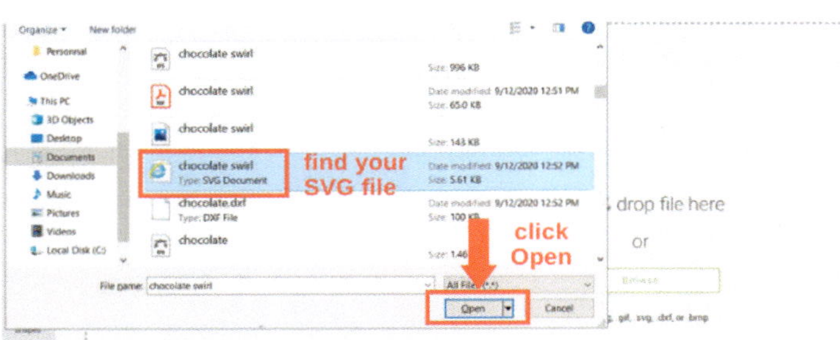

Step 3

Select your SVG file and click Open. Be sure it's the SVG version. When purchased some files come with multiple file types.

HOW TO UPLOAD SVG FILES

Step 4

Name your image and add some tags (optional). Whilst it is easy to skip over this step it will be really beneficial to help you search through all your files once you have a big library of uploaded images. **Click Upload.**

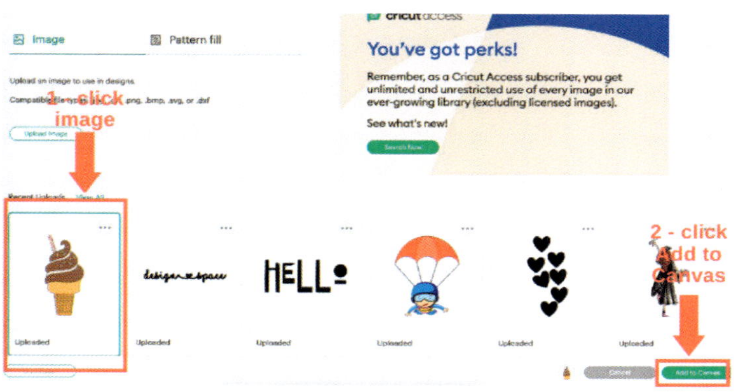

Step 5

To insert the SVG on to the Canvas, **select your uploaded SVG** and **click on Add to Canvas.**

Final Result

Your image will now be ready for editing. Your layers will be visible on the right. Click on a layer to highlight it so that you can change colors, resize it or hide it away completely (see page 10 to learn more about layers).

Notes

When you purchase an SVG file it will often arrive as a downloadable ZIP file. Cricut Design Space can not upload ZIP files, so you will first need to decompress the ZIP file. You can double click on the folder to view all the file options. It will typically contain an SVG, JPG, PNG, DXF, EPS and PDF version of the file. Make sure that you are uploading the SVG file only.

Commercial Use Image (PNG, SVG, EPS, & DXF) from Design Bundles (seller is Redearth and Gumtrees):
https://designbundles.net/redearth-and-gumtrees/496170-huge-summer-nautical-and-tropical-bundle-svg-merma

HOW TO FLIP AND ROTATE AN IMAGE OR SHAPE

How to Flip an Image or Shape

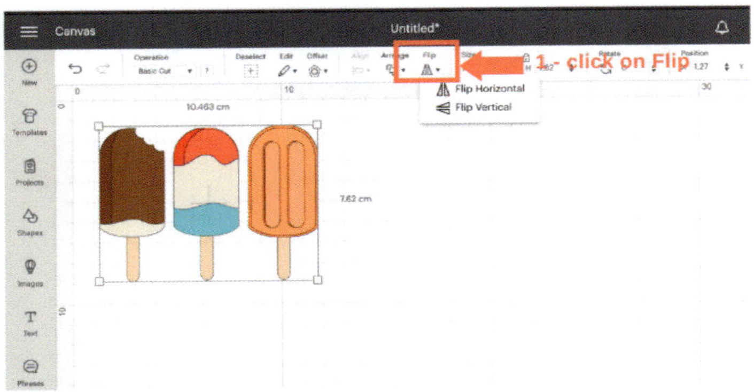

Step 1

Insert an image on your canvas and then **click Flip** in the Edit Bar. **A dropdown will appear** with the options to Flip Horizontal or Flip Vertical.

Step 2

Flip Horizontal will flip your image from left to right as shown. **Flip Vertical** will flip your image from bottom to top as shown.

How to Rotate an Image or Shape

Cricut Access Image: Summer Popsicles #MB5A6D9C

Step 1

Rotate an image precisely by using the Rotate tool in the Edit Bar and entering the number of degrees to rotate (example 90 degrees).

Rotate an image manually by hovering your mouse at the corner of the bounding box for the rotate icon. Click and hold the rotate icon and drag your mouse to rotate it.

HOW TO OFFSET AN IMAGE OR SHAPE

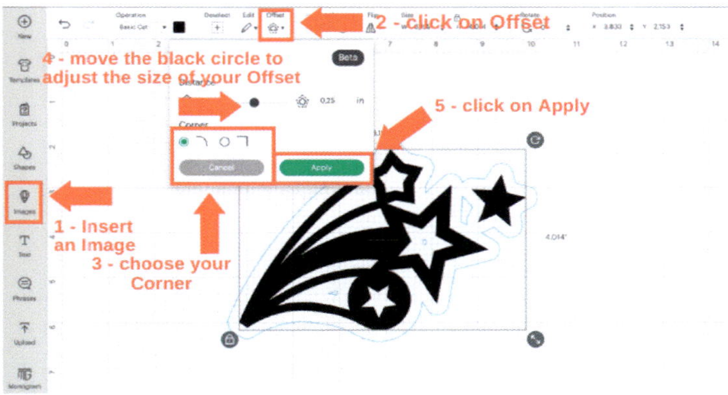

Step 1

Insert an image on your canvas. Select your image, **click Offset** and adjust the border size around your image by **adjusting the Distance** (black circle) on the slide bar. You can also change if the shadow layer is to be curved or angular. **Click Apply** and the shadow layer will appear to offset your image.

To Change Color

To change the color of the Offset layer, **select your Offset layer**. **Click on the color fill square** and select the color for the Offset (shadow) layer. To create multiple Offset layers, select the Offset Layer and repeat steps 2-3.

Add More Offset Layers

You can add as many Offset Layers as you want. Simply select both layers by clicking and dragging a box around both and then click on Offset to repeat the steps.

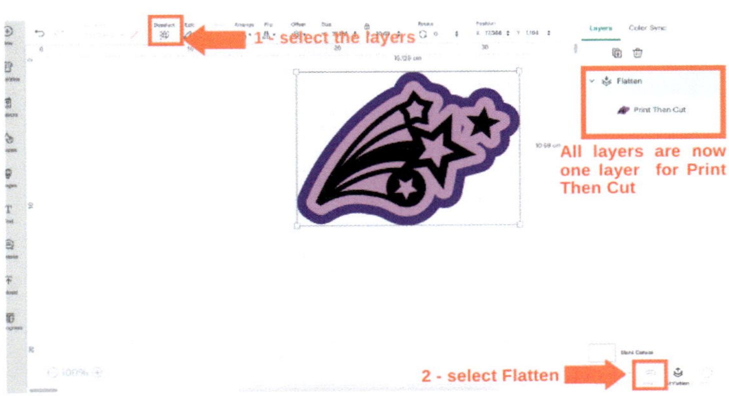

To Print-Then-Cut

For Print-Then-Cut projects, such as stickers, select all the layers and click Flatten. This will flatten the original object layer to the offset layer/s before printing.

Cricut Access Image: Shooting Stars #M472F3

HOW TO MAKE NEW SHAPES OUT OF THE CRICUT SHAPES

You can create unique shapes just by combining the basic shapes already in Design Space.

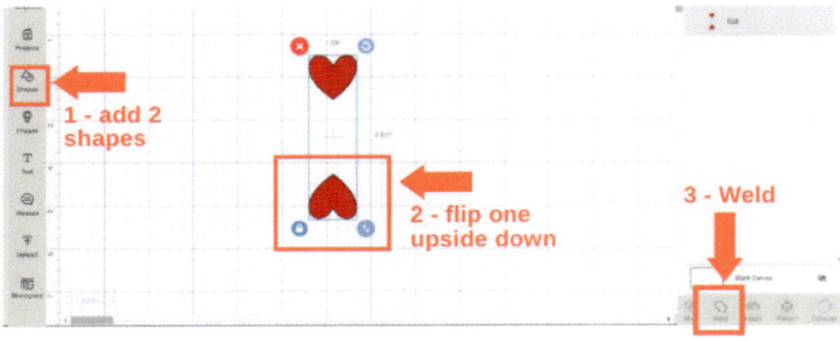

Step 1

Add 2 shapes to the canvas, **flip one of them upside down** (if needed - a circle doesn't need flipped), **align them both horizontally,** and **weld** them together.

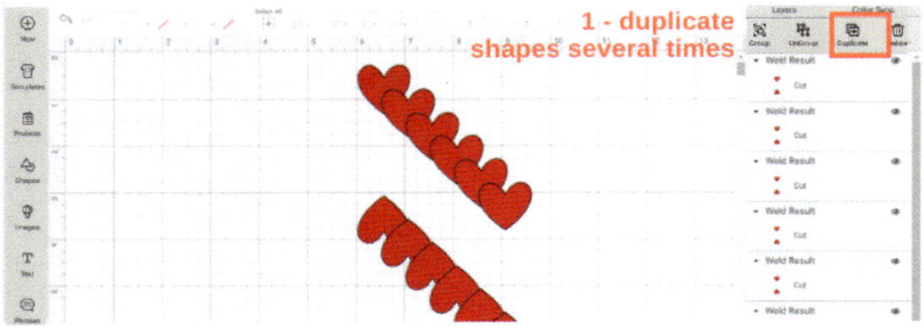

Step 2

Duplicate your welded shape several times (the number of copies will vary but you can add or delete copies as needed - it's a bit of trial and error).

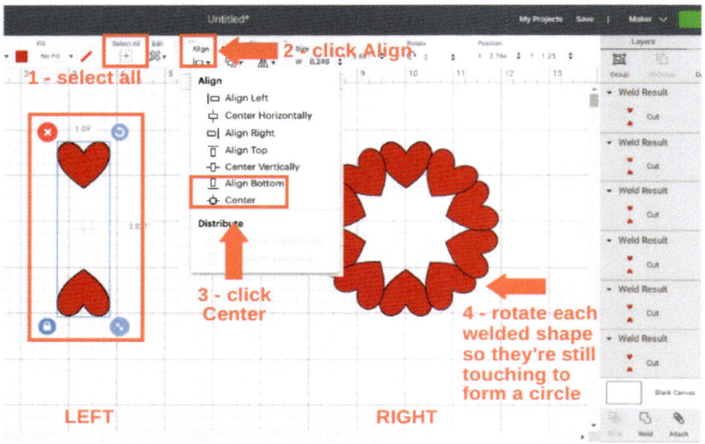

Step 3

Select all your welded shapes and click Align then click Center so they're stacked on top of each other (left side). **Click on each shape layer one by one and rotate them slightly so they're still touching** the vertical welded shape. **Repeat for each layer**, continuing to rotate them until you have them all touching in a circle (right side).

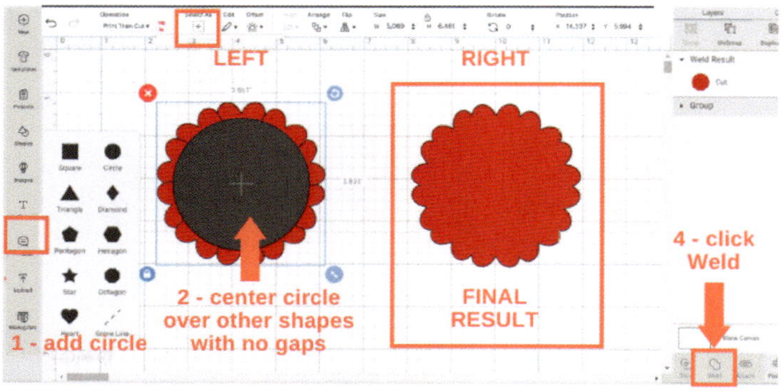

Step 4

Add a circle to the canvas and **center it over your grouping of shapes so it covers all the center part with no gaps** (left side). Select all then Weld and you'll now have a unique new shape (right side). *Try this will all kinds of shapes & you'll be amazed at the unique new shapes you can create!*

HOW TO CREATE FRAMES WITH SHAPES

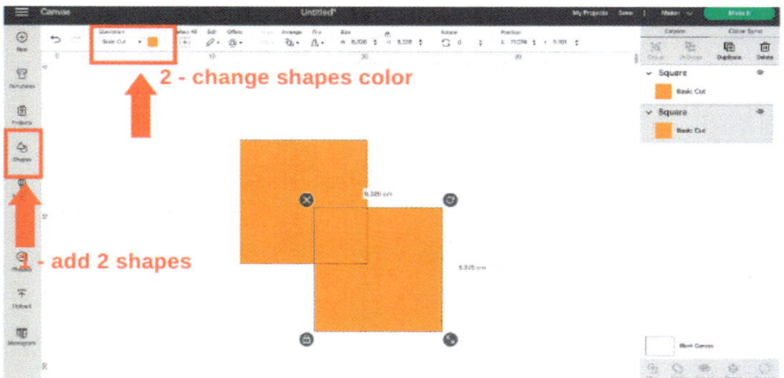

Step 1

Tap on Shapes in the Design Panel. **Add 2 shapes** to your canvas and **change their color** if you want.

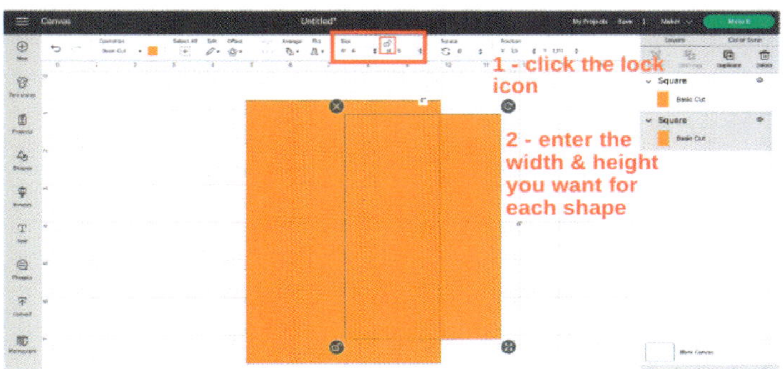

Step 2

Resize each square into a rectangle by **clicking the lock icon** between the width & height to unlock the proportions and **entering the size you want**. In this example, one rectangle is 5x7" and the other is 4x6".

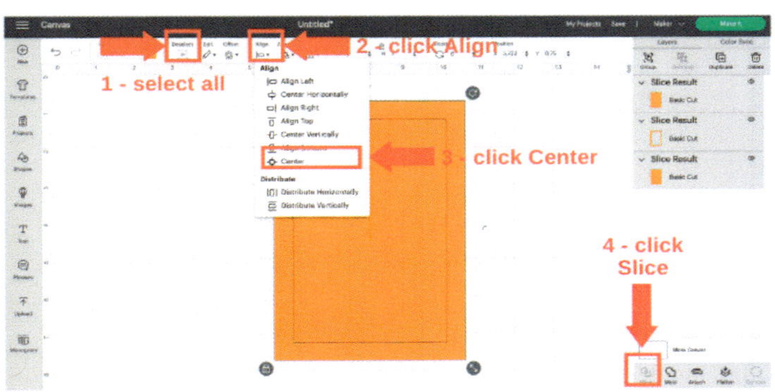

Step 3

Select both shapes by clicking Select All in the Edit Bar. Then align the shapes horizontally and vertically by **clicking Align & choosing Center**.

With all still selected, click on Slice in the Actions Panel.

Step 4

Delete the extra "slice result" layers that are in the center of your new frame by selecting them and clicking Delete so you can see the resulting frame. **This process works with any shape** so you can make lots of fun frames.

HOW TO SLICE A WORD OUT OF A SHAPE

Step 1

Click Shapes in the Design Panel and **add a shape** to your canvas. **Click Text** in the Design Panel and **add some text**. **Choose the font style** in the Font Edit Bar and move the letters closer together if needed (see page 63 for more details).

Step 2

Move your text over the shape and resize or rotate to get the look you want.

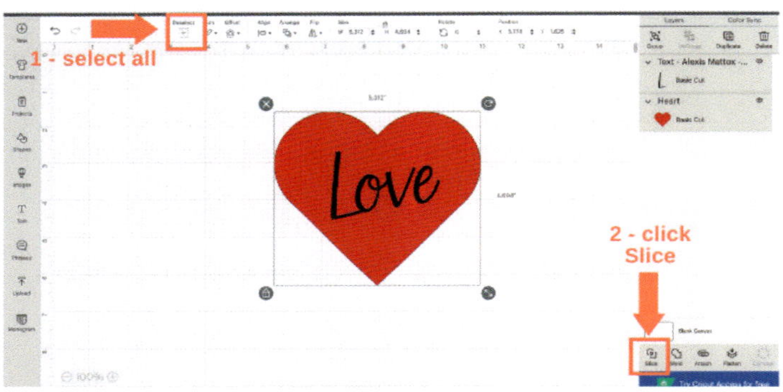

Step 3

Select the text and shape by clicking Select All in the Edit Bar.

Click on Slice in the Actions Panel.

Step 4

Delete or hide the extra "slice result" layers and you'll now have a shape with text cut out from it. **This process works with any shape or text** so you can make lots of unique projects.

Cricut Font Shown: Alexis Mattox - Emma Rae

HOW TO MAKE A PATTERNED SHAPE

You can combine shapes to create unique print then cut projects.

Step 1

Click Images in the Design Panel and **select 2 images** (one simple shape and one intricate one works well). Change both images to Print Then Cut by clicking Fill in the Edit Bar and change from No Fill to Print. Change the colors of each image.

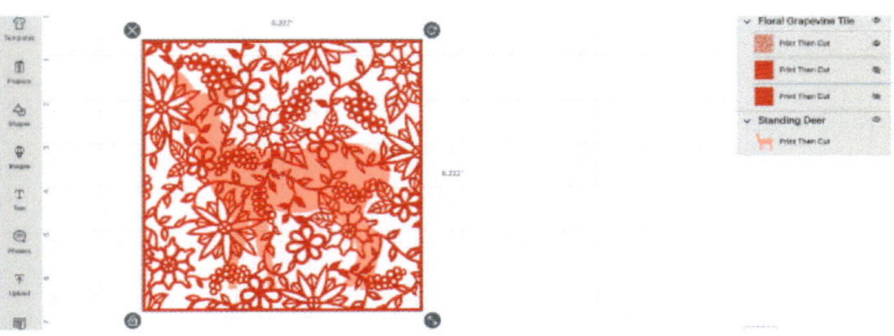

Step 2

Arrange the intricate image where you want it to be over the simple image. You can resize if needed.

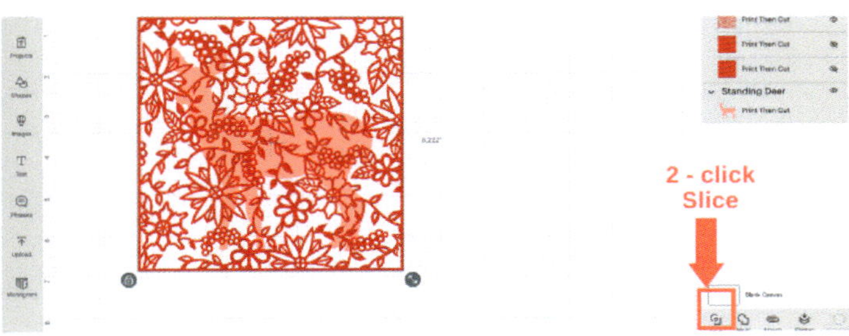

Step 3

Select both image layers and **click Slice.**

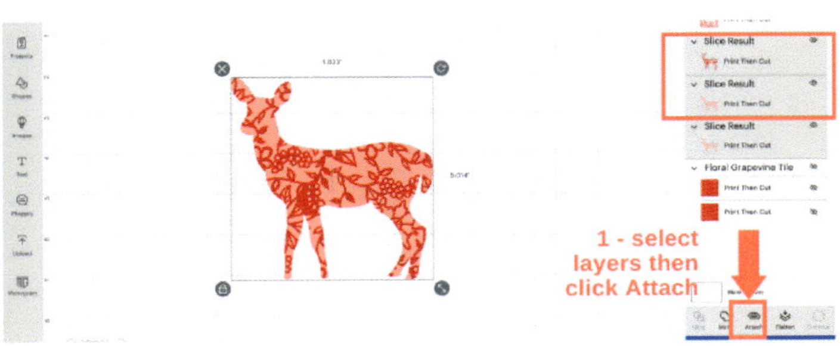

Step 4

Hide or delete the extra "slice result" layers and you'll have a patterned shape to Print Then Cut. **Select the layers you want** and **click Attach** so they'll stay together as one image.

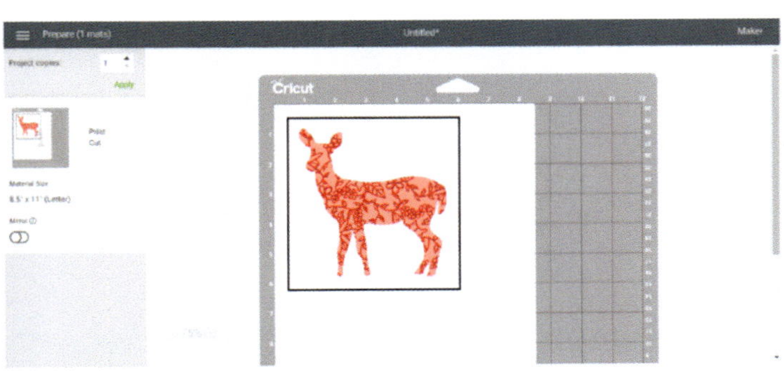

Step 5

Click Make It and you'll see your patterned Print Then Cut project on the mat.

Cricut Access Images:
Deer #M891040C
Floral Grapevine Tile #M232C61B

HOW TO FILL SHAPES AND/OR TEXT WITH PHOTOS

You can fill words or shapes with photos to create unique print then cut projects. Upload your photos to prepare for this project (see pages 47-48 for detailed instructions).

Step 1

Click Text in the Design Panel and **add words** to your canvas (thicker fonts work best, but experiment). You can also do this with shapes. **Click Upload** and **select a photo you've uploaded** and add it to the canvas.

Step 2

Send the photo to back by clicking Arrange and Send to Back. **Change the text (or shape) operation to draw temporarily** so you can see where to place the photo.

Step 3

Arrange the photo where you want it to be on the text (or shape). You can resize the text (or shape) if needed.

Step 4

Change the text (or shape) back to Cut in the operation dropdown. **Select both layers and click Slice** in the Action Panel.

Step 3

You can **hide or delete the extra "slice result" layers** and you'll now have text with a photo fill. The other slice results may be fun to use too though.

Cricut Font Shown: Close to my Heart - Artistry

HOW TO EDIT A MULTI-COLOR LAYERED SVG IN DESIGN SPACE

Note

You can remove, combine, group and/or change the color of any layer in your SVG files.

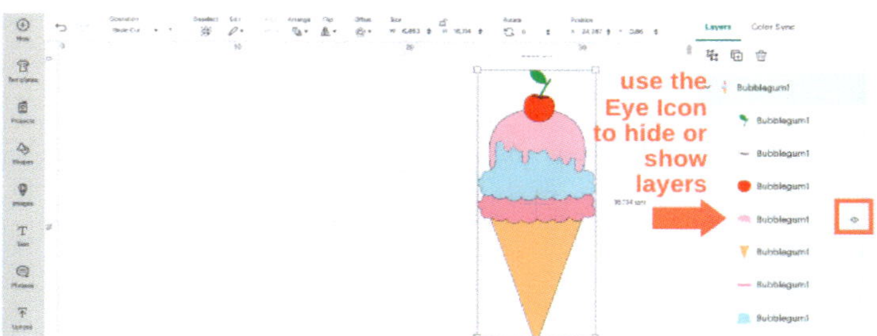

Hide/Show/Delete

Insert a layered SVG on your canvas. (see page 50-51 for upload instructions). To hide a layer from your workspace without deleting it, **click the Eye icon** in the Layers Panel. **Click the eye icon** again to show the image. To delete the layer permanently, **click to highlight the layer** and press the delete button on your keyboard.

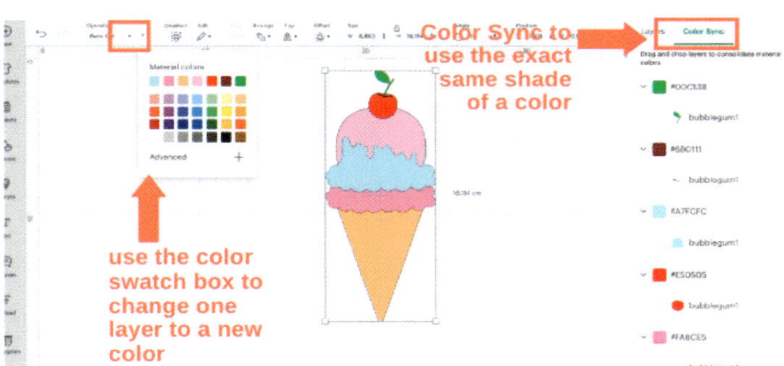

Changing Colors

You can change the layer's color either with the color box (next to Linetype in the top bar) or by using the the **Color Sync Panel**. You would use Color Sync to get the exact same shade of color and to quickly reduce down the number of colors you're using.

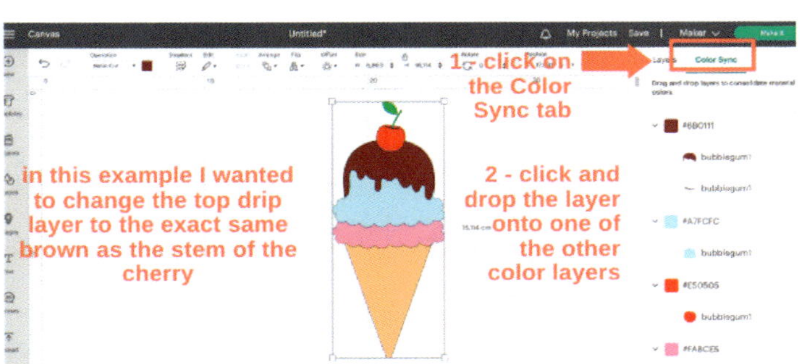

Combining Layers

To reduce the number or colors and layers, simply **click on the Color Sync tab** in the top right of your screen. **Click the layer you want to change** and drag it to the layer color you want to change it to.

Commercial Use Image (PNG, SVG, EPS, & DXF) from Design Bundles (seller is Redearth and Gumtrees):
https://designbundles.net/redearth-and-gumtrees/496170-huge-summer-nautical-and-tropical-bundle-svg-merma

HOW TO CHANGE A SINGLE LAYER IMAGE INTO MULTIPLE LAYERS

Note

Changing a single layer image into multiple layers will allow you create a more detailed design with multiple colors.

Step 1

Insert an image onto your canvas. Decide how many colors your completed image will be. You will need to **Duplicate** your image that many times. After you have duplicated your image choose one of your duplicate layers and **click Contour.**

Step 2

Here you can choose to **Hide All Contours** or manually hide each element individually. **Click all the elements of your image that will be the same color**. The darker shaded elements on your contour panel are the elements you will see after you contour. Once you've selected your elements simply **X out** of the contour screen. Repeat this step for each color set.

Step 3

Once all of your elements are contoured you will see all your layers in the layers panel on the right. You can now assemble your image to see the final project. Once assembled, select the entire image and group.

Cricut Acess Image: Bunny #MB02E9D7

HOW TO SAVE IMAGES FROM DESIGN SPACE TO YOUR DESKTOP

Note

Saving an image from Design Space is the only way you can share your designs with people who don't use Design Space yourself. It is also the only way to save things like logos that you may want to use outside out Design Space.

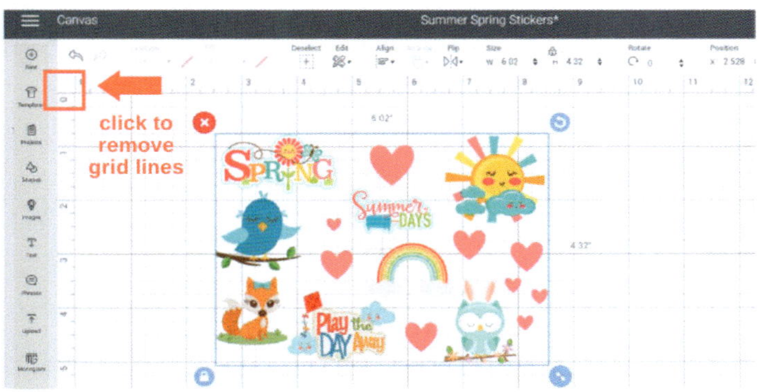

Step 1

Create your image/s in Design Space. **Remove the Grid Lines** from your canvas. To do so simply click twice in the small box (It is grey and unlabeled) at the top left corner of the canvas.

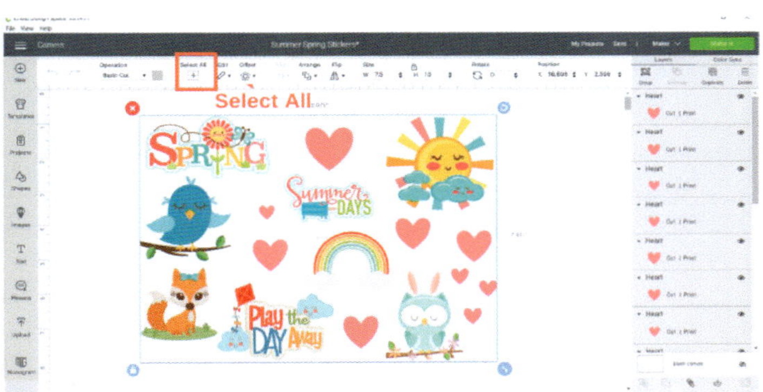

Step 2

Select your image (if you have multiple elements make sure to Select All the layers) **and adjust the size.** I like to make it as big as I can. You want to make sure that all elements are visible on the screen and that no edges are cut off.

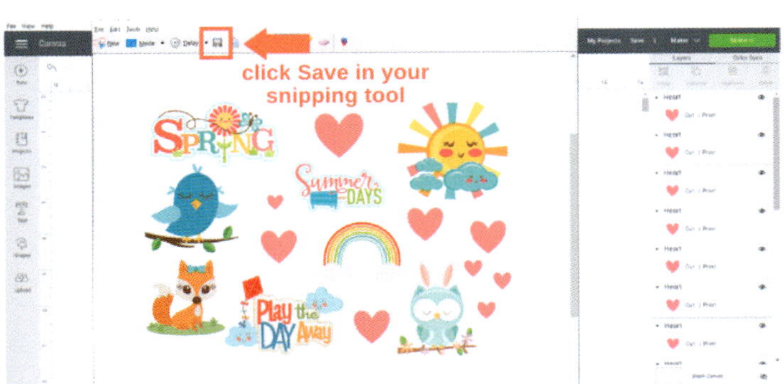

Step 3

Take a **screen shot of the image** using the **snipping tool on a PC or Cmd+Shift+4 on a Mac**. Save your screen shot to your computer.

Cricut Design Space Project Sharing Link Below:
https://design.cricut.com/landing/project-detail/5f1f78dc5380e90ef05d2a4a

HOW TO ADD FONTS TO CRICUT DESIGN SPACE

To Install Fonts on Your Computer

The term "add" fonts to Design Space is kind of misleading. Design Space only accesses the font files that are installed on your computer. Bear in mind that not all fonts work well in Design Space, including ones that are distressed or very uneven looking. Your best bet is to look for clean lines and simple font shapes.

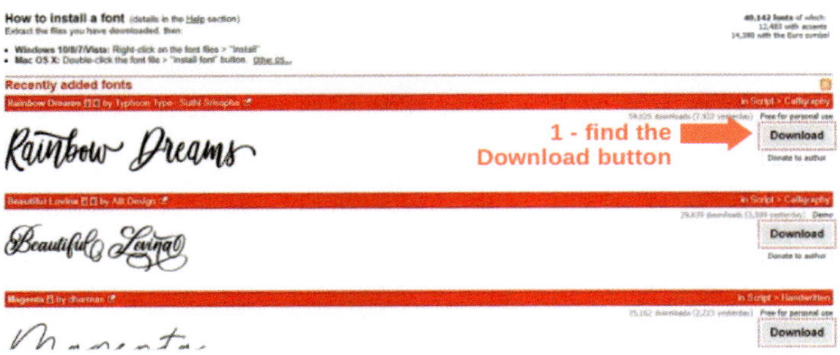

Step 1

Download the font from your chosen site. Most sites have instructions or a quick download button. Save it to your computer.

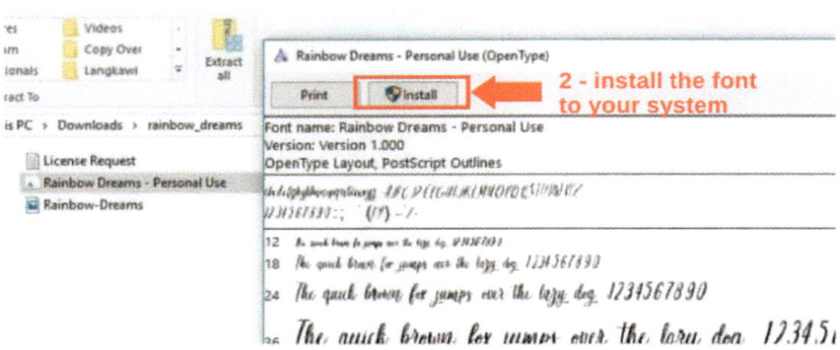

Step 2

Find the file on your computer, which will be zipped, and **unzip it**. Next, **double click on the font file with the .ttf extension** and **click on install** in the window that pops up.

To Use Fonts Installed on Your Computer in Cricut Design Space

NOTE: To make sure Design Space loads your new fonts, you must start up (or close and restart) Design Space or refresh Design Space and it will automatically load your new fonts.

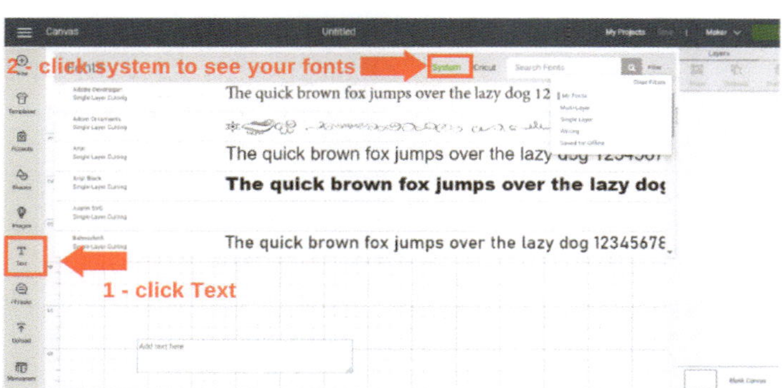

Step 3

Click Text on the design panel to the left of the Canvas to add a text box. **Click the Font dropdown menu & select System at the top** to see all the fonts installed on your computer - look or search for your new font (the list is alpabetical).

HOW TO EDIT YOUR FONT: CHANGING FONT, STYLE, SIZE, ETC.

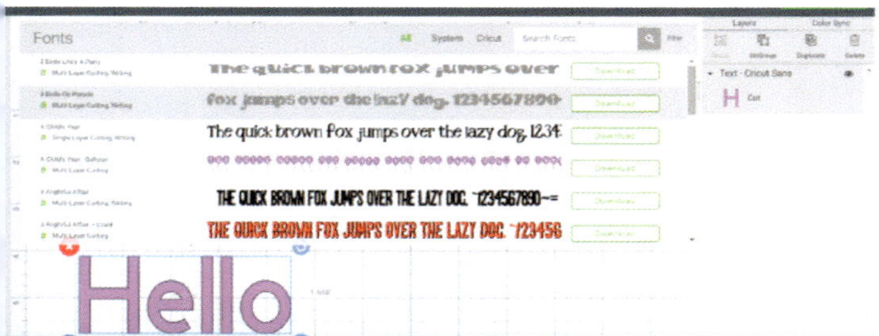

Cricut Font Shown: Cricut Sans

Changing Fonts

In the Text Edit Bar at the top, **use the Font dropdown menu to select the font of your choice**. Select **Cricut Access fonts** or **System Fonts**. Some fonts are not included in the Cricut Access subscription but can be purchased individually here as well.

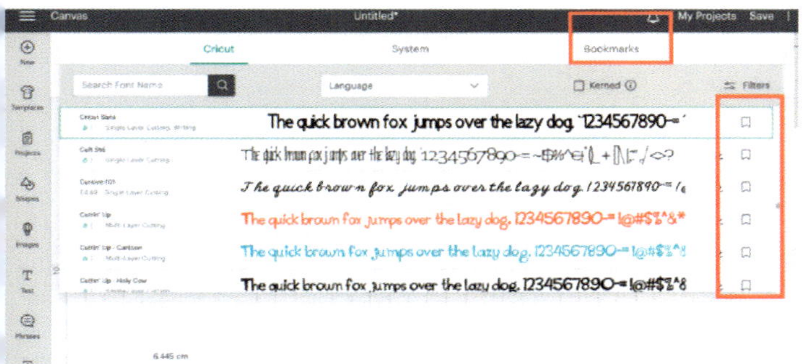

Bookmarking Fonts

Boomark your favorite fonts so you can quickly find them. **Select Text**, click the Font selector, then the Bookmarks tab. To bookmark fonts, **click the Bookmark Icon** next to the font. System fonts you bookmark will only be saved on that device.

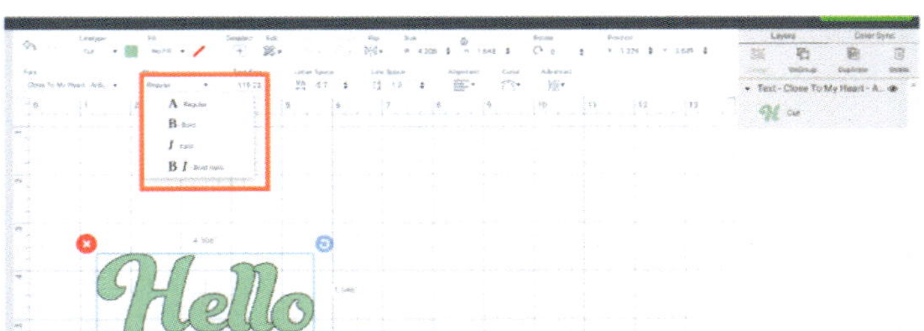

Cricut Font Shown: Close To My Heart - Artbooking

Changing Font Style

The font style allows you to change whether your text is bold, italic, etc. Note: If you use any system fonts, some may have separate fonts for bold or italics, etc. so they must all be installed to use them. Some fonts do not have any extra styles.

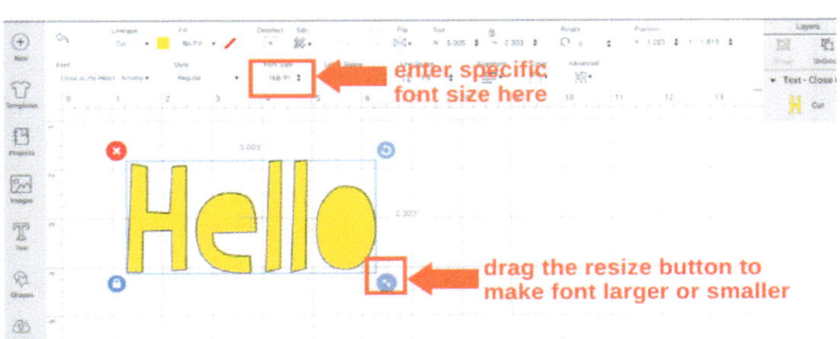

Cricut Font Shown: Close To My Heart - Artistry

Changing Font Size

You can **enter a specific font size in the Text Edit bar** at the top (use the up or down arrows or type in an exact size). You can also **left-click on the resize button by the font & hold the mouse button down while dragging** to make the font larger or smaller.

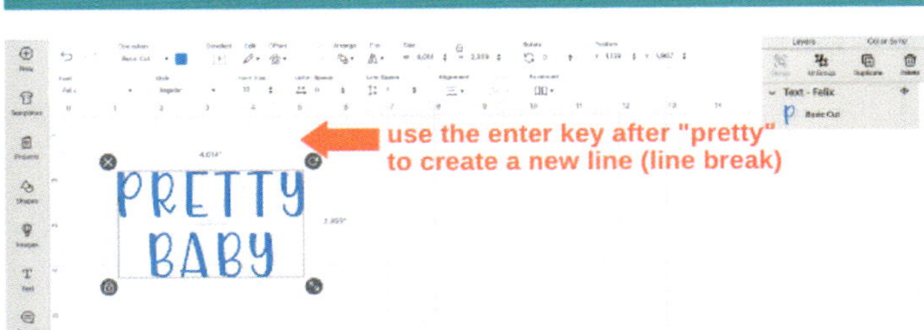

Cricut Font Shown: Felix

Creating Line Breaks

When typing, the text will automatically stay on a single line. If you wish to create a line break to add some words on a new row, use your Enter key where you want to create the new row of text in your text box.

HOW TO CHANGE LETTER AND LINE SPACING

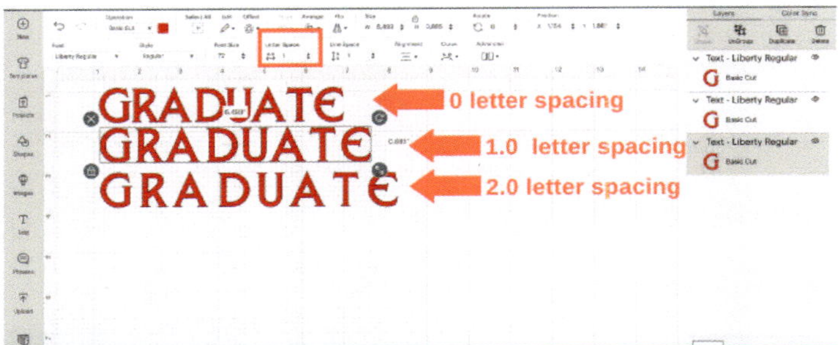

Cricut Font Shown: Liberty Regular

Changing Letter Spacing

To change the space between letters, **use the letter-spacing option in the Text Edit bar**. You can **type in an exact number** or **use the up and down arrow buttons** to move it pixel by pixel.

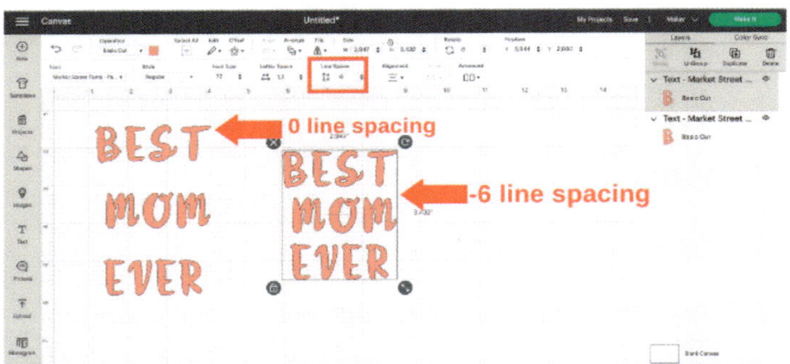

Cricut Font Shown: Market Street Fonts - Paint Can

Changing Line Spacing

Line Spacing allows you to close or expand the gap between each line break. **Click the Line Space arrow keys up or down to increase or decrease spacing. You can also enter a specific number** (even a negative number by using the "-" in front of the number).

HOW TO OUTLINE TEXT

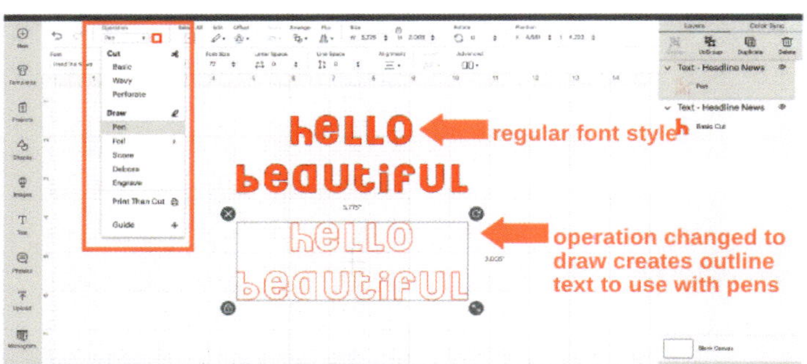

Cricut Font Shown: Headline News (Regular)

Step 1

You can change your text to outlines (with no fill). Cricut will automatically outline thick fonts when you use the "draw" function (because the pens can't color in elements to create the thick bold font). **Click on Operation** in the Edit Bar and **change from Cut to Draw**. Your font will now be an outline, and **you can select your pen color** from the swatch beside Operation.

NOTE: This method only works for draw because as soon as you change the operation to cut it fills in the text again.

HOW TO ALIGN AND CURVE TEXT

To Align Text

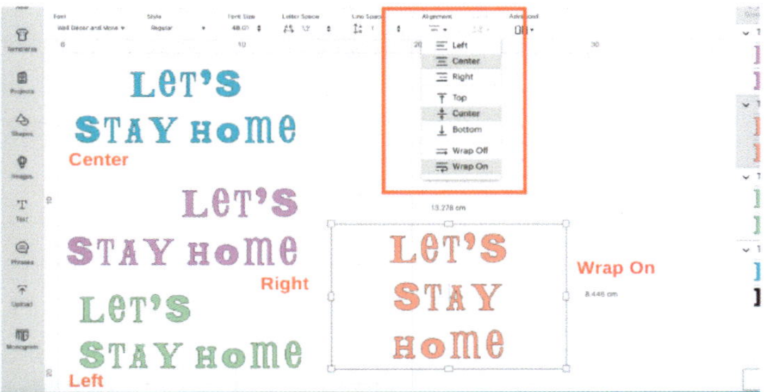

Cricut Font Shown: Wall Decor and More

Aligning Text

To change the text alignment, **select the Align dropdown** in the Edit Bar and **choose, left, center, right or wrap on.**

To Curve Text

Curving Text

To curve text, **click on Curve** in the Text Edit Bar. **Use the slider** to curve the words either up or down. A higher number creates a slight arch, a lower number creates a circle (drag all the way right or left). You can also enter a specific number for more control over the arch. To undo the curve, enter 0 (zero) in the Curve box.

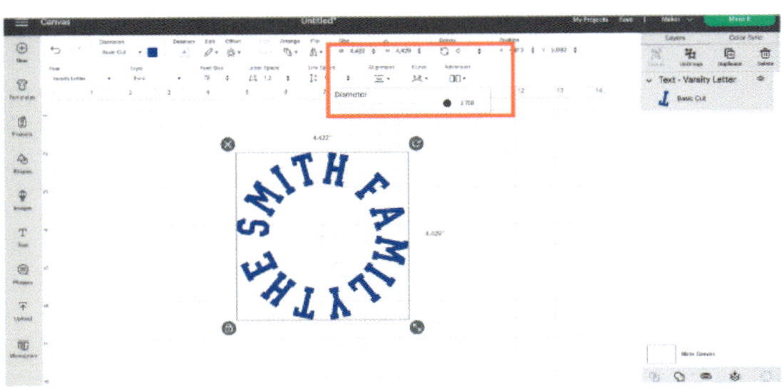

Cricut Font Shown: Varsity Letter Bold

Notes

- You may need to adjust the letter spacing as you arch or make a circle of your text to make it look better.
- Curve is only an option when you have a single line of text. If you make line breaks with your enter key the curve button will be greyed out and unusable.
- Some text does not look good curved, especially if you make it into a circle, so you might have to experiment to find the best font.

HOW TO CREATE VERTICAL TEXT

Step 1

Click Text to add text to your canvas.

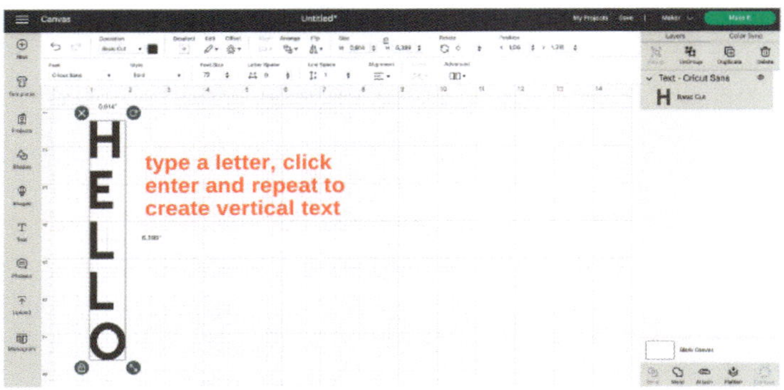

Step 2

Press the enter/return key on your computer after each letter you type to create vertical text.

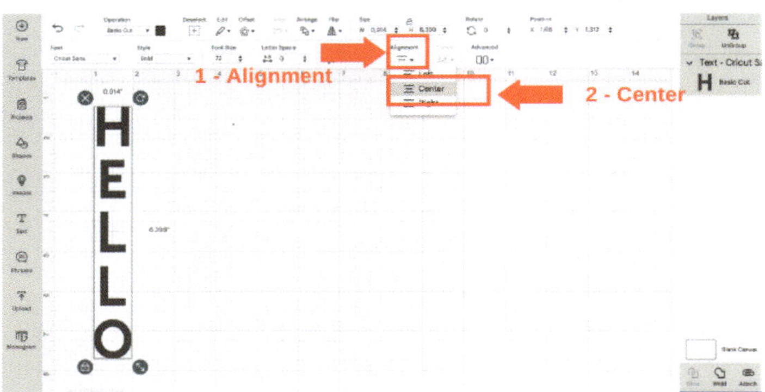

Alignment and Line Spacing

You might need to center align your letters and to fix line spacing issues.

Select your text and **click Alignment** and then **click Center.**

You can also increase or decrease the line space between the letters (see page 63 for instructions).

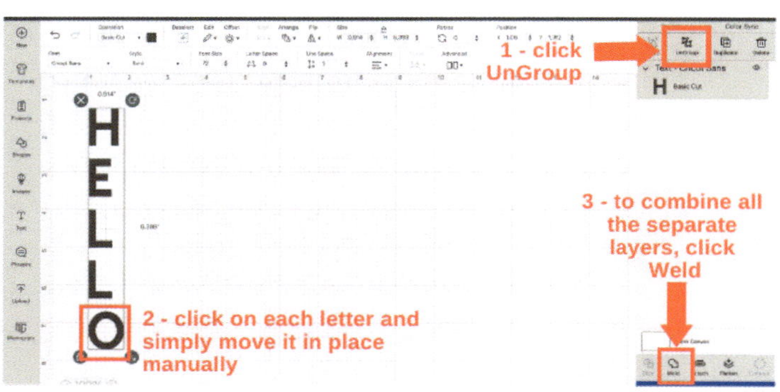

Font Shown: Cricut Sans Bold

Fixing Each Letter Individually

Sometimes the line spacing between the letters are really uneven. In this case you will need to **Click UnGroup** to separate the letters to individual layers. Next **click on each letter and move in it place** to fix the gaps. Next we need to merge all the letter layers to one single layer. To do so **click Weld** and now you have perfectly aligned vertical text.

HOW TO CREATE A MONOGRAM

NOTE: If you have Cricut Access you can use the Monogram Tool to create a Monogram. Use the steps below to create a Monogram if you do not have Cricut Access.

Step 1

Click Text and type one of your initials. Change the font to your favorite monogram font (you can find many free online). **Duplicate that letter 2 times** so you have 3 letters total on screen.

Step 2

Separate the 3 initials and **change the other 2 letters** to whatever you need for your names. **Increase the size of your last name letter. Put the letters in order** (first name, last name {big letter}, middle name).

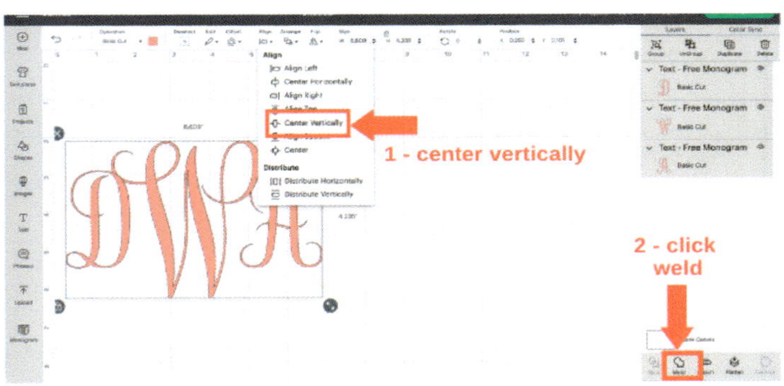

Step 3

Move the 2 smaller letters close to the larger letter so they overlap. **Select all** the letters and **click Align** in the Edit Bar and choose **Center Vertically.** With all letters still selected, **click Weld** in the Actions Panel.

Final Result

With your final monogram there are no overlapping cut lines like there were before welding. Once welded like this, you can resize the entire monogram without causing problems and when it cuts, it will all cut as one piece instead of separate letters.

Font Shown: Free Monogram Beta from dafont.com

HOW TO CREATE A SPLIT MONOGRAM

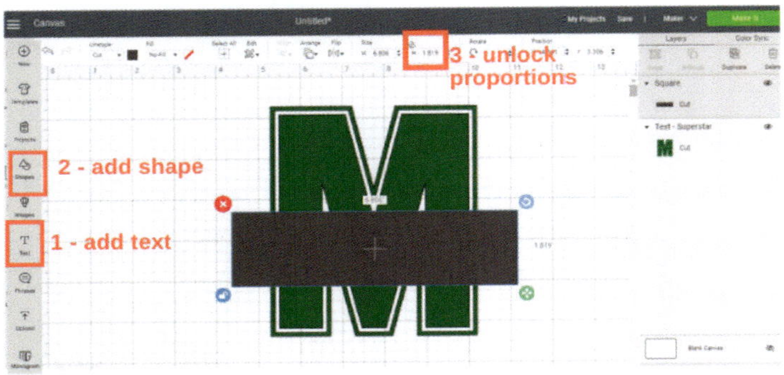

Step 1

Click Text and type the letter of your last name. Increase the size of your font so it will be easier to work with. **Add a square to the canvas** and unlock the proportions & change it to a rectangle. **Position where you want the monogram to split.**

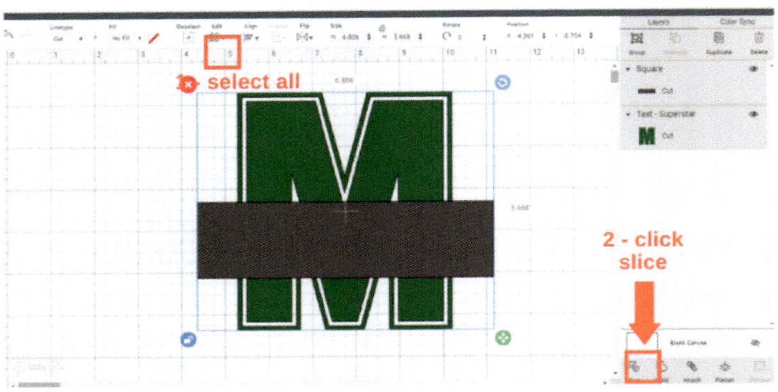

Step 2

Click Select all to select both the rectangle & your letter. **Click Slice** in the Actions Panel to cut the part where the letter and rectangle overlap.

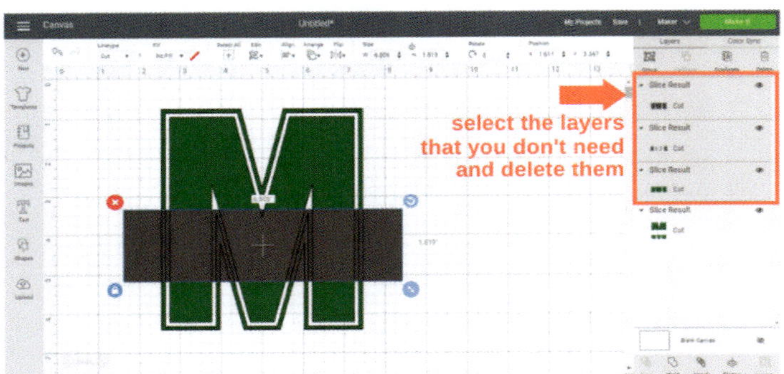

Step 3

Select the layers that you don't need in the Layers Panel and delete them. This will leave you with a nice cut out gap in your letter where you can add your last name in the next step.

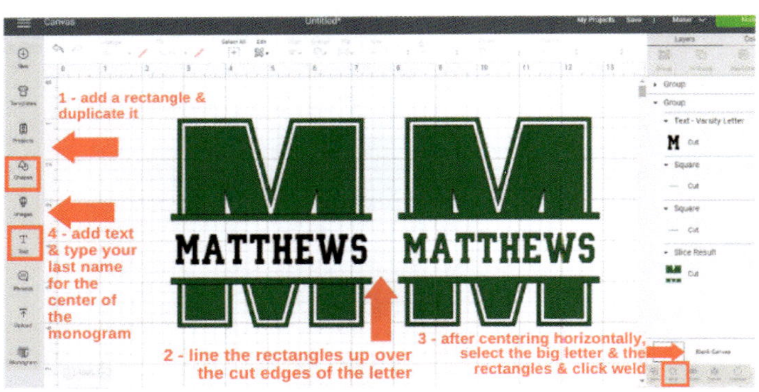

Step 4

Add a rectangle to the canvas and make it long and narrow. **Place it at the edge of the cut letter** to give it a nicer finish. **Duplicate the rectangle** for the other cut edge. **Select all, click Align & center horizontally then click Weld** so it will cut as one piece. **Click Text and type your last name in a matching font.** Center it in the open area of the cutout letter. Make sure to align horizontally again.

Cricut Fonts Shown:
for large letter M: Superstar
for last name: Varsity Letter Bold

HOW TO CREATE A MONOGRAM USING MONOGRAM MAKER TOOL

NOTE: Use the steps in pages 66 - 67 to create a Monogram and Split Monogram if you do not have Cricut Access.

Step 1

Click Monogram on the left hand side menu**. Change the font** to your favorite monogram font (you can find many free online). **Duplicate that letter 2 times** so you have 3 letters total on screen.

Step 2

Type in your initials or letters you wish to use for the monogram.

Step 3

Select the style of the monogram. Modern, Elegant, Handwritten or Vintage.

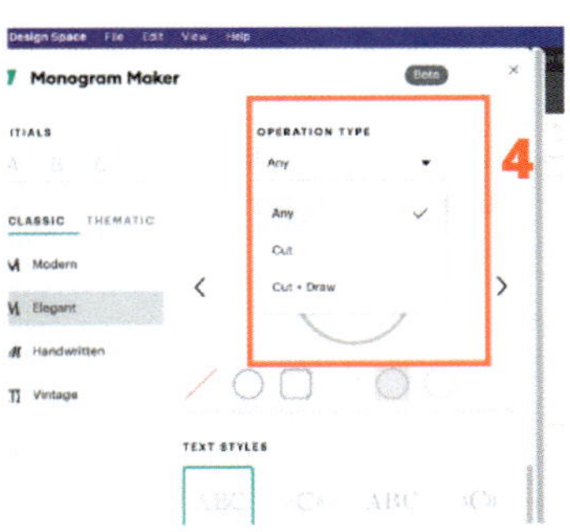

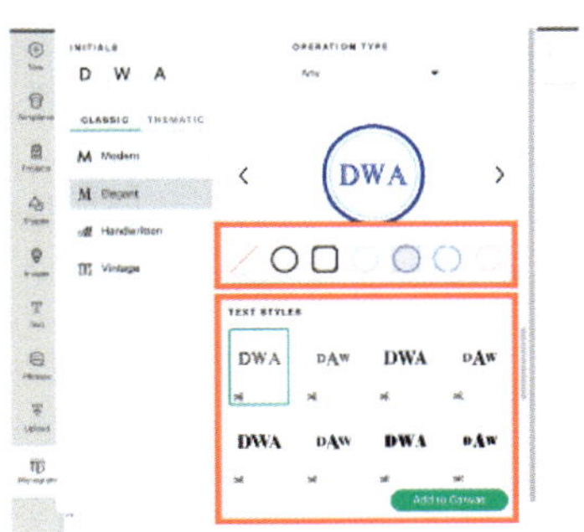

Step 4

Select the if you want to add a border.

Step 5

Select the Text Style. This changes depending on the style of Monogram chosen.

Final Result

When you are happy with what you have selected, click **Add to Canvas**. The monogram will appear on the project canvas. If you are happy click on Make It, the machine will cut or cut + draw depending on the operation type you have chosen.

HOW TO CUT SHAPES OUT OF YOUR TEXT LETTERS

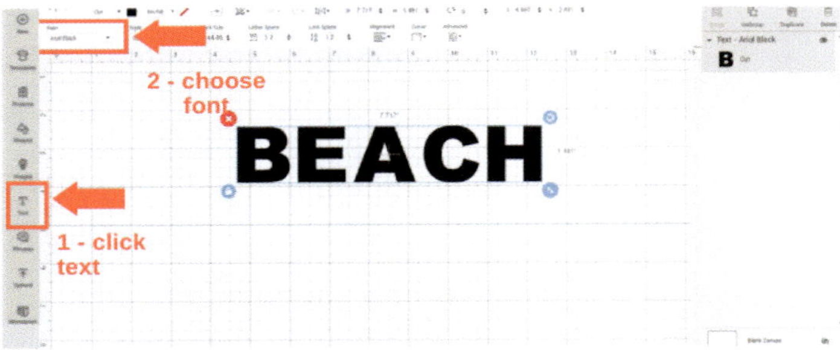

Step 1

Click Text to add your text to the canvas. Choose your font. A bold or chunky font works best for this. This is **Arial Black Bold.**

Step 2

Add SVG's, shapes or images to your canvas. You can use either a Cricut image or one you've uploaded. **Arrange** them on your text.
TIP: I find that it helps to change the color so you can see them easily.

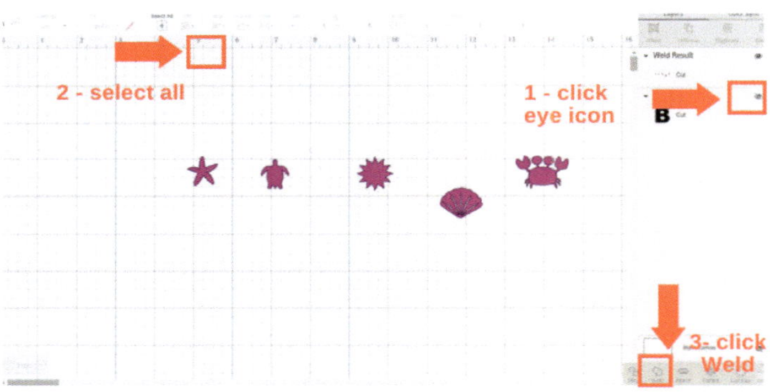

Step 3

Click the Eye icon to hide your text. You can only slice with two layers, so we need to weld the pieces together to create one single layer from all your elements.
Click **Select All** and **click Weld**.

Step 4

Click the Eye icon again to un-hide your text. **Click Select All** and **Click Slice.**

Once you move your sliced pieces you will have your text with the images cut out.

Font Shown: Arial Black Commercial Use Image (PNG, SVG, EPS, & DXF) from Design Bundles (seller is Redearth and Gumtrees):
https://designbundles.net/redearth-and-gumtrees/496170-huge-summer-nautical-and-tropical-bundle-svg-merma

HOW TO CREATE TEXT SHAPES

Step 1

Add your Shape or Image to your canvas. **Add your Text** to your canvas. Choose a font for your text.

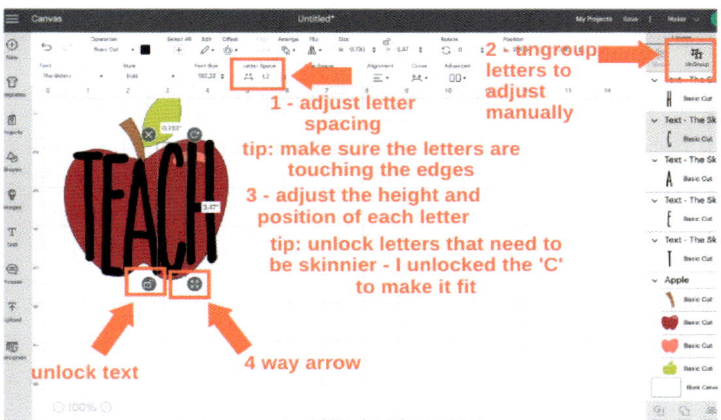

Step 2

Arrange your text on top of your shape/image. I love having both ends of my word on the edge of the shape. **Use Letter Spacing** to move the letters close together. **Click UnGroup** to seperate the letters. **Move and resize each letter** to fit the shape of your image. You can also unlock a letter to make it thinner or fatter.

Step 3

Once your text is where you want it, **hide the image/shape** by clicking on the eye. Next **click Select All** to select all your individual letters and then **click Weld**. This will join all the separate layers together to become one single layer.

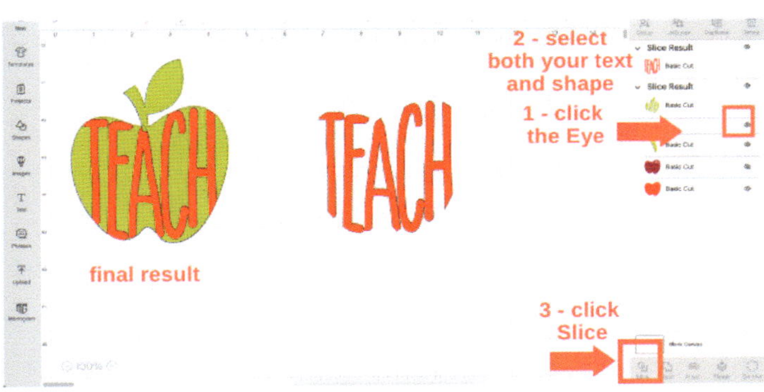

Image: Apple #M3B3B0 Font Shown: The Skinny Bold (free - dafont)

Step 4

Click on the eye to make your image/shape visible again. **Select the Text and one layer of your image** (you can only slice two layers). **Click Slice** to cut the text out of the shape. **Move your new layers to the side** to reveal your letters that are now shaped like your image/shape.

HOW TO USE FONT GLYPHS (FOR PC)

You can use font glyphs to add beautiful flourishes to your text. Character Map comes installed on most PC's, but there are other programs you can install like Main Type.

Step 1: PC Users

Click Text and **type your desired text** into the text box. **Choose the Font** you want to use. **TIP:** Not all fonts come with extra characters. The '*I Love Glitter*' font is one of the most popular font glyph fonts.

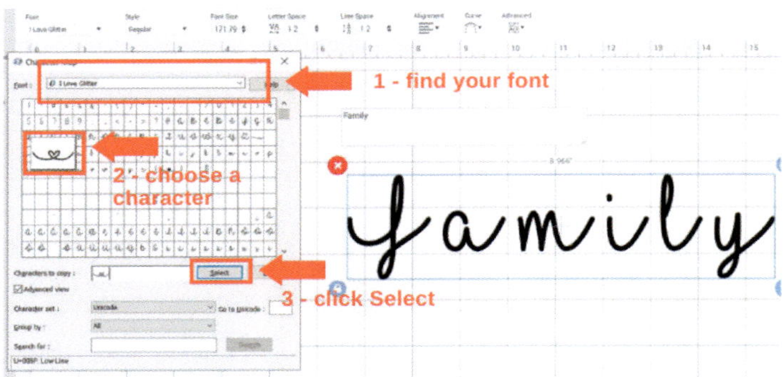

Step 2

Open Character Map on your computer. Find your font. **Click on the character** you want to use and **click Select**.

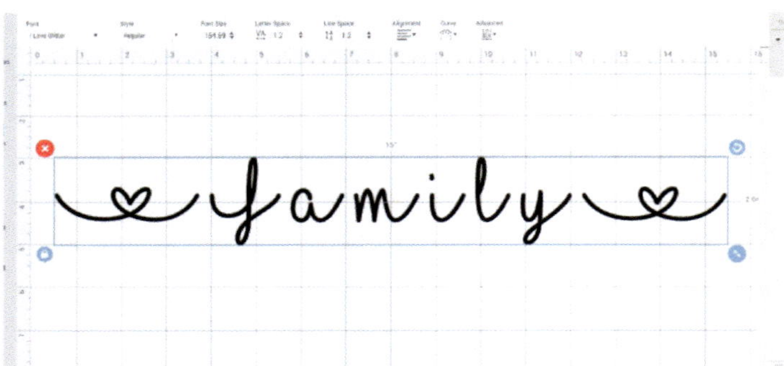

Step 3

Return to Design Space and **open your Text Box**. Place your cursor where you want to insert your character and **press Ctrl + V** to paste your character into the box. Repeat if necessary to add all the characters you need.

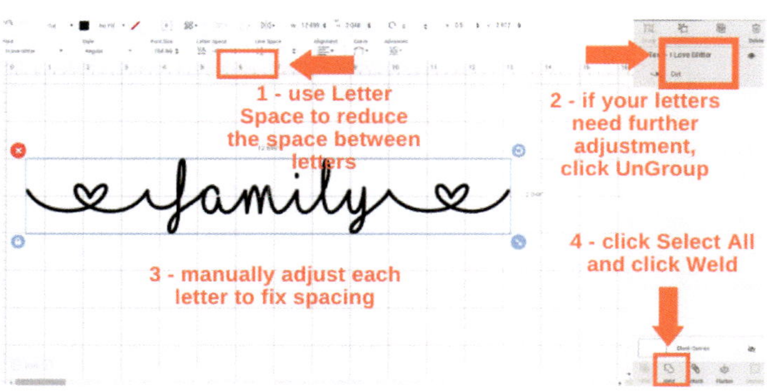

Final Result

You will need to fix the spacing. Use the **Letter Spacing** function in the top tool bar. <u>OR</u> **Click UnGroup** to seperate your letters into individual layers. You can now move each letter manually. **Lastly click Weld** to join all letters into one layer.

Font Shown: Free Version I Love Glitter from Dafont

HOW TO USE FONT GLYPHS (FOR MAC)

You can use font glyphs to add beautiful florishes to your text. Font Book comes installed on most Mac's and can be used to open and read font characters.

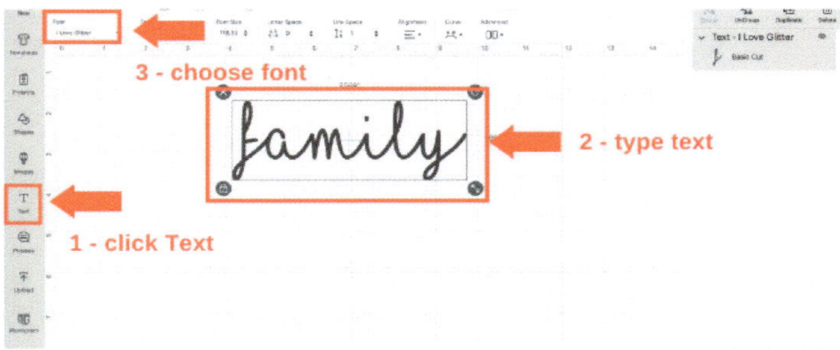

Step 1: Mac Users

Click Text and **type your desired text** into the text box. **Choose the Font** you want to use.

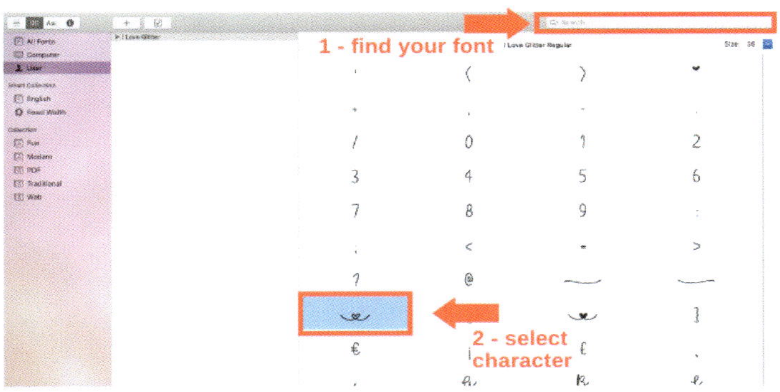

Step 2

Open Font Book on your computer. Find your font. **Click on the character** you want to use and **either click Edit then Copy** at the top of the screen or **CMD + C**.

Step 3

Return to Design Space and **open your Text Box**. Place your cursor where you want to insert your character and **CMD + V** to paste your character. Repeat if necessary to add all the characters you need.

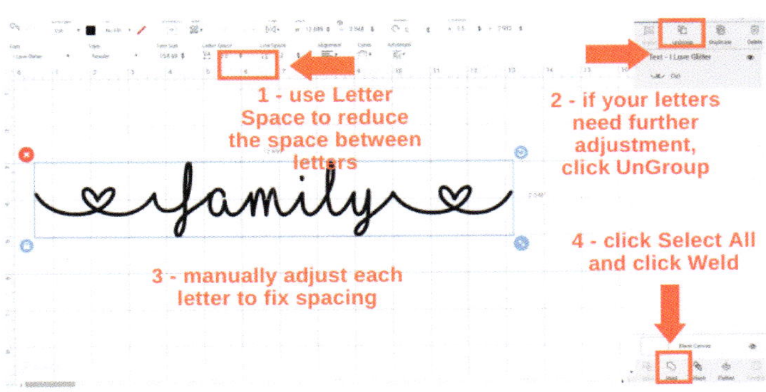

Final Result

You will need to fix the spacing. Use the **Letter Spacing** function in the top tool bar. OR **Click UnGroup** to seperate your letters into individual layers. You can now move each letter manually. **Lastly click Weld** to join all letters into one layer.

Font Shown: I Love Glitter from Dafont

HOW TO OFFSET TEXT

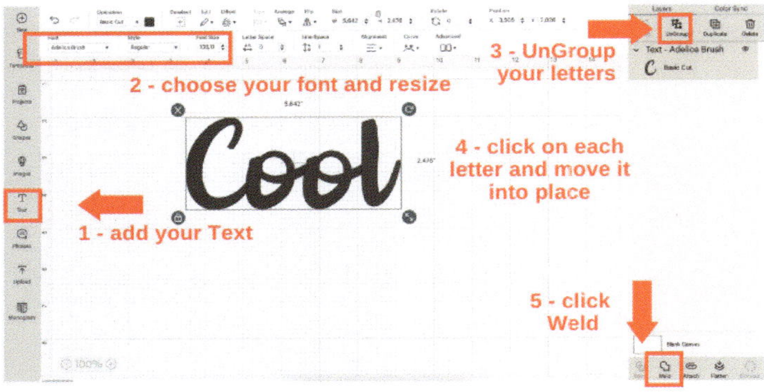

Step 1

Click Text and **add your text** to the text box. **Choose your font and resize** - see page 62 (if required). If you need to fix letter spacing, **click on UnGroup**, **move the letters manually**. Then **click Select All** and **click Weld**.

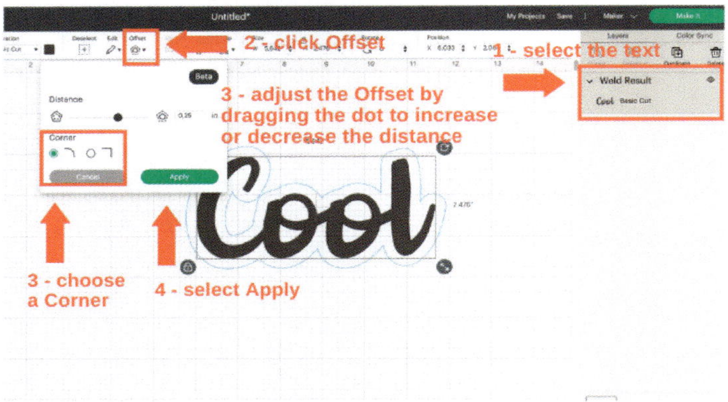

Step 2

Select your text, **click Offset** and adjust the border size around your text by adjusting the **Distance** on the slide bar. You can also change if the shadow layer is to be curved or angular. Click **Apply** and the shadow layer will appear to offset your text.

Step 3

To change the color of the Offset, select your Offset layer. Click on the color fill square and select the color for the Offset (shadow) layer. To create multiple Offset layers, select the Offset Layer and repeat steps 2-3.

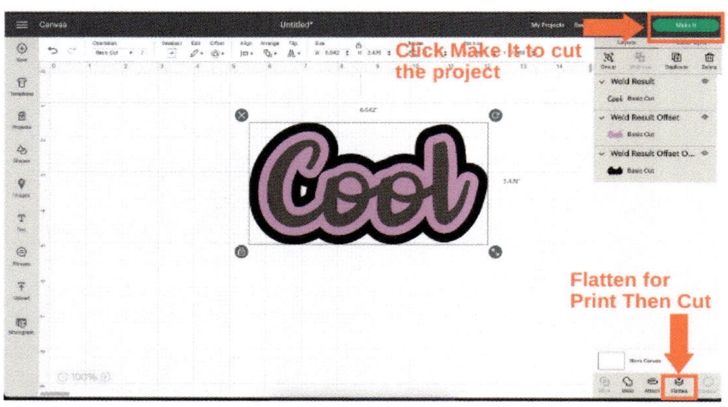

Final Result

For Print Then Cut projects, such as stickers, flatten the original object layer to the offset layer before printing.

For a cut project, you can go ahead and click on 'Make It' to cut out your pieces.

Font Shown: Cricut Access: Brush Script

HOW TO CREATE KNOCKOUT (WITH OFFSET)

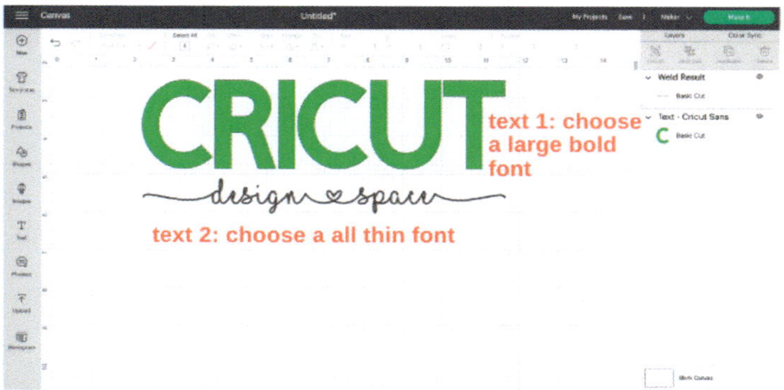

Step 1

Add your first text. Choose a thick font. Change the color of the text and resize for your project. **Add your second text. Choose a thin font** and if needed fix the Letter Spacing (see page 63). Add glyphs if you want (see page 71 & 72)

Step 2

Select your smaller text and then click on Offset. Use the slider to select your offset - I find 0.25-0.30 works well. Then click on Apply.

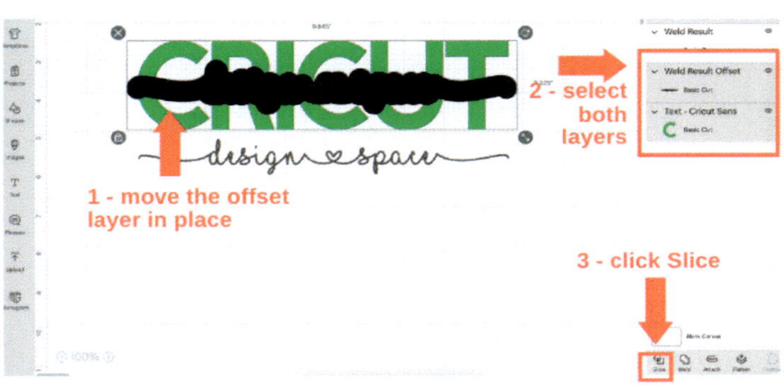

Step 3

Move the offset layer on top of the bold word. I like to center mine on the word. Then select both layers and click on Slice.

Step 4

And then simply delete the sliced layers that you don't need any longer. Move your small font in place to see what it will look like. Then click on Make It.

Font Shown: Cricut Sans and I Love Glitter from Dafont

HOW TO CREATE A 3D SHADOW FOR YOUR TEXT

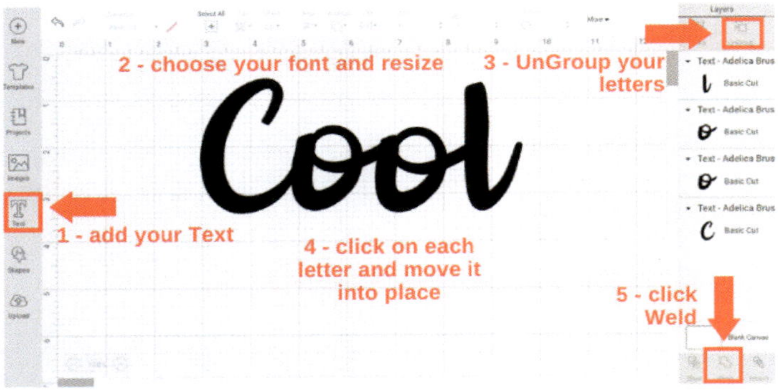

Step 1

Click Text and **add your text** to the text box. **Choose your font and resize** - see page 62 (if required). To fix letter spacing, **click on UnGroup, move the letters manually**. Then **click Select All** and **click Weld**.

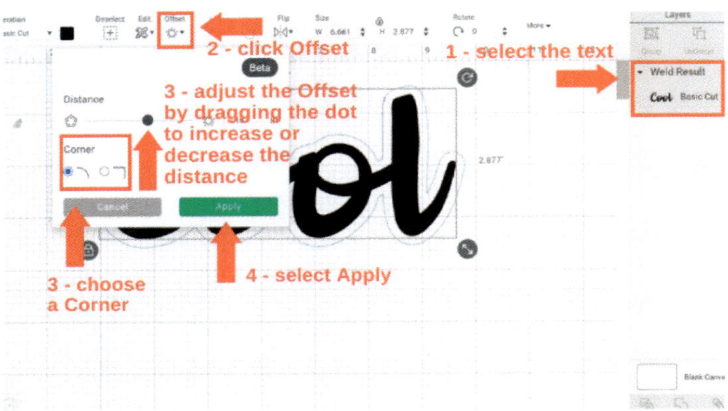

Step 2

Select your text, **click Offset** and adjust the border size around your text by adjusting the **Distance** on the slide bar. You can also change if the shadow layer is to be curved or angular. Click **Apply** and the shadow layer will appear to offset your text.

Step 3

Next, select the black text layer and simply click and drag it to the left and top to create a 3D shadow to your text.

How to Combine Offset with a 3D Shadow Background

Step 4

You can repeat the steps by adding another Offset layer and slightly offsetting the back shadow layer.

Font Shown: Free Font from DaFont: Adelica Brush

HOW TO CREATE WEEDING BOXES AROUND TEXT

Whilst a weeding box is NOT required for cutting text it definitely makes life easier. It helps you to use as little material as possible and it is much easier to weed a smaller piece of vinyl. You can also use the edges of the weeding box to help ensure that you adhere your text straight.

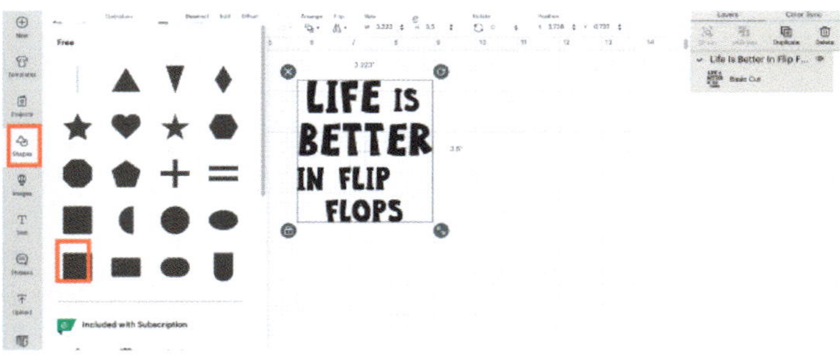

Step 1

Either create your design, upload a design or select one from the Design Space library. To create the weeding box, **click Shapes** and **select the Square.**

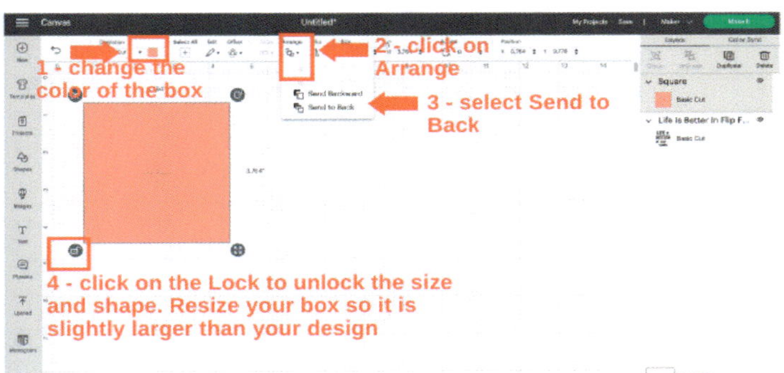

Step 2

Select the square, change the color so it's not the same color as your text. **Click Arrange then click Send to Back**. Next **click on the lock symbol to Unlock** the shape size. **Resize the box** so that it is only slightly larger than your design.

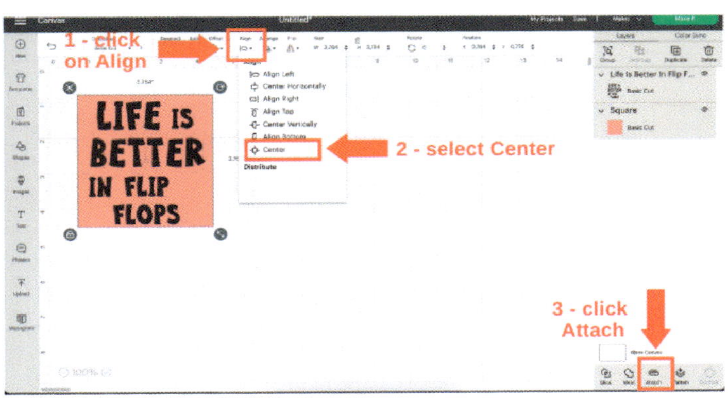

Step 3

Click on Select All to select both the box and your design. **Click on the Align dropdown box and select Center**. With both layers still selected **click Attach.** This will ensure you keep the position of both elements.

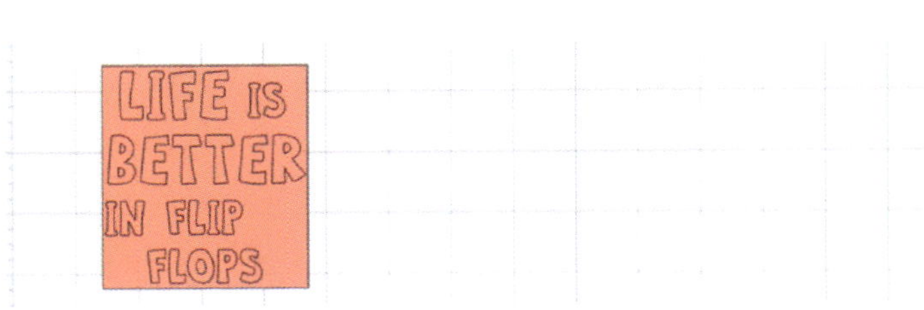

Final Result

After you attach the text/image to the shape you will see all the cut lines.

Cricut Access Image: Life Is Better In Flip Flops #MBE68016

HOW TO SCORE WITH A STYLUS OR SCORING WHEEL

Step 1

Open or create a project with score lines. You can add a score line to any project by **clicking Shapes, then selecting Score Line.**

Step 2

Make sure any lines you want to be scored are identified as "Score" (click the Linetype menu to change) **and are also Attached to the cut layer you want to score. Click Make It.**

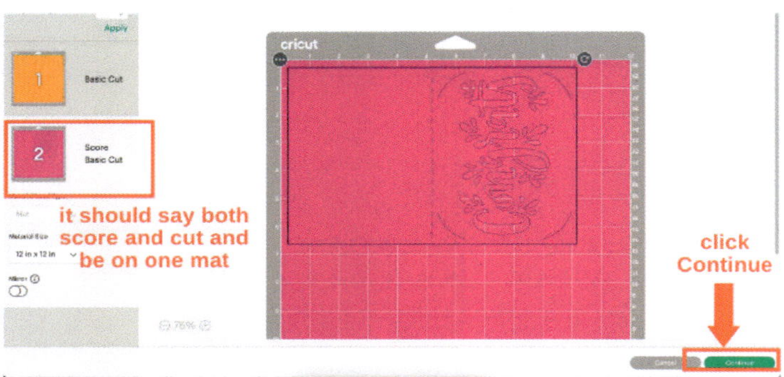

Step 3

Make sure the score line is on the same layer as the cut (so they both should be on one mat), then **click Continue**.

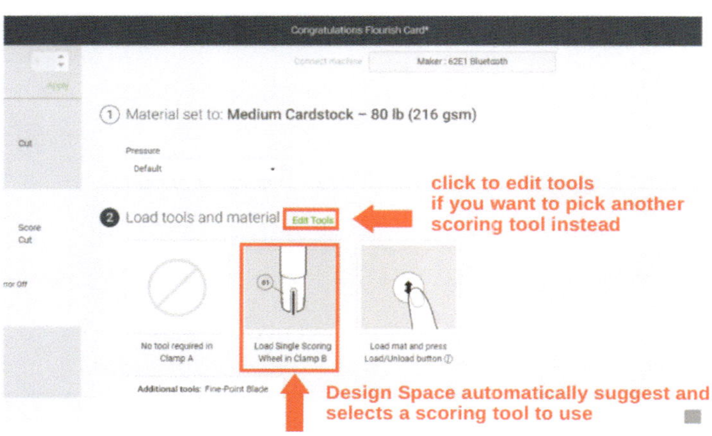

Note

You can score with either a scoring stylus, a single scoring wheel or a double scoring wheel. The Tool section will automatically recommend which one to use, but you can change it (you might not have the one recommended). **Click Edit Tools to see the options available.**

HOW TO SCORE WITH A STYLUS OR SCORING WHEEL

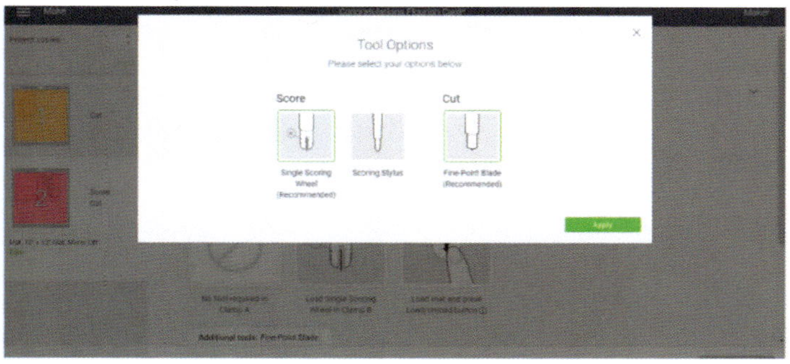

Step 4

Click on the scoring tool of preference, then **click Apply**.

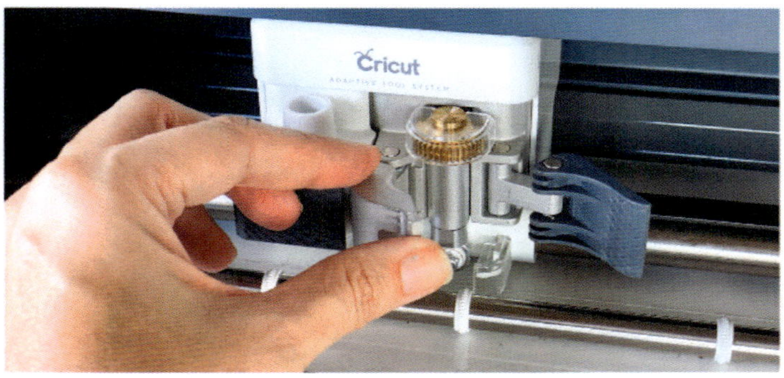

Step 5

Insert the scoring tool that matches step 5 (the scoring stylus goes in clamp A or the wheel goes in clamp B), then click the flashing icon on your Cricut to begin.

Notes

- The Scoring Stylus is available for Cricut Maker and Explore, but does not exert the amount of pressure that the Scoring Wheels do.
- The Scoring Wheels are only compatible with the Cricut Maker.
- The Scoring Wheel makes a deep, single score line – perfect for uncoated, light materials, including crepe paper, light cardstock, and even acetate.
- The Double Scoring Wheel creates two deep, parallel score lines – exactly what you need for coated or heavier materials like poster board and cardboard.
- The Double Scoring Wheel creates beautiful folds on coated and thicker materials; however it requires that you fold into the crease. If your material cracked at the fold, check to make sure that you didn't fold against the crease. This means you should plan your project with the "pretty" side of your material facing the mat. This may mean you'd need to mirror your project if using the Double Scoring Wheel so your words are on the correct side if you place your project face down (like cards, for example).

Cricut Access Project: Congratulations Flourish Card

HOW TO WRITE OR DRAW WITH A PEN

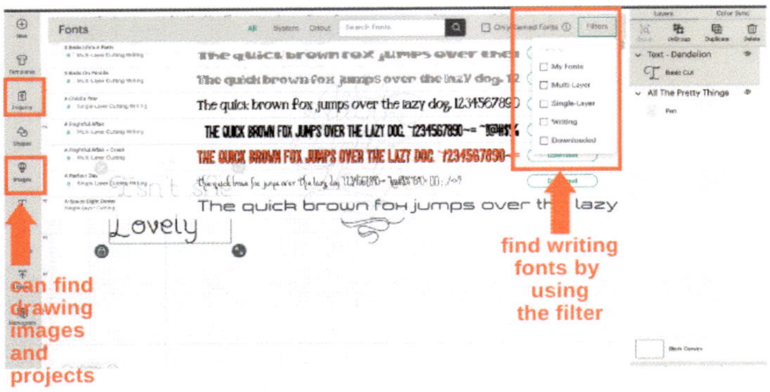

Step 1

Select a drawing image from Cricut Access or **add a writing font** to your project. **Click Text** to add a text box to the canvas, **click on the font menu**, click **"Filter" and select Writing Fonts**. Pick your favorite writing font & **type your text.**

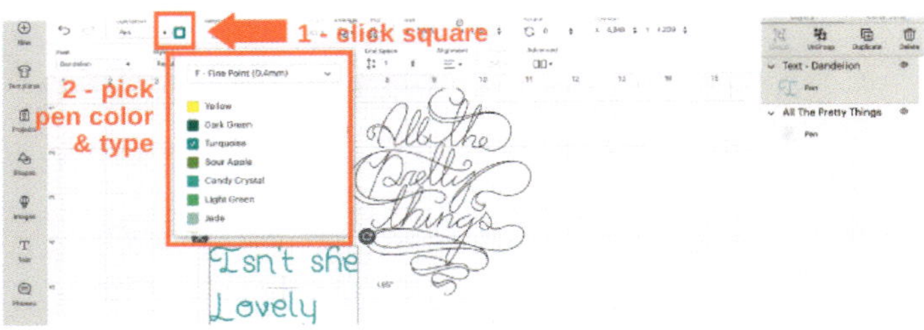

Step 2

Click the square to the right of Linetype (Draw), and **select a pen type and color** for your project.

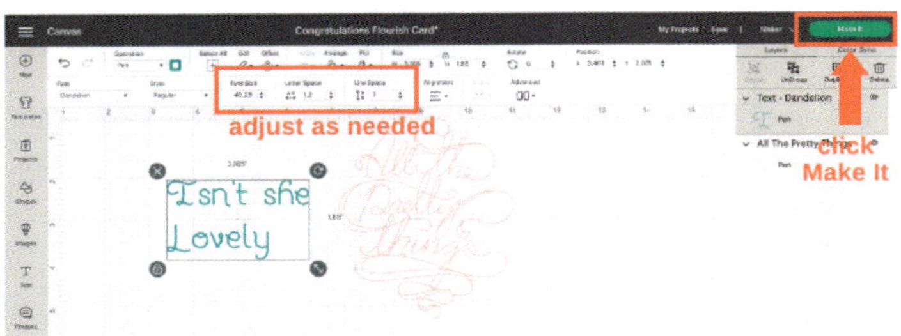

Step 3

Make sure to **adjust the font size, letter space & line space** (see page 62-63) as needed so it looks the way you want, then **click Make It.**

Step 4

Click and drag the text to the exact spot you want it to be written on your material on the cutting mat, then **click Continue**.

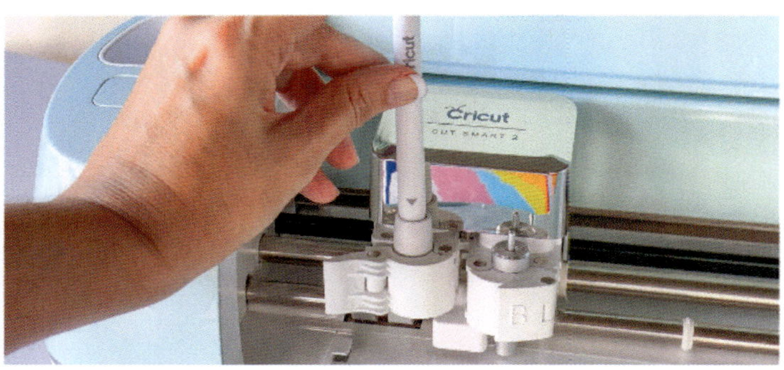

Step 5

Insert the pen in your Cricut's accessory clamp A (the little arrow on the pen should disappear when inserted properly), **load your mat** (with the material), and **press the flashing button** to start drawing your project.

Cricut Access Image: All the Pretty Things #M439FD0

Cricut Font Shown: Dandelion

HOW TO ADD FOIL HIGHLIGHTS WITH THE FOIL TRANSFER TOOL

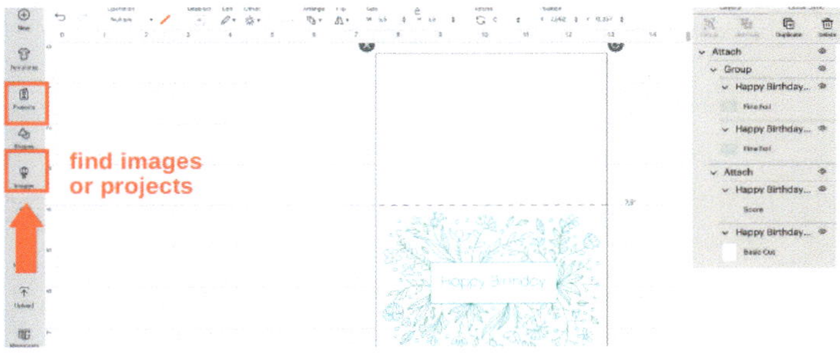

Step 1

Search Images or Projects in Cricut Design Space or create your own design. Some projects in the library already have Foil added to the design, but we will focus on customizing any design for the foil tool.

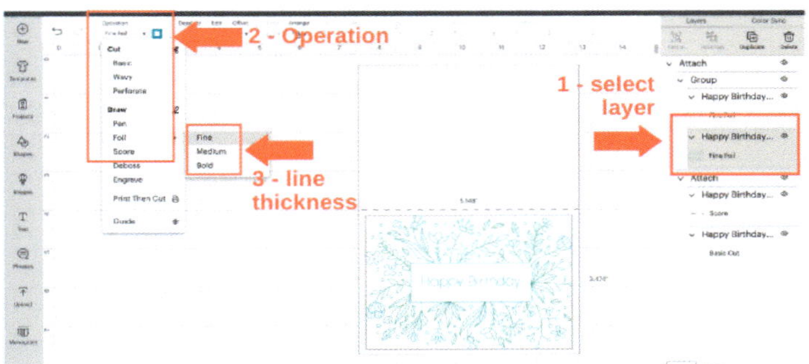

Step 2

Select the layer you would like to foil. Click Operation, go down to Foil and choose Fine, Medium or Bold. These options refer to how thick you want your foil lines to be. Repeat for each layer you want to foil.

Step 3

Select the layer you would like to change the foil color of. Go to Operation and choose the color you would like. Repeat for each layer you want to change.

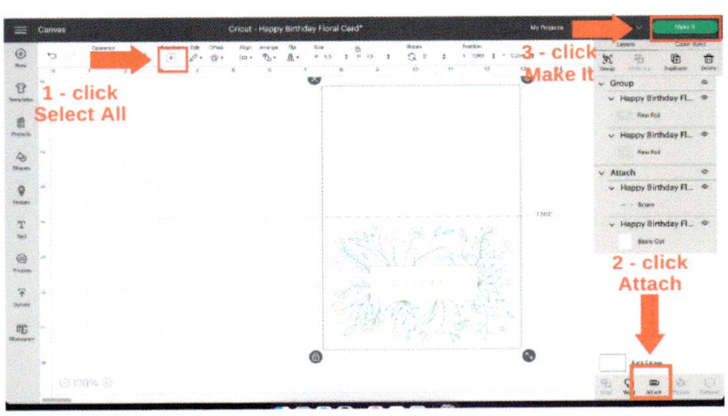

Step 4

In order for your project to be made the way you see it on your canvas, you will need to **Select All and click Attach**. This will ensure your score lines, cut lines and foil lines will keep their placement on the mat/s. **Click Make It.**

Cricut Design Space Project: Happy Birthday Floral Card

HOW TO ADD FOIL HIGHLIGHTS WITH THE FOIL TRANSFER TOOL

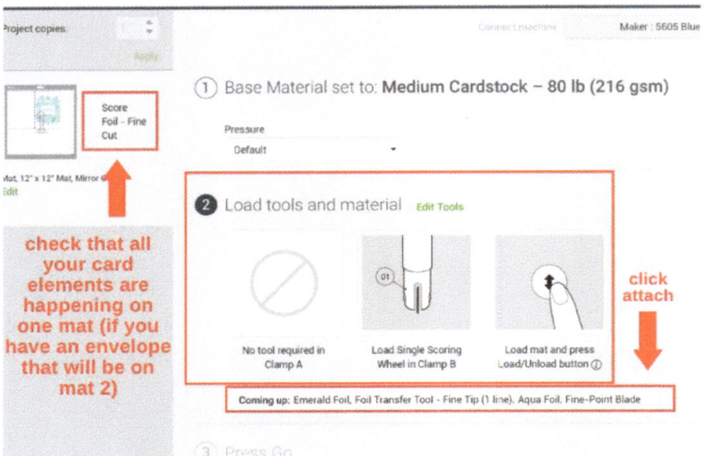

Step 4

This will bring you to the Cut Screen. **Check that all your steps for your card is on one single mat.** Choose your base material. Change pressure (if required). Last you will see a list of the tools required. Design space will prompt you when you need to change a tool. It also includes a list of what tool is coming next so you can get prepared.

Loading the Foil Tool

Find the size tip you will be using. Each tip has lines around the end indicating their thickness. One line is fine, two is medium and three for bold. **You can release the tip by pushing the plunger.** When prompted you will need to **insert your foil tool into clamp B** in your machine.

Attaching the Foil

Make sure **your piece of foil is more then large enough** to cover your design. You will need to place your foil over your design area (refer to your cut screen for your mat settings) and **use the white strips of tape** that came with your foil to tape down all four sides of your foil. Try to flatten your foil as much as possible. **Load your mat and press GO!**

Cricut Design Space Project: Happy Birthday Floral Card

PRINT THEN CUT VERSES SVG

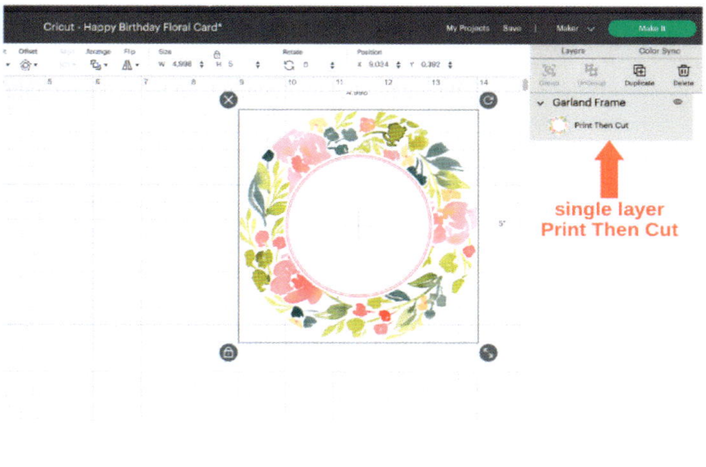

Cricut Access Image: Watercolor Garland #MC53453

Print Then Cut Images

- A Print Then Cut image is a printed image that Cricut will cut out for you by cutting around the outline of the image only.
- Your material will almost always be cardstock, paper, or printable vinyl since you're limited to materials that will fit in your printer.
- JPEG AND PNG image formats are automatically Print Then Cut when uploaded to Design Space.

- You need a printer to do a Print Then Cut project.
- The size of your project will be limited to 8.3 x 11.7 inches (A4) or 8.5 x 11 inches (Letter) as that is the limit of the Print Then Cut feature.
- Print Then Cut images are a lot more colorful and can be artistic like watercolor, since Cricut only cuts around the outline of your image.

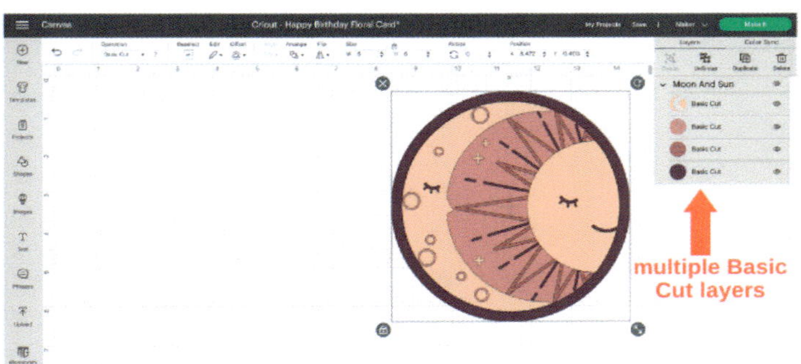

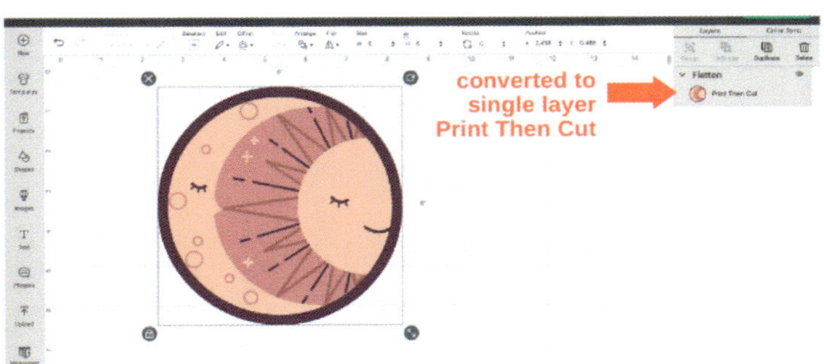

Cricut Access Image: Moon And Sun #M17CD23D8

SVG Images

- SVG stands for scalable vector graphic.
- An SVG image is a multiple layer image where all the colors are separate and can be cut individually.
- Your Cricut can use any materials with SVG images.
- You don't need a printer to use SVG files.
- You can cut projects at any size that will fit your mats.
- Your colors are limited by whatever material you are cutting.
- You can turn an SVG layered file into a Print Then Cut project by using Flatten. See page 38 for details.

HOW TO PRINT THEN CUT

Note: The maximum image size for Print Then Cut is 8.3 x 11.7 inches (A4) or 8.5 x 11 inches (Letter). Print Then Cut can be used with Cricut Explore and Maker models - but not with the Cricut Joy.

Step 1

Find or upload a printable image less than the sizes mentioned above.
Tip: I insert a square into my canvas matches the Print Then Cut size I use. That way I have a visible Print then Cut size guide that I can use when I organize all my elements.

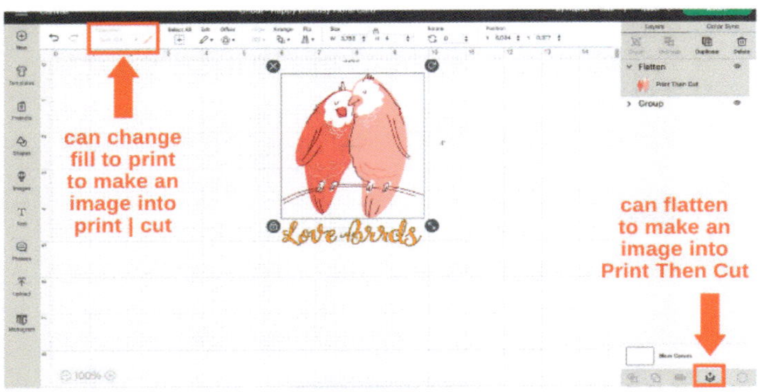

Images from Design Space

You can search for images in Design Space. You can use either printable images of cut images. **Cut images can be turned into Print Then Cut by flattening all the layers or changing Operation to Print Then Cut.**

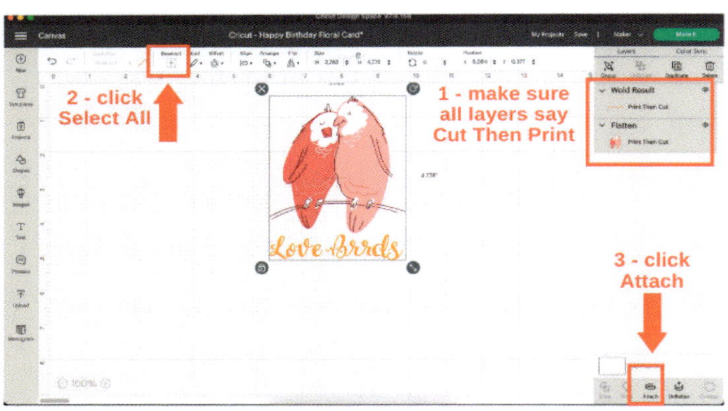

Step 3

Make sure all your layers says cut | print.
Click Select All to select all your layers.
Attach all your items so they stay in place on your mat, then **Click Make It.**
Note: If you used a rectangle as a size guide, delete or hide the shape before attaching.

Step 4

Confirm that you see "Print Cut" on the left, then **click Continue**.

HOW TO PRINT THEN CUT

Note

The preview screens can take a while to load, especially if you used many images.

Step 5

Select your Cricut (if necessary) then **click Send to Printer.**

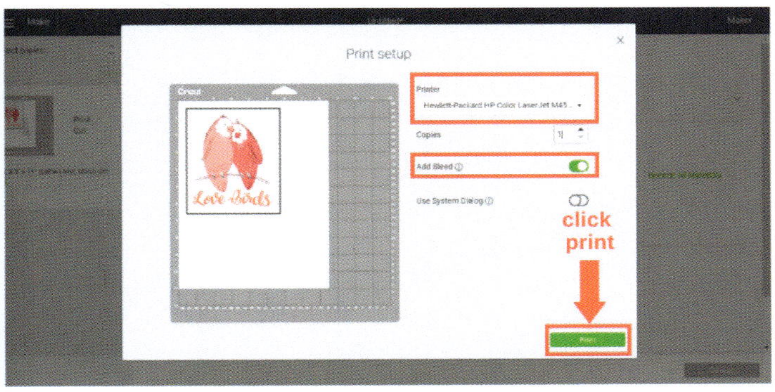

Step 6

Select your printer and turn on bleed if you want (optional, depending on what type of image you're using). Essentially the bleed is a small border around each image that allows for more precise cutting. **Click Print.**

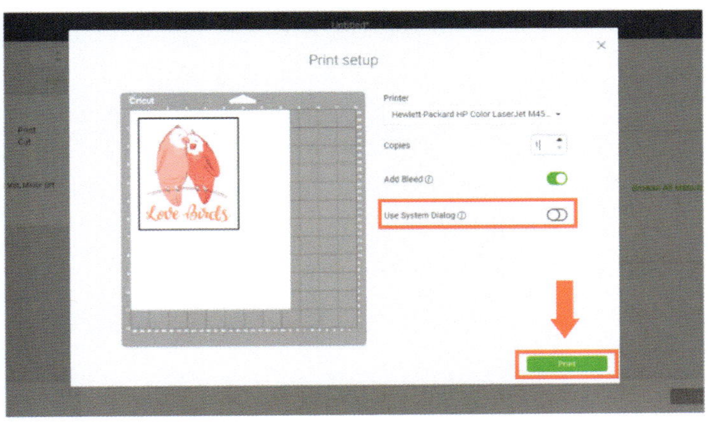

Note

You can also **toggle on "use system dialog**" if you want to select the quality of your print or different materials using your printer's menu. I typically select 'Photo Printing' and change my quality setting to 'High'. With these settings your printer will use more ink, but your images will be more vibrant and saturated.

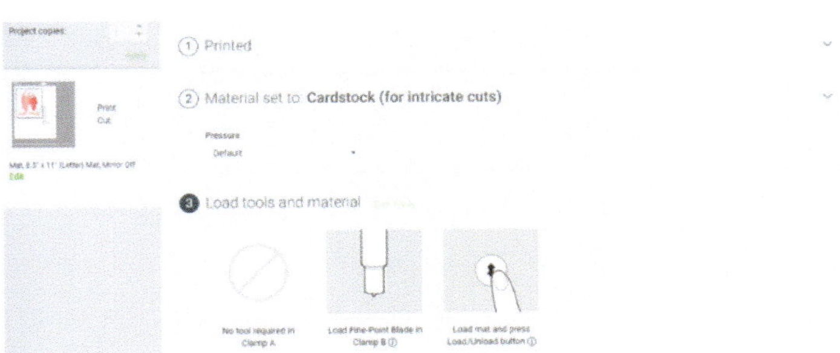

Step 7

Print out your sheet with an inkjet printer. **Select your material** and **place your printed page on your cutting mat. Load it** and **click Go.** Your cutting machine will automatically know where to cut.

Cricut Access Image: Bird Love #M13F6B2D4

Cricut Access Font: Friday

HOW TO COMBINE MULTIPLE PROJECTS ONTO ONE CANVAS

Note

You can combine a previously created image/design (in the example below: the heart spray) with a new image (in the example below: the elephant) to create a brand new project.

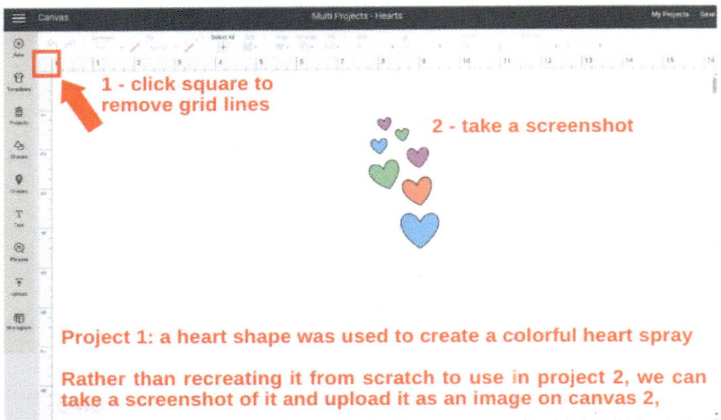

Step 1

Open the Project you want to add to another canvas. Make sure no pieces of the design are touching. **Turn off your Grid Lines** (see page 27 for how to remove grid lines). **Take a screen shot** of the image using the snipping tool on a PC or Cmd+Shift+4 on a Mac. Save your screen shot to your desktop.

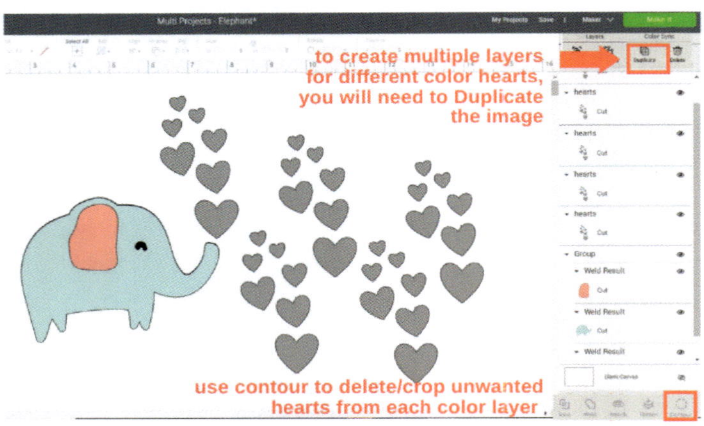

Step 2

Open the Project you want to add your other Project to. **Insert the image** on the canvas (see page 47-48 for upload instructions). **Duplicate your image** based on the number of colors you need. **Click Contour** and Contour your image (see page 42 for Contour instructions).

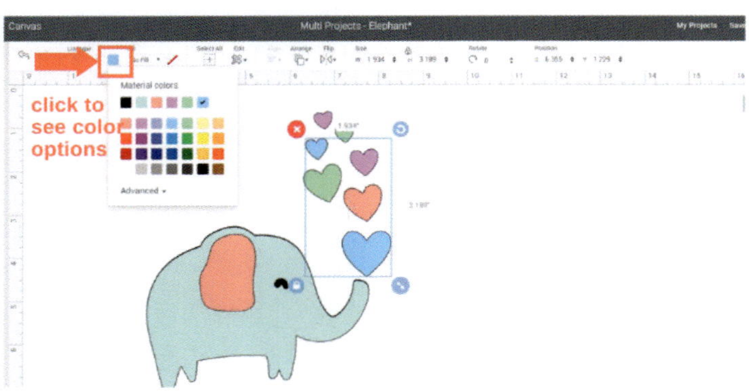

Final Result

As you Contour each element **change the color** so you can see the finished pieces.

Now you've combined both canvas's.

Cricut Acess Image: Elephant with heart #M14464424 and Heart #M369884

HOW TO MIRROR AND CUT IRON-ON (HTV) VINYL

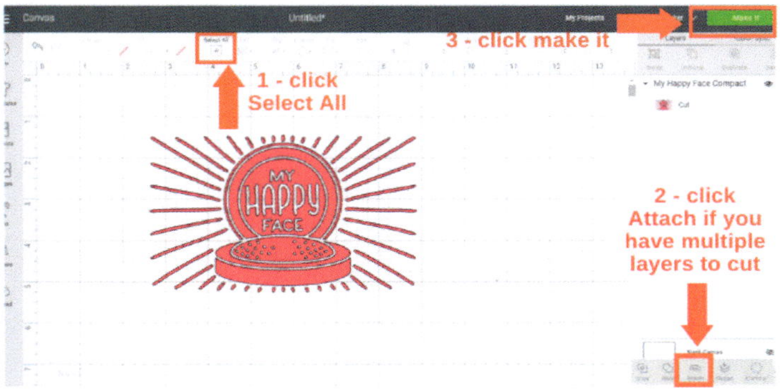

Step 1

Select all the objects you want to iron-on and **click Attach. Click Make It.**

Step 2

You need to reverse cut images when you work with HTV since the material is placed <u>face down</u> on the mat (otherwise text would be backwards). **Toggle Mirror to the on position**, verify that your image is now mirrored, and **click Continue.**

Step 3

Connect to your Cricut and **click on Browse All Materials**. Search for "iron" and **select the type of iron-on vinyl you plan to use**, then **click Done**.

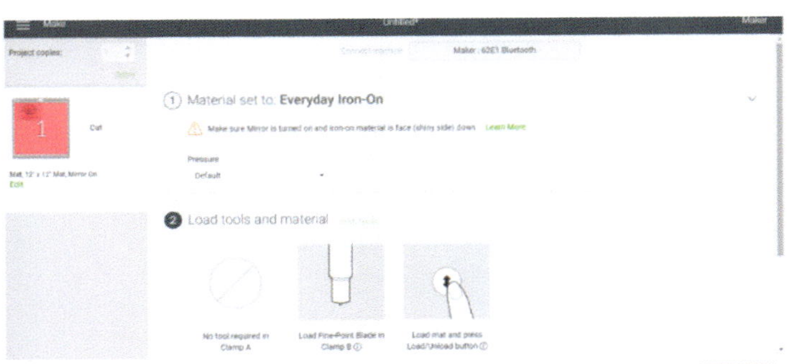

Step 4

Place your iron-on vinyl on your green StandardGrip cutting mat **FACE DOWN (or shiny side down)**, insert the mat, and **press Go.**

Cricut Access Image: My Happy Face Compact #M175786CA

HOW TO MAKE YOUR OWN STENCILS

Step 1

Add text and/or shapes that you want to use for your stencil. You can also **find images from Cricut Access** that will work well.

Step 2

Add a square to the canvas. Unlock the proportions to make it into a rectangle. **Size it the same size as your finished project** to make it easier to align the stencil. **Place the shapes behind your design. Be sure to align them** vertically and horizontally as needed.

Step 3

Select all the elements for one stencil (all the words, shapes, and background shape), then **click Attach**. Don't worry when the image "disappears" and you see only cut lines like the sample on the right. Once everything is attached, **click Make It**.

Cricut Access Image:
It's The Little Things That Matter Most #M13947D06
Cricut Font Shown: Paddington Regular

Step 4

Click continue, select your material (vinyl works for stencils for signs, etc.) **load your mat**, and **press the flashing button** to start cutting. Once complete, remove the excess vinyl from around the background shapes. Use a weeding tool to pull out the vinyl from the letters, but be sure to keep the centers of letters like 'o' or 'e' there. Use transfer tape to apply to your project.

HOW TO USE THE SLICE THEN SET TECHNIQUE FOR INFUSIBLE INK

You should not press the Infusible Ink multiple times (multiple layers) or the colors can bleed together or fade. Use this technique to cut out the elements & layer together before pressing.

Step 1

Add text and/or shapes that you want to use for your Infusible Ink project. You can create a duplicate of all items, group, & then hide to have a backup. **Have at least 2 of your elements overlapping** for this technique. **Weld your text** before step 2.

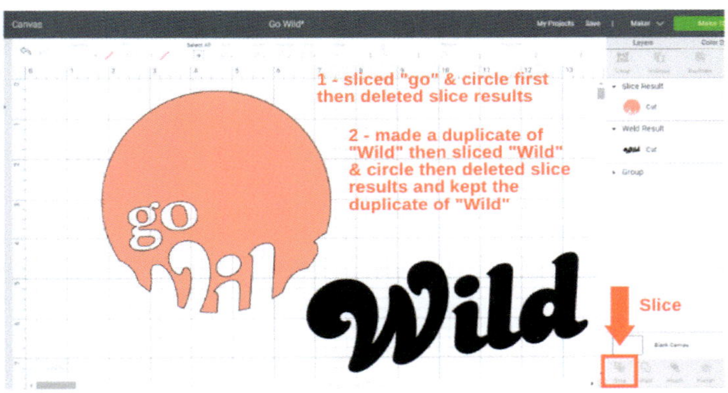

Step 2

Select 2 elements that you want to slice (you can repeat this for other overlaid elements), then **click the Slice Button** in the Actions Panel. After you Slice, new layers called "Slice Result" will appear. You can move, hide or delete these if you don't need them.

Step 3

Move the final overlaying elements back into place over the sliced background shape. **Click Make It.**

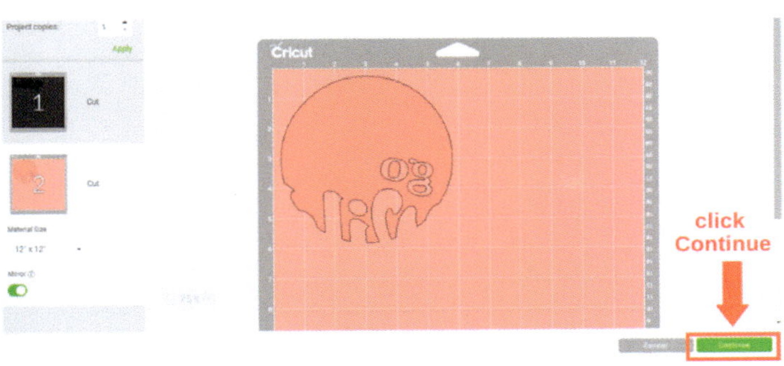

Step 4

Click continue, make sure to **mirror your images, select your material** (Infusible Ink Transfer Sheet) **load your green StandardGrip mat** (colored side up), and **press the flashing button** to start cutting.

HOW TO USE THE SLICE THEN SET TECHNIQUE FOR INFUSIBLE INK

Step 5

Gather your layers in one place, and **weed the Infusible Ink**. You'll notice that it is much thicker than vinyl and HTV iron-on and therefore weeds a bit differently.

Slightly bend and roll the backing paper until the smaller pieces "crack" away from the other pieces, and use your hands to weed away the excess.

Note: **Do NOT use traditional weeding tools to weed Infusible Ink!** Doing that may result in small amounts of ink being pressed into the plastic carrier backing, and that ink WILL still transfer to your blank!

Use the carrier backing sheet to layer the different elements together before pressing onto your project blank. You will press everything all at once. **Do not press the infusible ink multiple times (for multiple layers) or it can cause damage and fading.**

Use a lint roller to remove any lint, fuzz, or debris from the fabric of your project that might cause the ink to transfer improperly.

Place your Infusible Ink carrier sheet, ink side down, on top of your project (shirt, etc.).

Cover and press per the instructions.

Cricut Fonts Shown:
for "go": Close To My Heart - Art Philosphy
for "Wild": Candice Regular

HOW TO CREATE OVERSIZED PROJECTS IN DESIGN SPACE

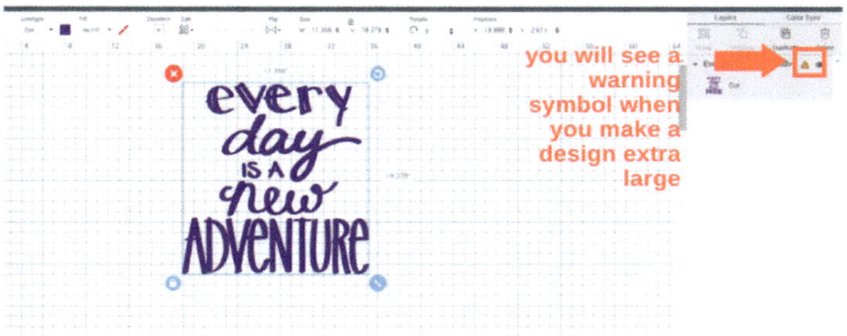

Step 1:

Load your SVG onto your Canvas. **Resize** to the size you would like. Due to it being too large to cut on one mat a small triangle with an exclamation point will show in your layers panel.

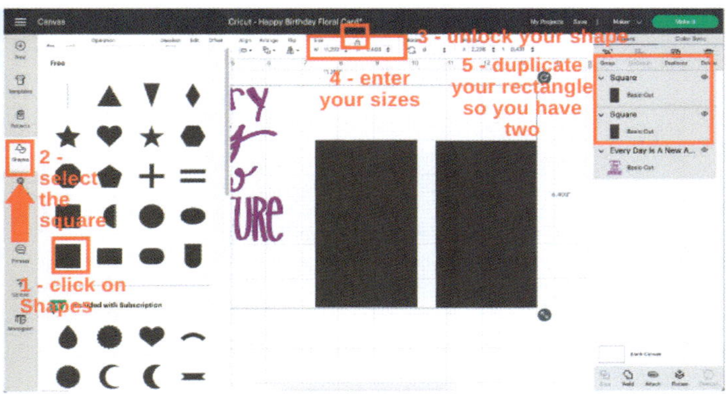

Step 2

Click Shapes and select the Square. It is helpful to have a visual guide of the mat size. For the regular mats resize the square to – 11.5 x 11.5'. For the large mats, you will need to **unlock the Square and then Resize** to 11.5 x 23.5'. **Duplicate** the square/rectangle for your second mat.

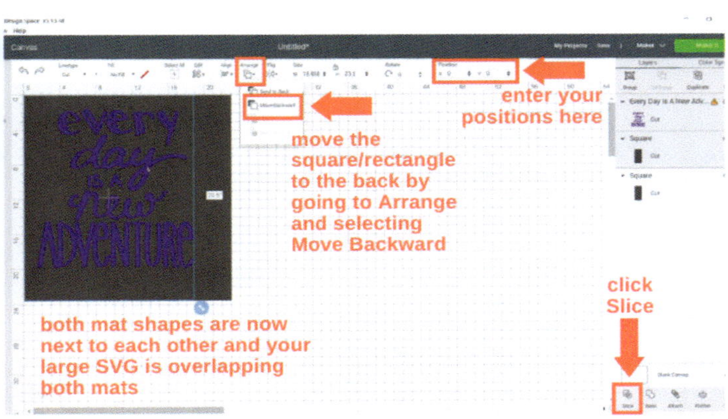

Step 3

Select your SVG and position it at x: 0 and y: 0. Do the same for one of your squares. **Select the other square and position at x: 11.5** (regular mats or 23.5' for large mats) **and y: 0**. Select the squares and **click Arrange and Send to Back**. Select the Square on the left and the SVG (you can only slice two layers t a time) and **click Slice**. **Repeat with the second square**. Now you can delete everything except your original SVG.

Step 4

When you **click Make It** and your Sliced image will show up on two mats.

Cricut Access Image: Every Day Is A New Adventure #M14236CA8

HOW TO CREATE CUT FILES FROM YOUR OWN DRAWINGS

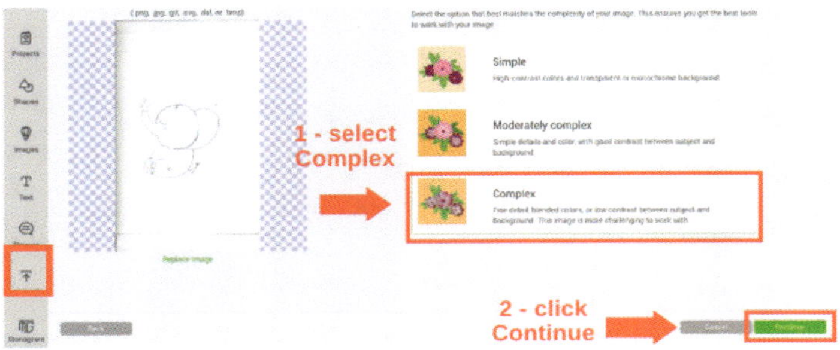

Step 1

Upload your drawing into Design Space (follow directions on page 47 - 48). **Choose Complex** as your image type and click **Continue**.

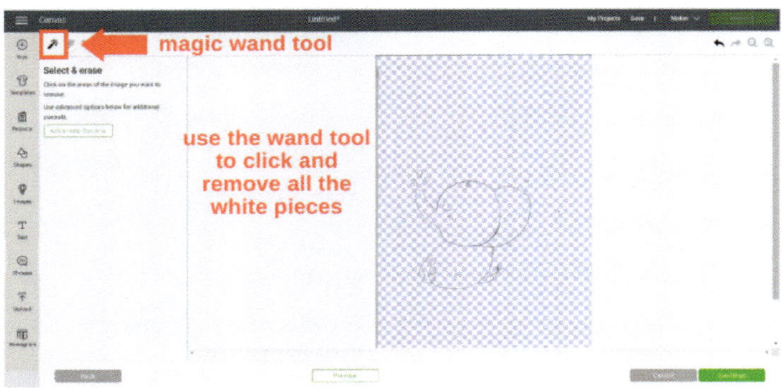

Step 2

Use the Wand tool (it will be automatically selected) to **click on all the white pieces** of your image.

Tip: Remember to check all the small spaces i.e. eyeballs, inside letters like a, b, d or e.

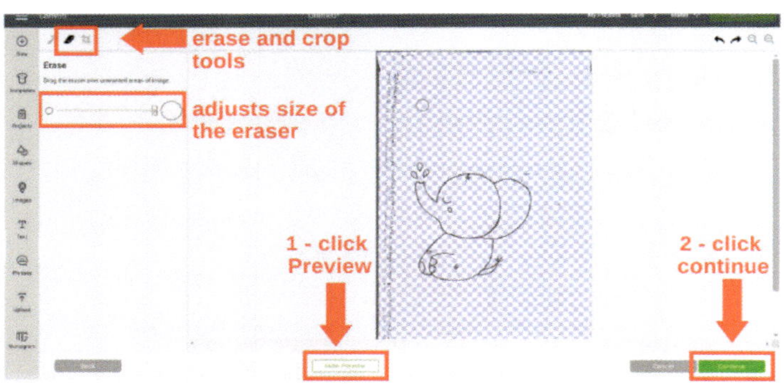

Step 3

Check your Preview to see if you've missed any pieces. If so, you can use the Erase tool to remove them. You can use the Crop tool to select just your image and remove any extra space from the background. When finished **click Continue**.

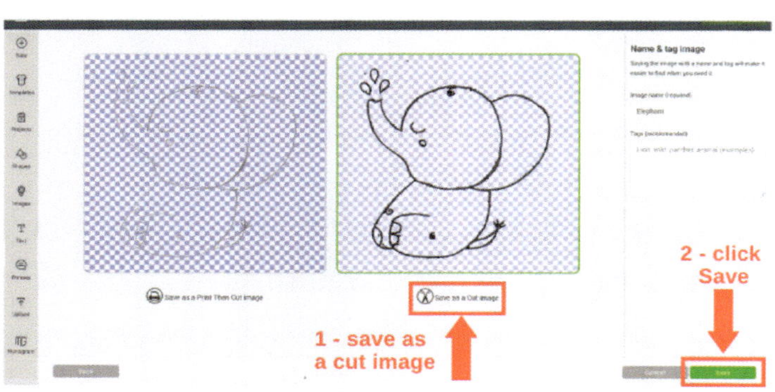

Font Shown: Free Monogram Beta from dafont.com

Final Result

Give your image a name and add some tags if you wish. **Select the option 'Save as a Cut Image' and click Save**.

CUSTOMIZE A READY-TO-MAKE MUG PROJECT OR IMAGE

How to Find Mug Press Projects in Cricut Design Space

Step 1

Click on Projects, in the Categories section type **"Mug Press"**. You will now see all the projects available in Cricut Design Space that you can use with your Cricut Mug Press.

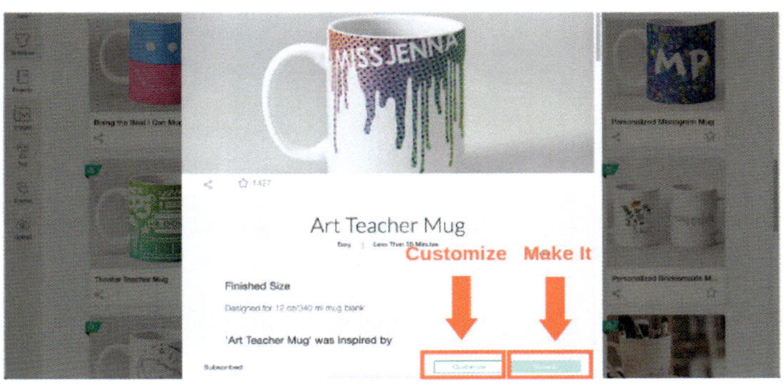

Step 2

Select the project template you wish to use. You can either click on **Customize to make changes to the Project Template or** you can click on **Make It and follow the steps** to cut out your design with your Cricut machine.

Customize a Ready-to-Make Mug Project

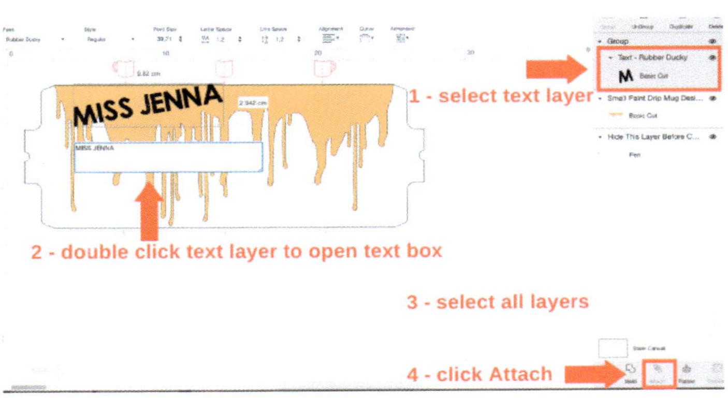

Step 3

Click Customize to add the project to your Canvas. If your design has a mug size option, choose the appropriate mug size choice.

Select the text layer, double click to open the text box so you can customize the text.

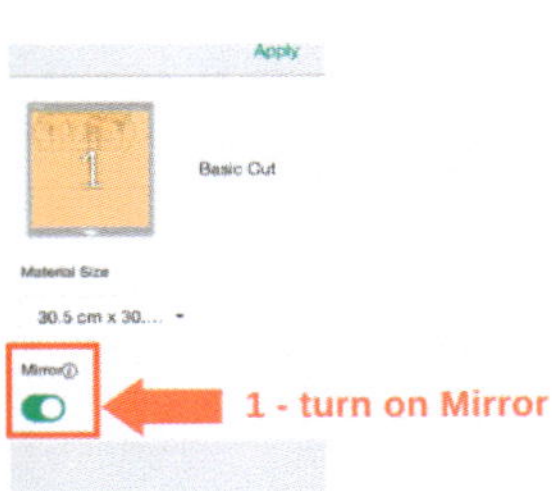

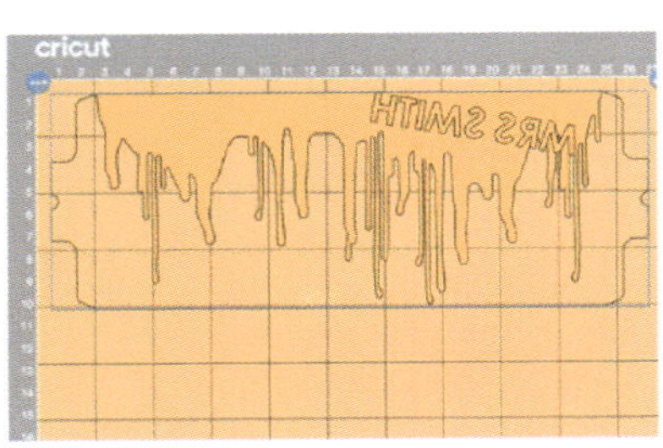

Mug Press Project: Art Teacher Mug

Step 4

Click on Make It. Use the mirror toggle to **turn on Mirror**. When the design is mirrored on your mat, **click on Continue** to send your design to be cut by your machine.

HOW TO CREATE YOUR OWN MUG DESIGN FROM A TEMPLATE

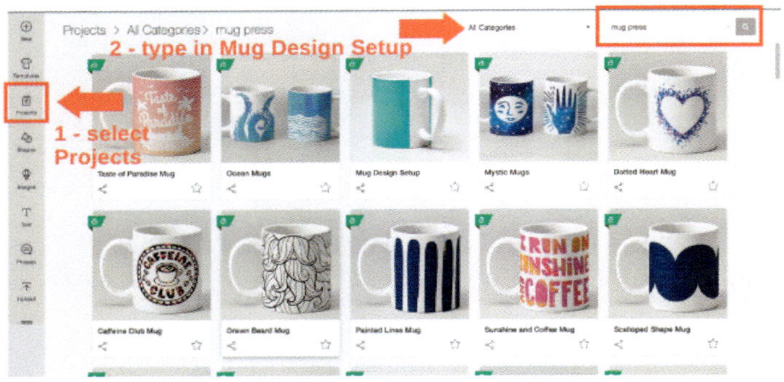

Step 1

Click on Projects, in the Categories section type **Mug Design Setup. Select the Mug Design Template Project.**

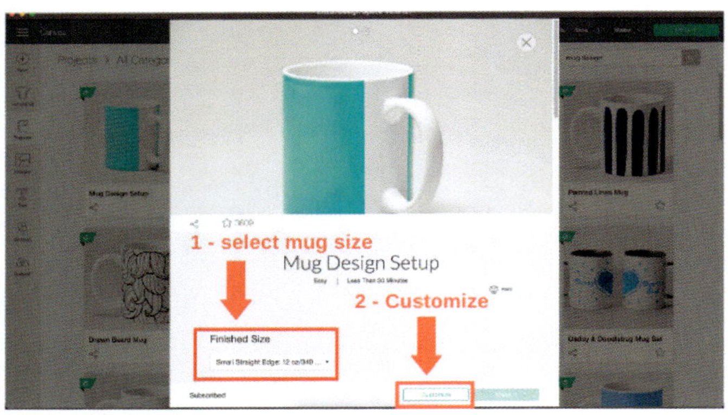

Step 2

Select your mug size from the drop-down menu. Click on **Customize** to make changes to the project template on a new Canvas.

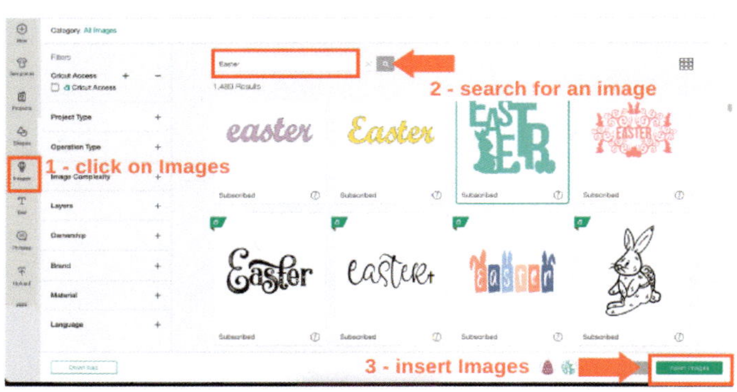

Step 3

Click Images to add your own images to the Canvas. Search for an image of your choice, we searched the word Easter.

Select the images you want to use then **click Insert Images**

Step 4

Resize and place the images on the template ensuring that the images are lined up with the Red Mug Guide and do not go outside of the blue area.

HOW TO CREATE YOUR OWN MUG DESIGN FROM A TEMPLATE

Step 5

When the design is complete **click the eyeball icon to hide the red mug guide layer.** I am also hiding the blue layer as I want the design from the Infusible Ink Sheets to be on the images and not the white of the mug.

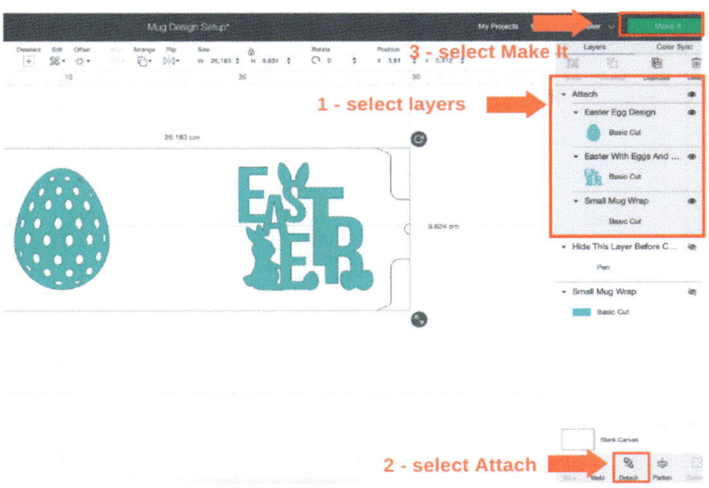

Step 6

Select the remaining visible layers and **click on Attach**. Once layers are attached **click on Make It**

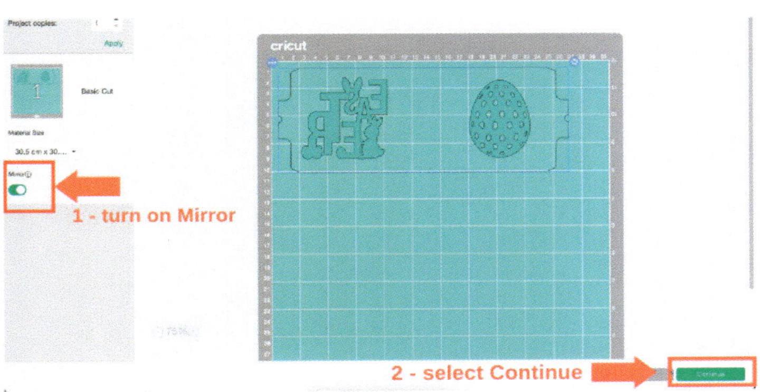

Step 7

Use the mirror toggle to **turn on Mirror**. When the design is mirrored on your mat, **click on Continue** to send your design to be cut by your machine. When cut remove from your mat and follow the guidelines for Heat Pressing Infusible Ink Transfer Sheets.

Mug Press Project: Mug Design Setup
Images Used: Easter with Eggs and Bunny #M238F53A1. Easter Egg Design #MB4DA975

Note

You can follow the same steps to create a design using Cricut Infusible Ink Markers. Use images from Cricut Design Space that are Draw images or your own words which you want your machine to write using Infusible Ink Markers.

BONUS RESOURCES

DESIGN SPACE FEATURES COMPARISON CHART FOR DEVICES(PART 1)

The following chart shows a comparison of Cricut Design Space feature availability across Design Space platforms (desktop, IOS and Android):

Feature	Windows/Mac	iOS App	Android App
Attach	✓	✓	✓
Bluetooth compatible	✓	✓	✓
Contour	✓	✓	✓
Cut & write in one step	✓	✓	✓
Flatten to print	✓	✓	✓
Writing style fonts	✓	✓	✓
Machine setup	✓	✓	✓
Print then cut	✓	✓	
Slice and weld	✓	✓	✓
System fonts	✓	✓	✓
Offline	✓	✓	

DESIGN SPACE FEATURES COMPARISON (PART 2)

The following chart shows a comparison of Cricut Design Space feature availability across Design Space platforms (desktop, IOS and Android):

Feature	Windows/Mac	iOS App	Android App
Photo Canvas		✓	
3D layer visualization		✓	
Smart Guides		✓	✓
SnapMat		✓	
Pattern fills	✓		
Templates	✓		
Image upload	✓	✓	✓
Link Physical Cartridges	✓		
Curve Text	✓		
Knife Blade cutting	✓		

CRICUT DESIGN SPACE SHORTCUTS

Keyboard Shortcuts

FUNCTION	PC USERS	MAC USERS
Select All	Ctrl A	CMD A
Copy to clipboard	Ctrl C	CMD C
Paste from clipboard	Ctrl V	CMD V
Cut to clipboard	Ctrl X	CMD X
Print/Cut/Go	-none-	CMD P
Undo	Ctrl Z	CMD Z
Redo	Ctrl + Shift Z	CMD +Shift Z or CMD Y
Save	Ctrl S	CMD S
Save As	Ctrl + Shift S	-none-
Exit Hide Contours & Edit Group modes	Esc	Esc
Nudge objects	Right/Left/Up/Down arrows	Right/Left/Up/Down arrows
Nudge objects Further	Shift + Right/Left/Up/Down arrows	SHFT + Right/Left/Up/Down arrows
Scroll down mat quickly	Spacebar	Spacebar
Send Forward	Ctrl +]	CMD +]
Send Backward	Ctrl + [	CMD + [
Bring to Front	Ctrl + Shift +]	CMD + Shift +]
Send to Back	Ctrl + Shift + [	CMD + Shift + [
Rotate an Object (45 degree angles)	Shift + Click and Drag	-
Scroll Down the Page	Mouse wheel	Use Tracking Pad Move Up or Down
Scroll Left or Right	Shift + Mouse wheel	Use Tracking Pad Move Left & Right
Brings up Options Menu	-	CTRL Click on Image

CRICUT DESIGN SPACE TERMINOLOGY QUICK REFERENCE SHEETS

Align	When multiple images and/or texts are selected on the canvas, the align function will allow you to align them either to the center, left, right, top, bottom, etc.
Attach	The attach tool will hold your SVG in place so it will cut exactly as it appears on your canvas. You can also use attach to attach score lines and text to images.
Arrange	Arrange will allow you to move a selected image/text in front of, behind, or in between other image layers on the canvas.
Canvas	In Design Space the Canvas refers to the visual work space on your screen. This is the area you will use to design and arrange your SVG's and image's.
Color Sync	When selected, the Color Sync panel allows you to consolidate the colors of a project to reduce the number of colored materials you will need.
Contour	The Contour tool lets you hide unwanted pieces of an SVG. Often used when creating a multi-layered image from a single layer design.
Cricut Cut/Go Button	The Cricut logo button on your machine is the Cricut Cut/Go button. Pressing this button will tell your machine to start creating.
Cut lines	The solid lines of an SVG image are the Cut Lines. These are the lines that will cut when initiated.
Cut Screen	When you click the Make It button, the Cut Screen will appear. This will show a preview of what's going to cut and show your layers sorted by mat.
Cutting Mat	The Cutting Mats are the surface your material will stick to prior to loading it into your Cricut machine. Use blue for lightweight materials, pink for fabric, green for medium weight materials and purple for heavy materials.
Deselect All	Deselect will deselect all items currently selected on the canvas.
Design Space	Cricut's cloud-based software for designing and doing your projects. Download it at https://design.cricut.com/
Draw Lines	You can select Draw in the LineType menu. Draw Lines are the lines you see on your canvas indicating the lines that will be drawn or written using a pen.
Duplicate	The Duplicate icon can be clicked numerous times to replicate any image on your screen as many times as you need.
Edit	Edit allows you to cut, copy, and paste any object on the canvas.

CRICUT DESIGN SPACE TERMINOLOGY QUICK REFERENCE SHEETS

Fill When an image is filled using a color or pattern it can be used for print then cut.

Flatten A multi layered SVG can be Flattened to create a printable image for the Print then Cut feature.

Flip You can rotate an image 180 degrees using the Flip feature.

Foil Add beautiful shiny metallic accents to your work with foil sheets. You can find this function under the LineType menu. The unique tool is a pressure-activated tool and works without heat.

Group In Design Space you can select multiple layers, images and texts and Group them together so they can be moved in sync with each other, thereby not disturbing the layout.

Images or Image Library The Image Library in Design Space houses thousands of pre-loaded images and SVG's. Some are free and others can be purchased.

JPG & PNG Files Files ending in .jpeg or .png can be uploaded into Design Space and used with the Print and Cut feature.

Layers Layers refer to one unified image on the canvas. Multiple images can be "layered" together or moved backward and forward using Arrange.

Linetype (Operation) Linetype tor Operation ells your Cricut machine which tool to use to create your project i.e. cut, draw, score, engrave, perforate, wavy edge, deboss or foil.

Load Button The load button is the double arrow button on your machine. You use this button to load and unload your cutting mat from the machine.

Material Settings Material Settings in Design Space, or on the dial if using Explore machines, is used to set the pressure the blade will use on the selected material.

Mirrored Image Mirroring reverses an image so it will be cut backwards. You want to mirror your image when working with heat transfer vinyl (iron-on) in order for the finished project to read correctly. You can mirror an image using the mirror toggle button on the Cut Screen.

No Fill No fill means that there is nothing on the canvas to be printed.

Print Then Cut The Print Then Cut feature is used to send your flattened image to your home printer via Design Space. Once printed, you can get your Cricut Machine to cut around the printed images.

Redo When working in Design Space you can Redo a recently undone action.

CRICUT DESIGN SPACE TERMINOLOGY QUICK REFERENCE SHEETS

Registration Marks When using the Print then Cut feature the Registration Marks are printed around your image and they to tell your Cricut machine where to cut.

Reverse Weeding Reverse weeding removes the vinyl that you would normally leave behind. This method is especially helpful when weeding tiny or skinny images.

Rotate Rotate will allow you to turn any image up to 360 degrees on the canvas.

Score Lines Score Lines are creases created in the material to help you create perfect folds. You can do this with either the scoring tool or scoring wheel.

Select All The Select All button allows you to select all visible images on the canvas.

Size The Size refers to the width and height of image or design selected on the canvas.

Shapes The Shapes button allows you to add a geometric shape to your canvas.

Slice When only two layers of an SVG are selected the slice tool allows you to create new cut paths from two layers. This will produce three or more new shapes as new layers.

SVG (scalable vector graphic) An SVG is a Scalable Vector Graphic. The benefit of an SVG file is it can be scaled larger or smaller and still retain its resolution. Use SVG cut files to cut colored materials with your Cricut and arrange a final layered design.

Text or Font Clicking Text will bring up a box for you to input your text. Once typed you can then change the Font and spacing selections. The LineType can be set to cut or draw your text.

Undo In Design Space you can use the Undo arrow to undo a recent action.

Ungroup Ungrouping a multi-layered image allows you to move each layer on the canvas individually.

Upload In Design Space you can Upload your own SVG's and images.

Weeding Weeding is the process of removing excess vinyl from a cut design.

Weld You can combine two single shapes or texts into one new seamless shape and eliminate unwanted cut lines by using the Weld feature. Welding is often used with text to create seamless cursive words.

TROUBLESHOOTING GUIDE

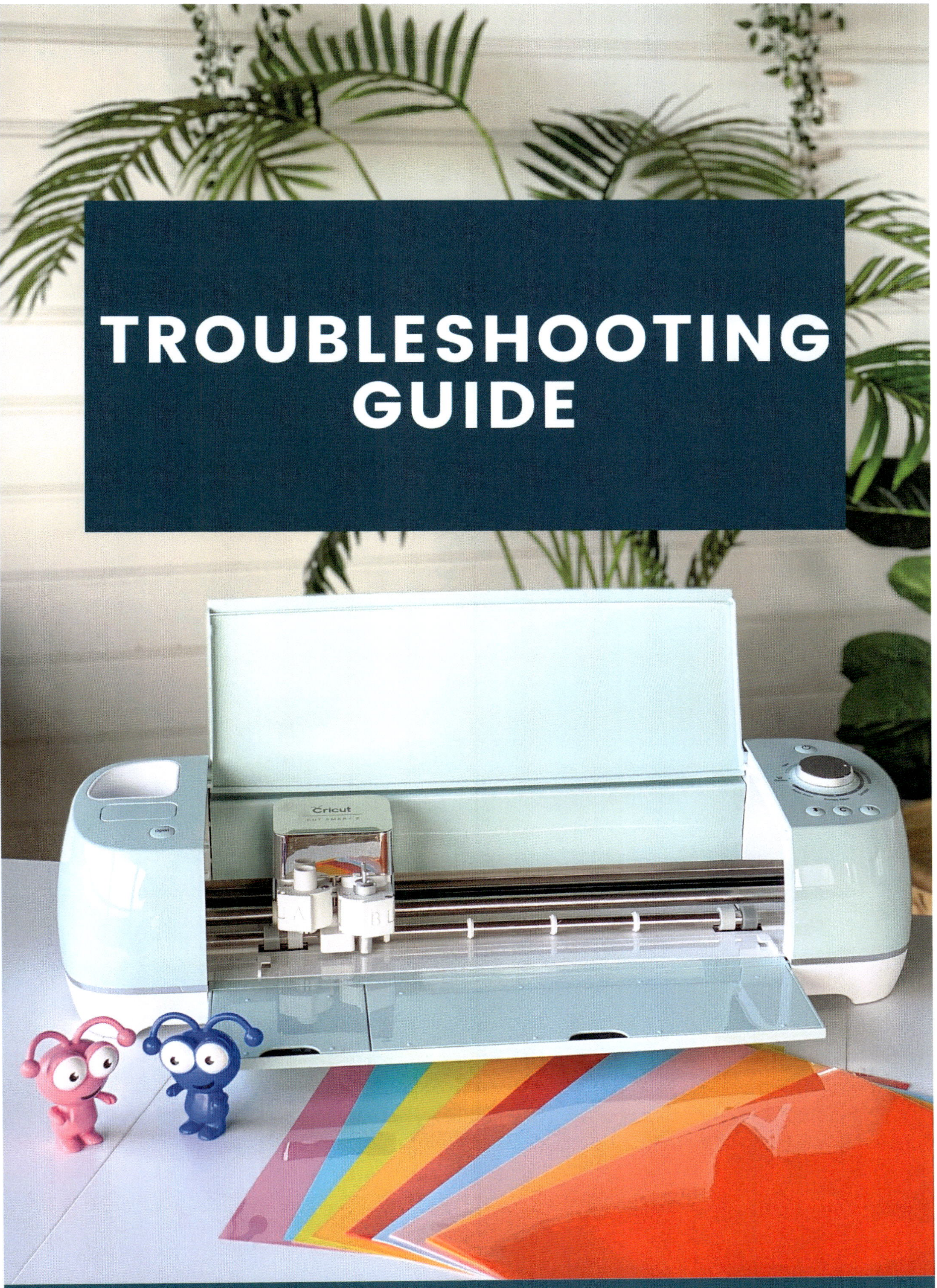

WHY DOES MY DESIGN JUMBLE UP WHEN I CLICK ON "MAKE IT"?

Step 1

Create your design in Cricut Design Space. You may want your design to cut exactly as it's paid out on screen if you're using different colored scrap materials on your mat or you don't want to piece it together on your project.

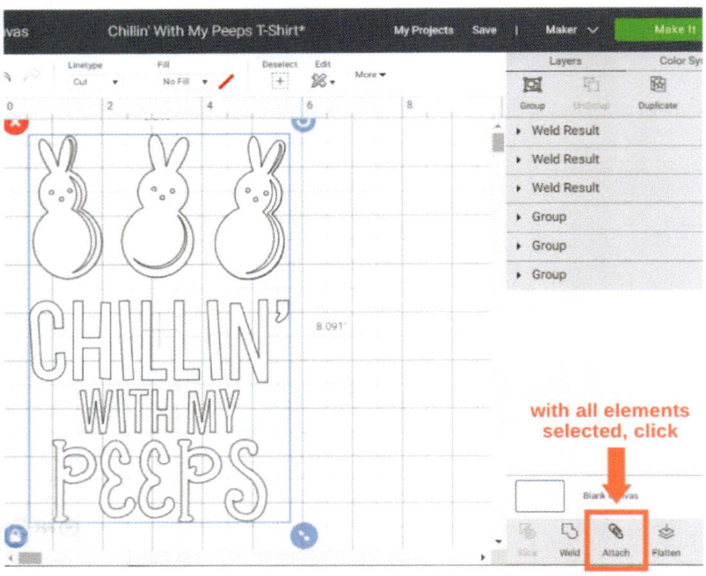

Step 2

To make everything stay in place, you will need to **select all your elements**, then **click on the "Attach" function** at the bottom of the layers panel to link them together.

Step 3

Now, when you **click "Make It"** the entire design will now stay on the mat exactly as you created it.

Cricut Access Project: Chillin' With My Peeps T-Shirt

WHEN I WELD MY FONT, WHY ARE SOME OF THE LETTERS FILLED IN?

This can happen when your letters are simply too close together. **Try moving the letters that filled in slightly away from the others.** It helps to enlarge your letters really big for this.

Cricut font shown: P.S.

I WELDED MY LETTERS TOGETHER BUT NOW I CAN'T REMEMBER WHAT FONT I USED! HELP!

If you open a project you previously completed and want to use the same font again, you won't be able to see the font name if you had previously welded the letters together. But don't worry, you can still find out which font you used!

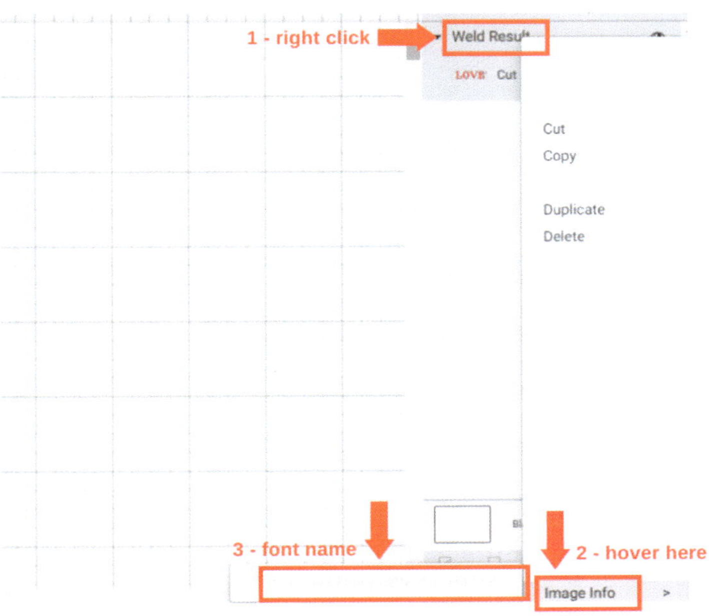

Step 1

Right click over "Weld Result."

Step 2

In the menu that pops up, look to the very bottom for **"Image Info."**

Step 3

Hover over "Image Info" and a little menu pops up with the font name in pale gray writing.

Cricut font shown: Candice Regular

HOW DO I REMOVE THE GRID LINES ON THE CANVAS?

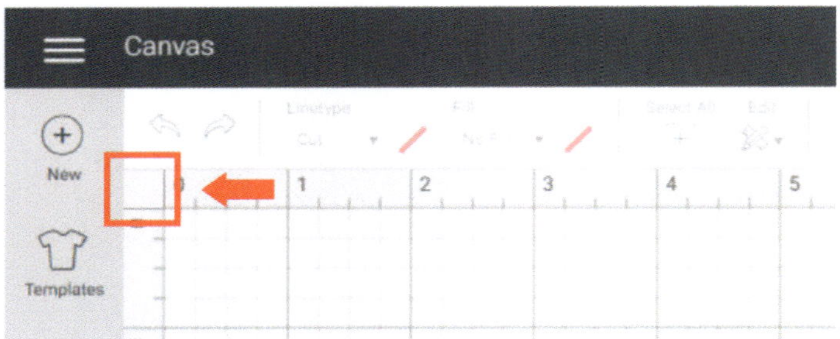

Click on the square in the top left corner of your canvas. It is grey and unlabeled, but when you click on it once the grid lines go bigger and when you click twice it will disappear.

WHY DOES MY FONT CHANGE TO ONLY OUTLINES WHEN I CHANGE THE LINE TYPE FROM CUT TO DRAW?

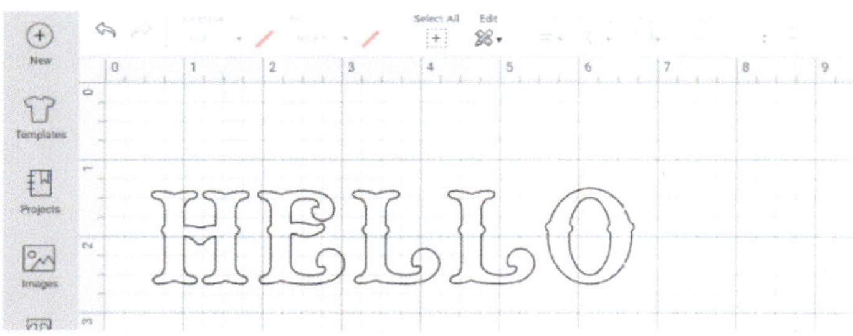

The pen tool can only follow the blade, so if you choose a thick font, the fine point of the pen will not be able to "color it in", and instead will only be able to draw the outline.

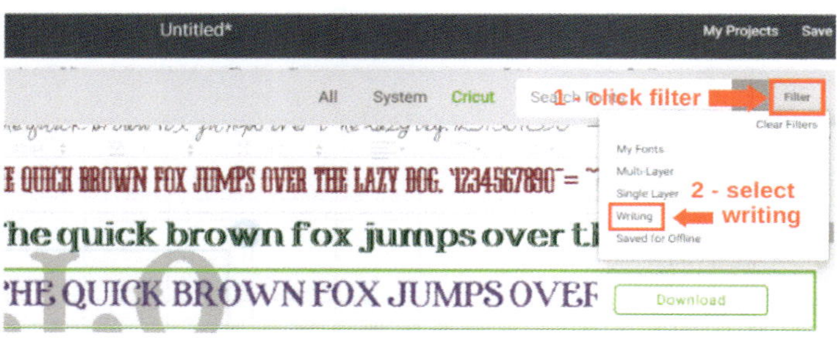

Tip 1

Filter for Cricut writing fonts by **clicking "filter" and then selecting "Writing."**

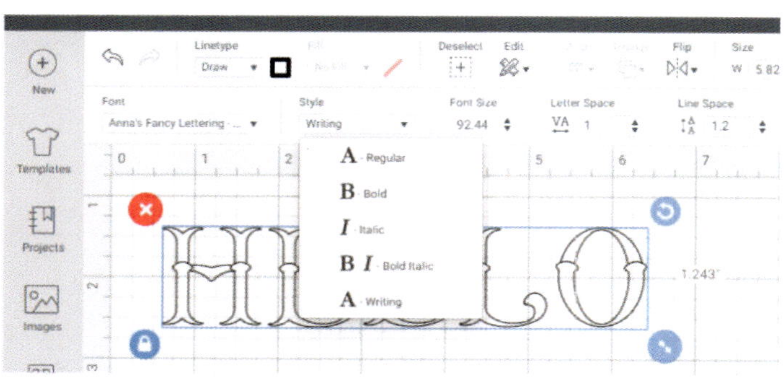

Tip 2

Some fonts come with regular and writing font styles that may look better than a normal "outline." To see if the font has a writing style, **click on "Style" beside the "Font" dropdown menu.**

Cricut font shown: Anna's Fancy Lettering - Hannah

WHY IS PRINT THEN CUT CUTTING OUT EVERY SINGLE LETTER?

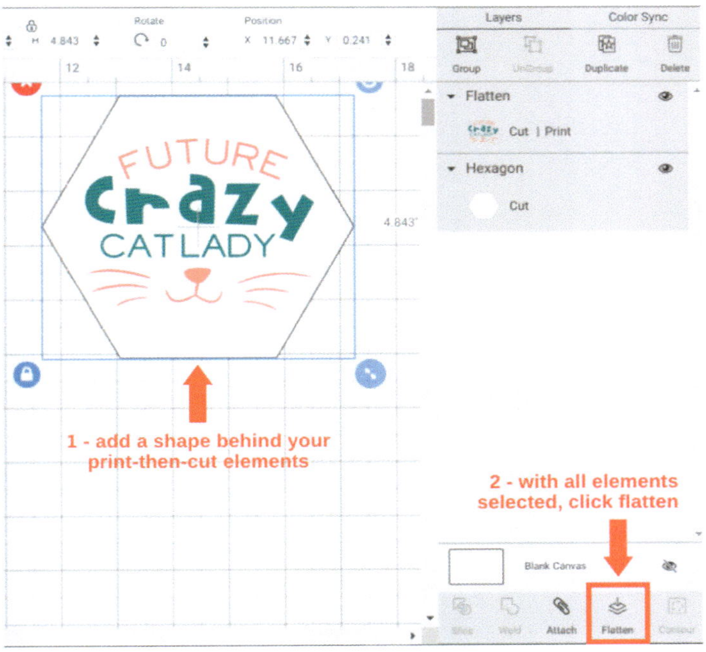

You need to flatten your text to a shape, that way it will only print out your text and cut only the shape instead. You can make the shape have no color if you don't want to see the shape printed (leave shape white if you are using white paper, for example) with your text, but still want just the shape cut out.

Step 1

Add a shape behind your print then cut elements. **Select everything**, then **click on the "Flatten" button** at the bottom of the layers panel.

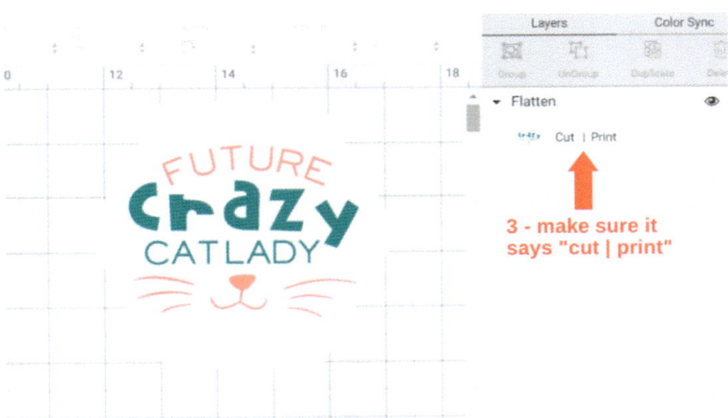

Step 2

Make sure the result says "Cut | Print" then **click "Make It"** to print the design and then cut around the shape.

Cricut fonts shown:
"FUTURE" & "CAT LADY": Sackers Gothic Std Medium
"CRAZY": Robotz

Cricut Access Image: Cat Face Mask #M15795B93

WHY IS MY CRICUT STRUGGLING TO READ THE PRINT THEN CUT REGISTRATION MARKS?

The sensor is a light, so a nifty trick is to close the lid of the cutter and to see if it does a better job.

WHY ARE THERE WEIRD SPACES IN BETWEEN MY LETTERS WITH SCRIPT FONTS?

Cricut wasn't designed to read fonts, so it struggles to read some fonts correctly. You can fix this by **ungrouping your letters and manually moving them in place** and then **welding them together**.

It might be easier to just use FontLab Pad or other software to **write your word and to save it as a SVG file** that you can upload to Design Space.

Cricut font shown: Emiline

WHY IS THE SLICE BUTTON GRAYED OUT?

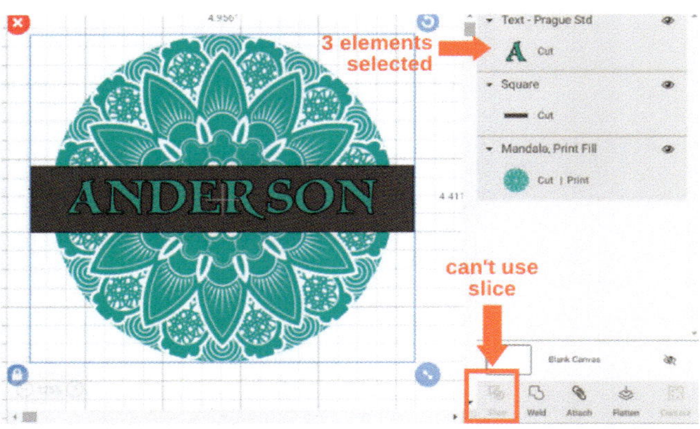

You can only use the slice tool on two elements. Double-check how many elements you are trying to use with the slice tool. **You can weld your letters together so that they are one layer** to reduce the number of elements you have so you can use the slice tool.

You can use the slice tool to create split monograms & other fun projects.

Cricut font shown: Prague Std

Cricut Access Image: Mandala, Print Fill #MC19E547

HOW DO I MOVE ELEMENTS FROM ONE MAT TO ANOTHER?

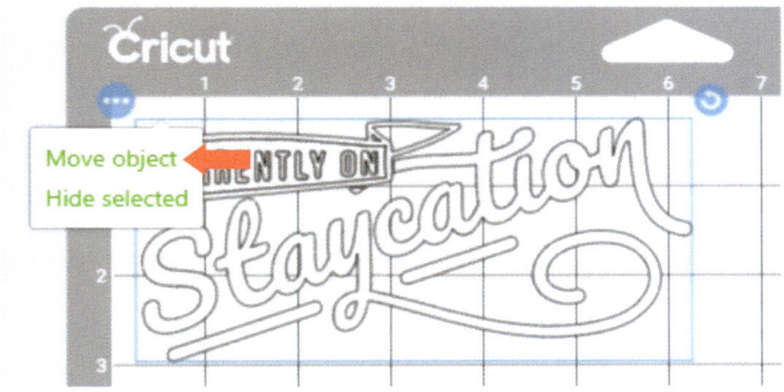

Step 1

After you click "Make It", **click on the element you want to move** and notice the three dots that appear. **Click on the three dots and choose 'move object'** and a new window will appear.

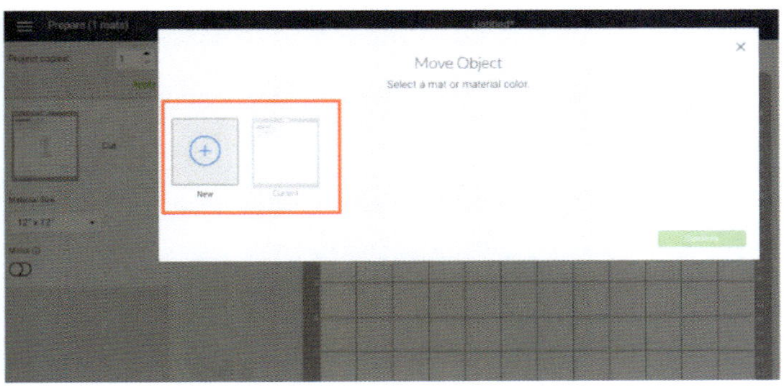

Step 2

Choose an existing mat you wish to move the item to or create a new one. If you create a new one, you will be asked to choose which color should represent the material you are cutting.

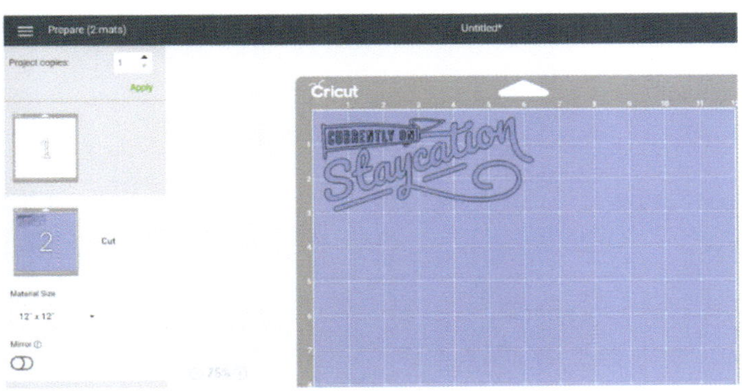

Step 3

Once you've chosen your mat or created a new one, **click the "Confirm" button** and your object will now appear on its new mat, and you can continue with your cut.

Cricut Access Image: Currently on Staycation #M16D115A0

THE NEW FONT I DOWNLOADED AND INSTALLED ON MY SYSTEM IS NOT SHOWING UP IN DESIGN SPACE!

Try refreshing or closing your Cricut Design Space application & opening it again so that it can load up all the fonts again. It should pick up any new fonts that were installed.

CONCLUSION

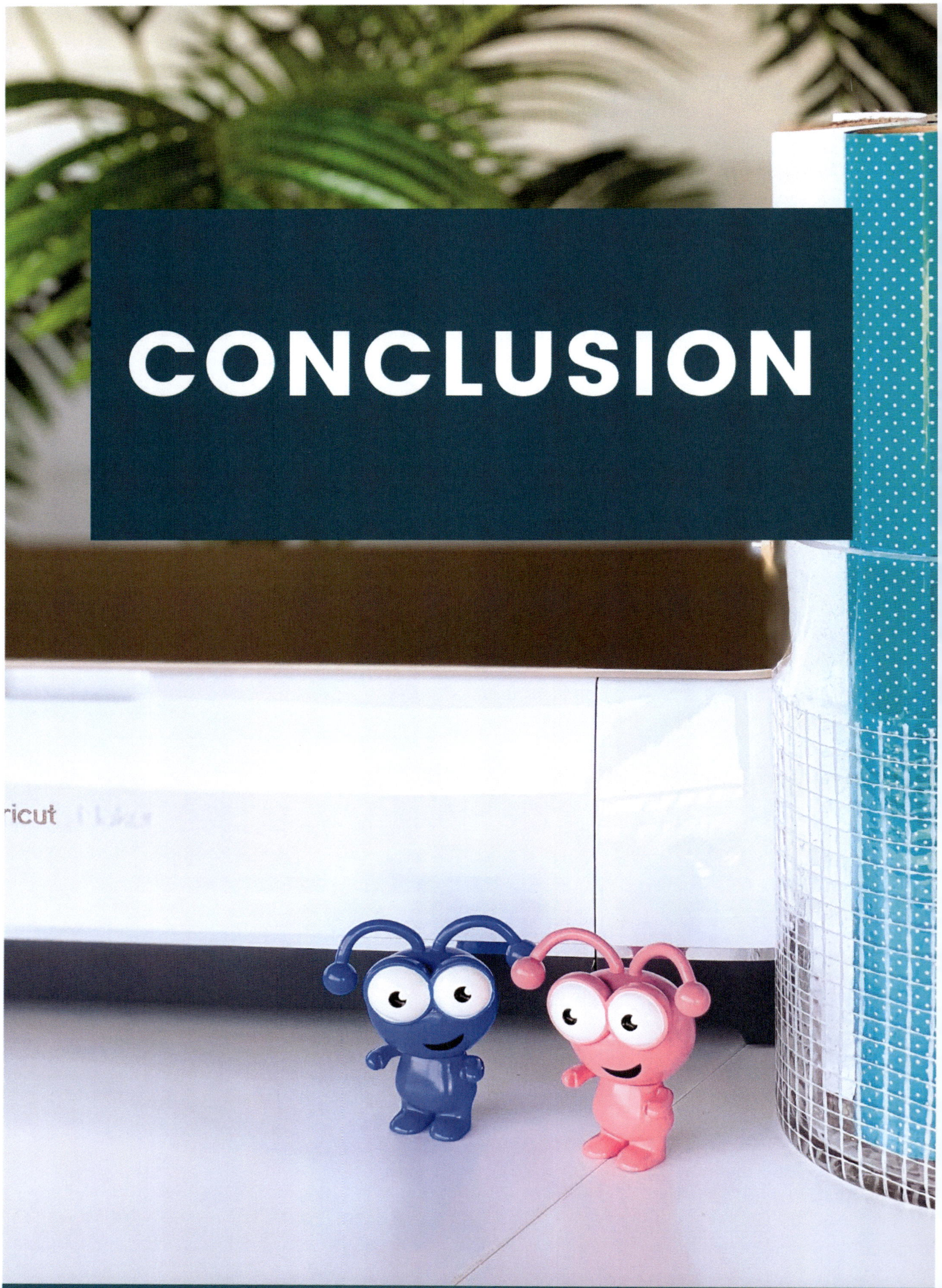

PRODUCTS

YOU MAY BE INTERESTED IN

I've been through the trenches with my Cricut machines. You don't have to go through the beginner phase alone. We get it, and we want to help you. Our Cricut Cheat Sheet Book is perfect for beginners!

01. The Mega Cricut Cheat Sheet Bundle Book

This book contains 80 cheat sheets with answers and walk-throughs to all your questions about working with a Cricut Maker, Cricut Explore, or Cricut Joy machine.

Simply pop the link below into your browser:
Digital Book:
https://www.thebestvinylcutters.com/cricut-cheat-sheet-pdf-book-2/

Digital Book:
https://www.amazon.com/Mega-Cricut-Cheat-Sheet-Book/dp/0645023221/

BEFORE

YOU GO!

I sure hope that you are aware that we have a wonderful website that is full of helpful resources for you: **https://www.thebestvinylcutters.com/**

We always share loads of inspirational photos, as well as video tutorials on our social media accounts. So make sure to follow us there as well (click the buttons below).

FIND US ON SOCIAL MEDIA

COPYRIGHT

AND RIGHTS OF USAGE

[CUSTOMER] agrees that you may not use any of these files for commercial or editorial purposes without the express written permission of TheBestVinylCutters.com. The Best Vinyl Cutters retains the copyright to all digital files.

The digital files that are being provided to you are licensed to you for any reasonable personal purposes, including but not limited to: printing, copying, and personal emailing (from one device to another).

Your license does not include use that results in financial gain, including but not limited to: advertising, stock photography, or resale of any nature.

Your purchase of the original files releases The Best Vinyl Cutters from any liability due to loss or damage of the files, and also releases us from any obligation to maintain copies of any digital file, image, or photograph.

The Best Vinyl Cutters may revoke this license at any time and for any reason.

The Best Vinyl Cutters retains all copyrights to the files and derivative works thereof.

By using any of these files, you are agreeing to the above terms.

---

xx, Jolene Ejmont

The Best Vinyl Cutters
support@thebestvinylcutters.com

Version 1 - updated November 2020
The Complete Guide to Cricut Design Space is copyright 2020 by The Best Vinyl Cutters (Operated under The Wanderlust Storytellers Pty Ltd). All rights reserved.

Cricut® and Cricut Design Space® are registered trademarks of Provo Craft. Use of them does not imply any affiliation with or endorsement by them.

Printed in Great Britain
by Amazon

21158377R00071